Studies in Contemporary Economics

Editorial Board
D. Bös
B. Felderer
B. Gahlen
H. J. Ramser
K. W. Rothschild

Gunther Maier

Spatial Search

Structure, Complexity,
and Implications

With 52 Figures

Physica-Verlag
A Springer-Verlag Company

Univ.-Doz. Dr. Gunther Maier
Vienna University of Economics
and Business Administration
Augasse 2-6
A-1090 Vienna, Austria

Published with Support of the *Fonds zur Förderung der wissenschaftlichen Forschung,* Vienna

---

ISBN 3-7908-0874-1 Physica-Verlag Heidelberg

Die Deutsche Bibliothek – CIP-Einheitsaufnahme
Maier, Gunther:
Spatial search: structure, complexity, and implications / Gunther Maier. –
Heidelberg: Physica-Verl., 1995
(Studies in contemporary economics)
ISBN 3-7908-0874-1

This work is subject to copyright. All rights are reserved, whether the whole or part of the material is concerned, specifically the rights of translation, reprinting, reuse of illustration, recitation, broadcasting, reproduction on microfilms or in other ways, and storage in data banks. Duplication of this publication or parts thereof is only permitted under the provisions of the German Copyright Law of September 9, 1965, in its version of June 24, 1985, and a copyright fee must always be paid. Violations fall under the prosecution act of the German Copyright Law.

© Physica-Verlag Heidelberg 1995
Printed in Germany

The use of registered names, trademarks, etc. in this publication does not imply, even in the absence of a specific statement, that such names are exempt from the relevant protective laws and regulations and therefore free for general use.

88/2202-543210 - Printed on acid-free paper

Preface

Two areas have fascinated me for a long time. One is the microeconomic theory of consumer behavior, the other one the role of space in economic processes. Usually, the two don't go together very well. In more advanced versions of microeconomic consumer theory its economic actor may face uncertainty, have to allocate resources over time, or have to take into account the characteristics of products, but rarely deals with space. He/she inhabits a spaceless point economy. Regional Science, on the other hand, describes and analyzes the spatial structure and development of the economy, but either ignores individual decision making altogether or treats it in a rather simplistic way.

In this book I try to bring together these two areas of interest of mine. I do this by use of the microeconomic concept of search and placing it in an explicit spatial context. The result, in my opinion, is a theoretical concept with fascinating implications, a broad set of potential implications, and numerous interesting research questions. After reading this book, where I lay out the basic idea of spatial search, describe its elements, and discuss some of its implications, I hope the reader will share this opinion. There are still plenty of unanswered research questions in this part of economic theory. Hopefully, this book will stimulate more work along these lines.

A number of people have contributed to this research. It all started with a collaborative research project with Peter Rogerson, State University of New York, Buffalo, financed by the Austrian "Fonds zur Förderung der wissenschaftlichen Forschung" and the "National Science Foundation" in the USA. Some of the major steps conceptualizing the research problem have been taken in this joint project. I am indebted to Peter Rogerson for his contributions and his permission to use his ideas in this manuscript. I would like to thank my colleagues at the Vienna University of Economics and Business Administration and the participants at various conferences for their criticism and suggestions. Also, my thanks go to colleagues at The University of North Carolina, Chapel Hill, for hosting me for a semester and giving me the opportunity to develop much of this material and discuss it with them.

Vienna, March 1995 Gunther Maier

Contents

1 Introduction   **1**
    1.1 Some Important Relationships 2
    1.2 Other Concepts of Search 5
    1.3 Basic Elements of the Analysis 10
    1.4 Aim and Structure of the Book 16

2 Economic Search Theory   **21**
    2.1 Basic Search Models 21
       2.1.1 The Sequential Search Strategy 22
       2.1.2 The FSS-Search Strategy 28
       2.1.3 Sequential and FSS-Strategy Compared 30
    2.2 Extensions of the Basic Search Models 32
       2.2.1 McKenna's General Search Model: Discounting, Utility, and Search Intensity 33
       2.2.2 Other Extensions of the Standard Economic Search Model 37
    2.3 Search Based Markets 40
    2.4 Summary 42

3 Prerequisites: Graphs, Routes, and Computational Complexity   **43**
    3.1 Graphs 43
    3.2 Routes 46
    3.3 Computational Complexity 48
       3.3.1 Types of Problems 50
       3.3.2 The Traveling Salesman Problem 53
    3.4 Summary 57

4 The General Spatial Search Problem   **59**
    4.1 Definition of the Spatial Search Problem 60
       4.1.1 Basic Assumptions 60
       4.1.2 An Algorithm for Solving the General Spatial Search Problem 63
       4.1.3 An Illustrating Example 69
    4.2 The Complexity of the General Spatial Search Problem . . 75

4.3 Incomplete Routes 78
 4.4 The Relevant Alternatives in a Spatial Search Problem ... 84
 4.5 Parameter Changes in the Search Problem 89
     4.5.1 Shifting and Scaling the Search Problem 89
     4.5.2 Changes in the Structure of the Search Problem:
           Stopping Effects vs. Routing Effects 91
 4.6 The Spatial Search Model and Economic Search Theory .. 96
 4.7 Summary 97

5 Tractable Spatial Search Problems   99
 5.1 Simplified Spatial Structures 100
     5.1.1 Linear Space 101
     5.1.2 Simplified Structures in Non-Linear Space 111
 5.2 Heuristics and Approximations 117
     5.2.1 General Aspects of Spatial Search Heuristics ... 118
     5.2.2 Heuristics for the General Spatial Search Problem . 122
 5.3 Summary 136

6 The Implication of Spatial Search for Market Areas and Firm Location   139
 6.1 Standard Location and Spatial Price Theory 140
 6.2 Search Based Location and Spatial Price Structures ... 148
     6.2.1 Consumer not Returning Home 150
     6.2.2 Consumer Returning Home 156
 6.3 Fetter's Law of Markets and Search 170
 6.4 Summary 176

7 Spatial Search and Agglomeration   179
 7.1 Hotelling's Principle of Minimum Differentiation 181
 7.2 Spatial Search and Agglomeration 189
 7.3 Summary 202

8 Spatial Search and Spatial Interaction Models   205
 8.1 The Gravity Model 206
 8.2 The Intervening Opportunities Model 212
 8.3 Discrete Choice Models 214
 8.4 Search, Spatial Interaction, Discrete Choice 222
 8.5 Notes on the Econometrics of Spatial Search 232
 8.6 Summary 235

9 Conclusions and Future Research   237

References   243

Chapter 1

Introduction

When we shop for consumer durables like furniture, some electronic equipment, a car etc. we usually have to make a number of interdependent decisions. We decide about which store to check, what characteristics we want the product to have, what price we are willing to accept. If we cannot find the product we want at an acceptable price at the first store, we will have to think about another store, and maybe have to revise our aspirations about characteristics and price. When we fail at the second store as well, we will have to decide about a third, fourth, fifth store, and so on.

This type of step by step decision making is usually called a *search process*. Search processes will be an important element in the discussion in this book. The spatial structure of the area we are in has some implications for the decisions we make in a search process. In a metropolitan area, where there are many shops close together offering the type of product we are looking for, chances are good that we will be able to find the respective product with the required characteristics at an acceptable price. In a remote rural area, where there may be only one supplier, we will have to accept what is available there. At the same time, our behavior as customers has important implications for suppliers and helps to structure our spatial environment. When we increasingly go to suburban shopping malls, because of their agglomeration of shops and the large collection of products they offer, small neighborhood stores will find it more and more difficult to attract enough business to break even. At the same time, developers will realize the potential for profits in shopping mall development, and build additional shopping centers.

In this book we will be dealing with questions and problems of this type. We will use search processes in a spatial context, and try to understand the relationship between spatial structure and the search behavior of economic agents. Therefore, we will use the term "spatial search". Although we have phrased the argument above in a shopping context, shopping is by no means the only type of economic process to which our discussion applies. The basic structure of a search process applies also when we are looking for a job, for college education, for an apartment, just to give a few additional examples. Again, we have to decide where to start looking, what terms we can get, at what wage, tuition, or rent level. When we cannot get what we want, we will have to decide where to continue looking. Although we will continue to use shopping as our main reference activity, we should keep in mind that the arguments we will develop may apply to the other areas as well.

It is our intention to develop a consistent modeling framework for spatial search and its implications. As we will see in the next section, although there is only limited literature about spatial search per se, our attempt fits into a considerable body of existing, well developed and highly formalized literature. However, our perspective adds considerable complexity to these already quite complex formal structures. In order to keep the complexity of our discussion at a manageable level we will have to simplify other aspects of these theories, and will have to sacrifice certain aspects for inclusion of the concept of spatial search.

In our view, introducing spatial search is definitely worth these cost. It brings about insight into a number of behavioral processes which are hard to grasp otherwise. We will be able to demonstrate some of the forces behind agglomeration and to show the transition between a dispersed and a concentrated locational structure. We will be able to show why in some cases small changes in the system may have dramatic implications for some economic agents; a collapse of their market, for example. Most of these results are immediately connected to the fundamental structure of spatial search and seem to be quite stable as far as our simplifying assumptions are concerned.

1.1 Some Important Relationships

The type of search process we have sketched above, and which we will be using throughout the presentation, has been prominent in economics for some decades now and rests soundly in the microeconomic tradition (Hey, 1979; Lippman and McCall, 1979; McKenna, 1985). Particularly in labor economics the idea of job search, i.e. workers trying systematically to find jobs that pay an acceptable wage, has become an integral part of the theory (e.g., Mortensen, 1986; Blau, 1991).

Economic search theory allows an economic agent to draw a series of offers from agents at the other side of the market. Each draw reveals the value of the respective offer, but also has some cost associated with it. The problem of the economic agent is to search for that particular offer,

1.1. Some Important Relationships

the value of which exceeds the cost of searching by a maximum amount[1]. The economic search problem is usually modeled as a series of decisions, where after each draw the agent has to decide whether the respective offer is good enough to be accepted or whether it is preferable to reject the offer and invest into a new draw.

Spatial search can be viewed as an attempt to place the economic search model into an explicitly spatial framework. This means that instead of being generated from within a spaceless point economy, in spatial search the offers can be found at specific locations in space. This places them in some relationship to one another. When the searcher goes to an alternative to draw an offer, he/she may have come closer to one alternative but may have moved away from another. This seemingly minor extension of the economic search concept introduces complications and new phenomena. We will investigate them in the later chapters of the presentation.

Despite the attention the search concept has found in regional science in the seventies and eighties, until recently there have been no attempts to place the search concept in a spatial framework. The earlier search models in regional science (e.g., Rogerson, 1982; Huff, 1984; Pickles and Rogerson, 1984) assume that search takes place within a spaceless point economy. The search component therefore does not differ from the search concept of standard economics. The spatial component only appears between these point economies. In a migration application, for example, search processes within the region determine the wage level a migrant can expect in a potential destination. Space, however, only appears as a cost of moving to this respective region. Some of the migration literature using a search concept has been summarized by Molho (1986) and Maier (1990).

Only recently regional researchers realized that "the alternatives to be searched in many cases will have not only a price distribution, but also a *spatial* distribution" (Rogerson, 1990, p. 337). This notion of the search process occurring within space adds a new dimension to the search problem and raises a number of new research questions most of which will be discussed in this volume. Important steps in the direction of modeling search within a spatial context have been undertaken by Harwitz et al. (1989), Rogerson (1990), Jayet (1990a,b), Maier (1991, 1993a), and Miller (1991, 1993). Their approaches differ in some basic assumptions and will be discussed later on in this presentation.

Instead of looking at spatial search as an attempt to put the economic search concept into a spatial framework, we may also view it as an extension of a routing problem. The problem of routing and scheduling of vehicles and crews received considerable attention in the transportation science and operations research literature. Summaries of this literature are

---

[1] For a more elaborate discussion see chapter 2.

provided by Bodin and Golden (1981), Bodin et al. (1983), Christofides (1985). More recent attempts to the vehicle routing problem and specific versions of it are e.g. by Gilbert (1989) and Pooley (1992).

In vehicle routing a set of alternatives on a graph need to be served by a fleet of vehicles along a route that fulfills some performance characteristics. Additional requirements and constraints, e.g. about service time, vehicle capacity, number of vehicle, lead to many specific instances of the routing problems. One version of a routing problem that is of particular importance in our context is the well-known Traveling Salesman Problem (see section 3.3). It can be thought of as the routing problem for *one* vehicle that has to pass through each alternative exactly once at minimal cost. We will investigate the relationship between the Traveling Salesman Problem and the Spatial Search Problem in more detail in chapter 4.

Practically all versions of the routing problem have in common, that all the alternatives need to be served, or at least until a certain threshold criterion is met (e.g. the vehicle is empty or full). In this sense, the various alternatives are of the same level of importance in the routing problem.

In the spatial search problem, the route may terminate at each alternative. The searcher may find the offer drawn attractive enough, terminate search, and return home. Moreover, the probability for this to happen depends upon the stochastic characteristics of the remaining alternatives. The spatial search problem can therefore be viewed as a routing problem with an endogenous trip termination process. It is important to note that this termination process contains not only a stochastic component, but also a decision to be made by the individual (searcher or vehicle operator).

Whether in a spatial or in an a-spatial context, search activities are not performed for the sake of entertainment. With each search process the searcher tries to achieve some market transaction, where he/she is either on the supply (e.g., job search) or demand (e.g., shopping) side of the market. When the alternatives from which to search are distributed over space, this brings us close to spatial price and location theory (Beckmann and Thisse, 1986; Maier and Tödtling, 1992, ch. 3).

In spatial price theory, prices are usually assumed to be given and known to the other economic agents. With the usual assumptions about individual behavior of the agents and given prices, in a shopping model, for example, we can assign each customer to a specific supplier and thus determine market areas for each supplier. Each customer visits only this one supplier and there are no shopping-trips across the boundaries of market areas. With the deterministic price assumption of spatial price theory, additional suppliers have no impact upon the behavior and economic well-being of a customer, as long as he/she is not captured by the market area of one of these suppliers.

In a search based shopping model, on the other hand, searchers move through space carrying along potential demand for the respective product. This potential demand becomes actual, when the searcher considers the price offer he/she received to be acceptable, buys the product and terminates search. As a consequence, the searcher's potential demand may become actual at various alternatives, and we can derive probabilities for this to happen at the various locations (choice probabilities). Quite clearly, market areas may overlap, and additional suppliers mean more choices for a specific customer.

The concept of spatial search can be used as a behavioral basis for a stochastic version of spatial price and location theory. Despite the simplifying assumptions one has to make in order to derive versions of manageable complexity, a stochastic spatial price and location theory yields insights that go way beyond those that can be derived from its deterministic version. We will discuss the relationship between the deterministic and the stochastic spatial price and location theory, and some of the insights in chapter 6 of this volume.

The close relationship between spatial search and spatial price and location theory brings about another important relationship: that to the economics of imperfect competition. In recent years, theories and concepts developed in the spatial literature have been used increasingly to understand the relationships between economic agents in an imperfectly competitive market (Greenhut et al., 1987). In this literature, space is reinterpreted in a more general sense as the distance between suppliers, their competitors, and customers in terms of product characteristics, service strategies etc. In the same way as spatial price and location theory feeds into the economics of imperfect competition, some of the additions provided by spatial search may carry over to this branch of theorizing as well.

1.2 Other Concepts of Search

The economic search concept is not the only one available in the literature. The terms "search" and even "spatial search" are used in some other contexts which differ substantially from ours. In order to distinguish the approach we use in this presentation from these competing approaches, and to avoid confusion we will briefly discuss three of the more important competing concepts. We will point out what distinguishes them from the economic search concept. In particular, we will discuss

1. the secretary problem,
2. search theory of operations research, and
3. the spatial search concept of Brian H. Massam.

The Secretary Problem

"In the late 1950's and early 1960's there appeared a simple, partially recreational, problem known as the secretary problem, or the marriage problem, or the dowry problem, that made its way around the mathematical community." (Ferguson, 1989, p. 282). The standard form of the secretary problem can be stated as follows: "A known number of items is to be presented one by one in random order, all $n!$ possible orders being equally likely. The observer is able at any time to rank the items that have so far been presented in order of desirability. As each item is presented he must either accept it, in which case the process stops, or reject it, when the next item in the sequence is presented and the observer faces the same choice as before. If the last item is presented it must be accepted. The observer's aim is to maximize the probability that the item he chooses is, in fact, the best of the n items available." (Freeman, 1983, p. 189).

As we will see in chapter 2, the secretary problem has a lot in common with the economic search problem[2]. Most importantly, both concepts are based on a sequence of decisions, where, at least in the basic versions, recall of already rejected alternatives is not possible. The fundamental difference between the economic search problem and the secretary problem lies in the objective of the process, a difference which reflects the scientific heritage of either problem. While the economic search concept is aimed toward some economically meaningful goal like minimizing cost or maximizing return, the goal upon which the secretary problem is based is purely statistical: to have the best chance for finding the best of the n alternatives (or "items" in Freeman's terminology). Besides the relative comparison to previously drawn alternatives, the value of each alternative is of no importance in the secretary problem. Choosing the second best alternative, even if it is only marginally worse than the best one, is as bad as choosing the worst alternative.

The searcher in the secretary problem does not invest into the search process. Because the objective in not expressed in financial terms, it is difficult to integrate cost components. At each alternative the searcher faces the risk of (1) rejecting the best alternative, or (2) accepting an

---

[2]Both the secretary problem and the economic search problem have been developed into many different variants. We will only compare the most basic versions here. For a more detailed discussion of the economic search problem see chapter 2.

1.2. Other Concepts of Search

alternative that is not the best one. In either case, he/she has failed to solve the problem.

The economic search problem, on the other hand, is based upon maximization of returns or minimization of costs. At each alternative, the searcher has to make an *economic* decision: Is the value of this alternative good enough to accept it, or is it better to reject this alternative and incur the additional cost of continued search. Search cost are an essential part of the economic search problem. When search cost are zero, the economic search problem actually disappears.

Another important difference between the secretary problem and the economic search problem lies in their information assumptions. The searcher in the secretary problem only knows the number of alternatives, but has no knowledge about the distribution of their values. So, when the best alterative comes along the searcher usually cannot identify it. In the economic search problem we usually assume that the searcher has perfect knowledge about the distribution of the relevant values (see section 1.3). Therefore, he/she can identify the best value whenever it comes along, although it is not the aim of the economic search to find the best alternative.

The solution of the secretary problem is surprisingly simple (Gilbert and Mosteller, 1966). It can be shown that the searcher has the best chance for finding the best alternative if he/she

1. rejects the first $r - 1$ alternatives,
2. accepts the first alternative which is the relative best of all the alternatives investigated so far.

The correct value of r depends upon the number of alternatives n. According to Ferguson (1989, p. 283) the probability, $\phi_n(r)$, for selecting the best alternative based on the above rule is $1/n$ for $r = 1$, and, for $r > 1$,

$$\phi_n(r) = \left(\frac{r-1}{n}\right) \sum_{j=r}^{n} \frac{1}{j-1} .$$

"The optimal r is the one that maximizes this probability" (Ferguson, 1989, p. 283). When n is large, the optimal value for r is approximately

$$r = \frac{n}{e} \approx 0.37 n .$$

The searcher's optimal strategy in the secretary problem is therefore to reject the first 37% of alternatives and accept the first one afterward that is better than the best one rejected thus far. The chance for actually accepting the best of the n alternatives is also about 37%.

Samuels (1985) discusses an interesting variant of the secretary problem that allows to integrate a spatial component as well as recall of previously rejected alternatives. Samuels assumes that an infinite number of alternatives is independently and uniformly distributed on the unit interval. The searcher starts at location 0 and has to bear search cost of c per unit of distance traveled. Samuels integrates search cost – and overcomes the above mentioned problem – by assuming a unit loss if the selected alternative is not the best one. This translates the objective of the secretary problem – find the best alternative – into a monetary measure. Thus it can be combined with search cost to form a new objective, namely to find a strategy that minimizes cost. This objective is quite similar to the one of the economic search problem. The fundamental difference lies in the fact that the searcher's penalty depends only on whether the selected alternative is the best one, whereas in the economic search model the value of the alternative enters the objective function. In this way the basic structure of the secretary problem is retained in Samuels' model, despite its similarity with the economic search model.

The optimal strategy in Samuels' version of the secretary problem[3] "parallels that for the classic problem: Pass a certain proportion of the applicants, then stop with the first 'candidate' (i.e., applicant that is relative best so far), if any; if none, return to the best after passing all of the applicants" (Samuels, 1985, p. 461). There are two limiting cases, however. When search cost is too small the searcher will pass all the alternatives and return to the best one. When search cost is too large, it is best to stop at once.

The Search Theory of Operations Research

Search theory of operations research has grown out of military oriented research conducted during World War II (Morse, 1977; Koopman, 1980). Since then the theory has developed in many different ways and has been applied in a wide set of circumstances (see, e.g. Haley and Stone, 1980).

Search theory is concerned with the problem of locating a specific object or an object with specific characteristics in search space. The object may be a missing airplane (e.g. Mattson, 1980), deposits of natural resources (e.g. Field, 1980; Fergusson, 1980), a disease in a human population (Kolesar, 1980), a defective component in a machine (Kadane, 1980), information in a computer storage (Ahlswede and Wegener, 1987) etc. Consequently, search space may be, for example, some area on the globe (or in the universe as in the case of search for new stars), a group of people, the set of components of a machine, records or bytes in computer

---

[3] Samuels uses the term "applicant" for what we have called "alternatives".

memory or on a disc. Search theory attempts to generate effective strategies for detection of the target. Some important measures of effectiveness[4] are (Richardson, 1989, p. 2)

1. Probability of detection
2. Expected time to detection
3. Probability of correctly estimating target "whereabouts"
4. Entropy of the posterior target location probability distribution.

Search models in operations research can be categorized in a number of other ways in addition to the objective they use. One particularly important distinction is whether the target is stationary or moving (Stone, 1989). When the target is moving, its movement may be unrelated to the search efforts of the searcher (e.g., a satellite), or the target may be reacting to the searcher's attempts of detecting it. The latter case raises problems similar to those discussed in game theory. Therefore, models that take into account reacting moving targets are often referred to as "search games" (e.g., Alpern, 1974; Gal, 1980).

The searcher in search theory is after a specific target similarly to the searcher in the secretary problem. This target either can be found at a specific location or not (the searcher in the secretary problem may succeed or fail in selecting the best alternative). Similar to the economic search model, the objective in search theory is often economical: The target should be located in the shortest period of time, at least cost, or with highest probability. As in the case of the secretary problem, the major difference between the economic search model and search theory lies in the fact that search theory does not take into account any tradeoff between the values of alternatives and resources invested into search. In most of the problems with which search theory deals, such a tradeoff does not exist because the search goal is of binary nature. An airplane wreckage, a submarine, a specific record in computer memory is either found or not. The searcher cannot be satisfied with being "close enough" to the target, as is the case in the economic search model.

Massam's Spatial Search

The work by B.H. Massam (1980) is related much less to our discussion than the previous two fields of research. We discuss it here mainly because

---

[4]"In a 'whereabouts' search, the objective is to estimate correctly the target's location in a collection of cells given a constraint on search cost" (Richardson, 1989, p. 3). The last measure in the list is concerned about the amount of information available about the target's location after the search effort.

of its title – Spatial Search: Applications to Planning Problems in the Public Sector – which is very close to the title of our own work.

Massam does not provide a clear definition of what he means by spatial search. Under the heading "What is Spatial Search?" he writes: "This book is concerned with the location of public facilities. A selection of procedures which have been used and are currently used for locating facilities will be discussed, together with procedures which could or should be used. It is suggested at the outset that the location chosen for a facility is the outcome of a search process which typically involves a consideration of alternative locations, hence for the main title of the book we have chosen *Spatial Search*" (Massam, 1980, p. 2). He distinguishes two types of spatial search problem: "first, the type of problem outlined above, that is, the search for the best *location* for a facility; second, the problem of the consumer's search for and selection of a facility for his own use" (p. 2). Massam concentrates on the first type of problem.

Despite its title, Massam's book deals with *choice* rather than search. The potential locations for the public facility under consideration are usually available at the same time and the decision maker selects one element from this set of alternatives. However, Massam's concern is not even the choice itself: "The extensive literature in psychology, sociology, and political science on choice and decision-making cannot be included in this study, other than in a superficial way. If our concern were primarily to explain the ways spatial search occurs and the ways location decisions are made, we would need a thorough review of the literature on choice and decision-making, but this is not the case here." (Massam, 1980, p. 9). Massam's concern is with the political and planning process that leads to a location decision for a public facility and with techniques for supporting this process. This is a legitimate research topic. However, it is usually not associated with the terms "search" or "spatial search". Massam's work is much closer to behavioral location theory (e.g. Schmenner, 1982) and public policy than to the problems that constitute the topic of our own work.

1.3 Basic Elements of the Analysis

Space

One basic element of our discussion of spatial search problems is – of course – space. All our analysis focuses at the question of how spatial relationships between various locations influence the behavior of economically optimizing agents. To be able to evaluate this relationship, we have to have a clear understanding of what is meant by space.

1.3. Basic Elements of the Analysis

While mainstream economic theories occupy "a wonderland of no spatial dimension" (Isard, 1956, p. 25), geography as a spatial science has developed various concepts of space (see, e.g. Bartels, 1974). The following two are of particular importance in our context:

- In theories of regional development the various regions – the basic units of analysis – are usually treated as "point economies" with no internal spatial dimension. "Space" in this sense only occurs between the regions and influences their exchange of goods and resources. Basic neoclassical regional development theory (see e.g., Richardson, 1973) even eliminates this space by assuming free mobility between regions.

- Spatial price and location theories take into account the spatial separation of various economic activities, but simplify space in another respect. They usually reduce it to one dimension (linear space) and employ a linear homogeneous relationship between distance and transportation cost. Overcoming one unit of distance always requires the same amount of resources. When space is not collapsed into one dimension – as in the model of von Thünen (see, e.g. Maier and Tödtling, 1992, pp. 125ff)– transport occurs on a featureless plane. In this sense spatial price and location theories are based on euclidean distance as their concept of space.

The concept of space we use in our discussion of spatial search processes is more general and encompasses the above mentioned concepts as special cases. As discussed in more detail in chapters 3 and 4 we use graphs for representing spatial structure. The edge-weights of the graphs that represent the costs of going from one vertex to another are not confined to any a-priori relationship as are euclidean distances. Graphs are flexible enough to describe any structures between the vertices.

Linear space as used in spatial price and location theories can be considered as a very special form of a graph. We will come back to this point in chapter 3. The idea of "point economy"-type regions can be represented in a special graph as well. We only have to set the edge weights between all pairs of vertices that belong to the same region to zero.

Although we will be dealing basically with prices and cost, space is not represented by monetary costs alone. The edge weights which represent the costs of going from one vertex to another may also contain time cost, costs in terms of effort, social distance, political and administrative barriers, or any other component that separates the two vertices. However, because we need to combine the costs of distance with the search process, we have to have a common unit of measurement for representation of both of them.

Uncertainty

An important element of our discussion is the introduction of uncertainty into economic processes occurring in space. Uncertainty[5] can be conceptualized in a number of different ways, all of which have been used in spatial analysis. Their common denominator is that the decision maker does not have full control over the outcome of all his/her actions. When the actor chooses one type of action (a specific location, to shop at a specific store etc.) the final result of this action depends upon some other force over which the actor has no control.

This other force may be another economic actor or an anonymous force that exerts some random influence. The difference lies in their motives: the economic actor will usually attempt to take an action which is in his/her self-interest, and which might itself be a reaction to the action taken by the original actor. The anonymous force, on the other hand, generates one of various *states of the world* at random, not based on any apparent objective function.

The first type of situation is typically dealt with in game theory. In its simplest form it takes into account two players, each of them knowing exactly the possible actions for both players and the respective result for each of them. Each player will take into account the other player's options and will base the decision upon the assumption that the other player will try to optimize his/her own outcome. When there is a predetermined sequence in the decisions and each decision is immediately revealed to the other player, the strategy is trivial: The first player will choose the option for which the other player's best conditional decision provides his/her best outcome[6]. But even this simple situation leads to fairly complicated strategic problems when we allow for repeated decisions or assume that the second player has to decide without knowing the first players decision. In the first case the players will have to anticipate a whole series of interdependent decisions with questions of stability of solutions and of short term vs. long term optimality arising. In the second case the players may be caught in a prisoners' dilemma (see, e.g. Hirshleifer and Riley, 1992, pp. 431ff).

In a spatial context, situations of this type have been analyzed first by Stevens (1961), Isard and Dacey (1962), Isard and Reiner (1962). Al-

---

[5]Following McKenna (1986, p. 9) we use the term "uncertainty" in a fairly general way meaning "absence of certainty". In a more narrow sense the term uncertainty is used only for those situations, when no probabilities are assigned to the states of the world. Situations where probabilities are assigned are termed as involving "risk" (see e.g. Kahle, 1990).

[6]In a problem of this type there is no uncertainty involved.

though it was not presented in this way originally, the adjustment mechanism (see also section 7.1) in Hotelling's famous model represents a repeated game with two players. The stability problems in this context have been pointed out by d'Aspremont et al. (1979). Greenhut (1957) argues that the classical von Thünen-Weber location theory leaves out an important aspect by ignoring game-like interdependencies. Isard (1967, 1969) and Isard and Smith (1966) are the first to address this problem. Webber (1972) uses the interdependencies between competitors in a spatial market as a source of uncertainty and analyzes some of its consequences.

Although a considerable part of our presentation is concerned about locational questions and the corresponding interdependencies between actors, we will not treat them in a game-like fashion. In order to focus upon the spatial search component, we will have to keep this aspect of location at a fairly simple level. This is one of the sacrifices we will have to make in order to include the uncertainty resulting from the second type of situation; uncertainty resulting from a random influence.

This second type of situation is of greater importance in our case than the strategic behavior resulting when a game is played against another economic agent. The economic theory dealing with this situation is known as the *economics of uncertainty* (Hirshleifer, 1989).

In the economics of uncertainty we usually distinguish between the actor who chooses from a set of *acts* and a random component, often called *nature*, that chooses one from a number of possible *states of the world*. Both together, the actor's acts and the states of the world chosen by nature, determine the consequence for the actor. The relationship between acts, states, and consequences is described by the *consequence function*.

Since the actor has no control over the states, he/she has to take into account all the possible consequences a specific act may have. However, some states may be more likely to occur than others. The actor's believes about how likely various states can occur are captured in a probability function defined over the various states. These believes may be based either on some objective knowledge about the process generating the states (e.g. when states are determined by rolling a dice) or on the actor's subjective experience. Assumptions about the probability function are critical elements of the theory and we will discuss them in more detail below.

It can be shown that under certain postulates of rational choice (see, e.g., Friedman and Savage, 1948; Luce and Raiffa, 1957; Markowitz, 1959; Marschak, 1968) a cardinal preference-scaling function can be assigned to the consequences such that the preference ranking of any pair of acts coincides with the rankings under the expected-utility rule (Hirshleifer, 1989, p. 158). Let $a = (1, \ldots, A)$ be the set of possibe acts, $s = (1, \ldots, S)$

the possible states of the world, c_{as} the consequence of act a and state s, and π_s the probability that state s occurs. We can write the expected-utility rule (von Neumann and Morgenstern, 1944) as

$$u(a) = \sum_{s=1}^{S} \pi_s v(c_{as}) ,$$

with u being a utility function over actions and v being the cardinal preference-scaling function. The shape of v determines the actor's preference toward risk (Pratt, 1964; Arrow, 1965).

When one act yields the same consequence irrespective of the state that occurs, the actor will receive this consequence with certainty. In this way we can combine acts with certain and uncertain outcomes in a single decision. Moreover, one of the possible consequences may be the right to make another decision under uncertainty. The value c of this consequence will depend upon the structure (acts, states, probabilities, consequences) of the lower level decision, which in turn may depend upon another decision, and so on. In this way we may link a whole sequence of decisions under uncertainty together to form an interdependent structure of decisions.

The (non-spatial) search model (see chapter 2) represents such a structure. The searcher has two acts to choose from: (1) accept the current offer, (2) reject the current offer, pay search cost, and draw another offer. The consequence of the first act is known with certainty, whereas the consequences of the second act depend upon the value of the next offer drawn (states). The wage or price offer distribution describes the probabilities for the various states.

While we can view the search model as a sequence of decisions under uncertainty, the possibility to repeat decisions adds new dimensions to the problem. Since the searcher can reject a bad consequence and repeat the decision, the searcher can expect a better result than when he/she faces the equivalent one-time decision. On the other hand, repeated decisions raise questions about the quality of the probability distribution.

It is quite common in search theory to assume that the searcher knows the probability distribution (wage/price offer distribution) perfectly well. We will rely on this assumption throughout this book. Despite its popularity in the theoretical literature, this assumption raises a number of questions. For example, where does the information about the probability distribution come from? If the searcher has acquired it, he/she must have invested a tremendous amount of resources. Why did the searcher not acquire additional information about the offers of specific suppliers? If the searcher has sampled suppliers to accumulate this information, he/she must have detected very attractive offers. Why didn't the searcher accept

1.3. Basic Elements of the Analysis

these offers? Was he/she unaware of the ultimate goal of the information and search activities, namely to find a good alternative? If so, why did he/she acquire this information in the first place?

Acquiring perfect information is economical only when this information is completely free. As soon as it takes time, money, effort etc. to collect this information, a rational decision maker will never achieve a state of perfect information (about the probability distribution). He/she will invest into information collecting activities only as long as the marginal benefit of the information exceeds the marginal cost, where the marginal benefit depends upon the decision for which the decision maker accumulates the information.

Some of these arguments are brought forward by the *economics of information* which deal with the economic problems involved in transmission and accumulation of information. Dropping the assumption of perfect information about the probability distribution in the context of decision making under uncertainty leads us to a range of new and interesting problems: how confident is the decision maker about the information he/she has accumulated; how will new information be combined with prior knowledge; is there an incentive for economic agents to keep some information private and to make other information publicly available; how can decision makers get access to information other agents do not want to make available ("screening"; see, e.g. Hirshleifer and Riley, 1992, p. 405ff); how can agents pass information to the other side of the market when other agents transmit distorted information ("signalling"; see, e.g. Nelson, 1974, 1975; Spence, 1974; Cho and Kreps, 1987; Hirshleifer and Riley, 1992, pp. 424ff); how will markets – and the market for information in particular – be influenced by the strategic options imperfect information allows?

Although we will not go into any details, two aspects of imperfect information are worth mentioning. First, when the two sides meet in the market, information is often asymmetric. Suppliers of a product may know more about its quality and characteristics than the potential customers. Of course, when the information is favorable for their product the supplier will try to use this information to distinguish his/her product from the "average" product in the market and to get a higher price. When the information is unfavorable the supplier will try to keep the information private to be able to charge the (unjustified) market price. When the market does not reflect all the information – some information cannot be passed on, some can be kept private – suppliers of high-quality products will drop out of the market while suppliers of low-quality products will be attracted. This consequence of informational asymmetry is known as *adverse selection*. It leads to Akerlof's famous "lemon principle" (Akerlof, 1970) stating that under some conditions the quality of products transacted in some markets will be biased toward the lower end[7].

The second aspect we want to note is that in a world of imperfect information economic activities usually carry information. When agents who possess a specific piece of information which is not available to others try to capitalize on their knowledge by some market transactions, their behavior reveals some of their information to other actors ("information leakage"). Similarly, in a search process with imperfect information about the price/wage offer distribution, the searcher's draws not only represent options he/she may accept or reject, they also provide additional information about the price/wage offer distribution (DeGroot, 1970). The searcher will incorporate this additional information into his/her knowledge about the distribution (Axell, 1974; Rothschild, 1974; Rosenfield and Shapiro, 1981; Janko et al., 1993). A search model of this type, i.e. with imperfect knowledge about the distribution, has been used in a migration context by Maier (1985) (see also Maier, 1990).

Imperfect information as an extended version of uncertainty has a lot of theoretical appeal. However, using this more realistic concept of uncertainty (in a general sense) in a modeling context, adds considerable to the complexity of the formulations. The analyst has to make a decision whether imperfect information is likely to add that much to the understanding of the problem under investigation that it is worth the additional complexity (and necessary simplifications in other areas). Although we generally acknowledge the theoretical superiority of imperfect information over the assumption of perfect knowledge about the distribution, and recognize the conceptual problems of the latter, in the present context we chose to stay with the more manageable assumption. In the rest of this presentation we will always assume the searcher to have perfect knowledge about the distribution from which he/she is drawing.

1.4 Aim and Structure of the Book

Although the discussion above has shown that spatial search is closely related to a number of well established theoretical concepts, the idea of spatial search is fairly new. Only recently analysts have begun to investigate the implications of spatially distributed alternatives on search behavior. This attempt has led to a number of conference papers and journal articles (Harwitz et al., 1989; Rogerson, 1990; Jayet, 1990a,b; Maier, 1991, 1993a; Miller, 1991, 1993) that typically focus upon specific, narrowly defined aspects of search behavior. A comprehensive treatment of spatial search

---

[7]The name "lemon principle" is derived from an American expression for poor-quality used cars.

1.4. Aim and Structure of the Book

is still missing.

It is the main goal of this book to provide this missing comprehensive discussion of spatial search. We follow this goal by providing a rigorous definition of the "spatial search problem", and by looking at it from different theoretical perspectives. In chapter 4 we will present a list of assumptions that define the "spatial search problem". These assumptions are being used throughout the presentation. Based on this definition of the spatial search problem we also discuss a basic procedure for solving it and illustrate it with a numerical example. In chapter 4 we derive a number of theoretical results about the spatial search problem. Among them are results about the relevant alternatives, about the reaction of the problem structure to parameter changes, and results about incomplete routes.

In order to lay the ground for this treatment of the spatial search model and to provide a point of reference, in chapters 2 and 3 we present some basic prerequisites for our analysis. Chapter 2 deals with the standard search model as it is frequently used in Economics. The spatial search model can be viewed as an extension and generalization of this model. In chapter 3 we present some basic concepts of graph theory and provide a brief introduction to complexity theory. In both cases we restrict our attention to those elements that are needed for the main argument of the book.

The structure of the algorithm we derive for solving the spatial search problem immediately raises concerns about the computational complexity of the spatial search problem. A major part of chapter 4 is devoted to discussing this question. By relating the spatial search problem to the well known traveling salesman problem, we can show that the spatial search problem belongs to a class of highly complex optimization problems.

Chapter 5 builds on this result about the complexity of the spatial search problem. Since the theorem derived in chapter 4 indicates that the spatial search problem in its most general form may be difficult to handle, chapter 5 tries to find computationally tractable versions of the spatial search problem. This is done in two ways: first, we try to impose additional constraints upon the spatial structure of the general spatial search problem; second, we give up the goal of finding the optimal solution, and analyze nearly optimal – heuristic – solutions instead. Both approaches yield additional insights into the structure of the spatial search problem.

Spatial search, as defined and discussed in chapter 4, can be viewed as a microeconomic theory of the optimal behavior of economic agents in a spatial setting. The question arises, what implications this type of behavior may have for the space economy. We will provide a few answers in chapters 6 to 8. In each of these chapters we select one well established concept from Regional Economics, incorporate the concept of spatial search, and analyze to what extent the spatial search based version differs from the standard one. In general, the introduction of spatial search opens up a broad scope of interesting aspects. In some cases it allows us to deal with spatial phenomena that are known to be of great practical relevance but cannot be dealt with satisfactorily in the standard theories.

Chapter 6 concentrates on questions of market areas and firm location. In section 6.1 we review the classical, transportation cost based spatial price theory and the type of spatial competition this model implies. When we introduce spatial search on the side of the consumers (section 6.2) we find that one of the strong theoretical implications of the standard theory disappears: market areas are no longer clearly separated. Instead we get overlapping areas that are usually dominated by one supplier but may be served by other suppliers as well. Even simple mill-pricing may lead to a non-linear relationship between distance and expected costs[8] where the shape of the function depends upon the position of the supplier in the spatial market. While these questions are discussed in linear space in section 6.2, in section 6.3 we briefly extend the analysis to two-dimensional space. The main point of reference there is Fetter's law which states that under the usual assumptions of spatial price theory the boundaries between the market areas of two adjacent suppliers are hyperbolas. Under the search based model this result only holds in a special case.

In chapter 7 we turn to the relationship between spatial search and agglomeration. Although an important and well established concept in Regional Science, agglomeration factors are difficult to derive from standard microeconomic models. In section 7.1 we investigate Hotelling's model. It gave rise to the famous "principle of minimum differentiation" that is commonly interpreted as a microeconomic argument for the spatial clustering of activities. However, when we look into the recent literature on the Hotelling model and when we investigate its basic assumptions in detail, it turns out that the forces toward concentration are the result of a very specific set of assumptions that have some dubious theoretical implications. When we drop any of Hotelling's basic assumptions the model yields a deconcentrated locational pattern rather than a concentrated one.

In section 7.2 we introduce spatial search into a Hotelling-type model. We employ a set of assumptions that has been found to produce a dispersed locational pattern in Hotelling's original framework. When allowing for search we introduce another mechanism in addition to transportation costs: the option for a lower price quote from another supplier. It is the relationship between these two factors that determines the outcome of the model. When transportation costs are high relative to price variation, suppliers will find it optimal to locate apart from one another. When

---

[8]The equivalent to delivered price in a search based model.

1.4. Aim and Structure of the Book

the importance of transportation costs declines relative to price variation, suppliers will be drawn closer and closer together. From a certain point on they will find it optimal to cluster at the same location. By introducing spatial search we can derive an agglomerated location pattern, as well as observe the transition from dispersion to agglomeration.

Section 8 turns to spatial patterns of interaction at a more aggregate level and asks whether frequently observed interaction patterns may be the result of spatial search processes. We analyze this question by comparing the spatial search concept to three important families of spatial interaction models: gravity models, intervening opportunities models, and discrete choice models. In section 8.1 we review the most important structural features of the gravity model and discuss its relationship to entropy maximization. Section 8.3 briefly reviews the intervening opportunities model. The main focus of section 8.3 is a discussion of discrete choice models. We concentrate on their microeconomic foundation and the transition toward empirical application. Rather than discussing different types of discrete choice models we concentrate on the logit model and the nested logit model.

Section 8.4 traces the relationships between the three models discussed so far in chapter 8 and the spatial search model. As it turns out, the intervening opportunities model can be viewed as a specific and highly restrictive version of a spatial search model. The relationship between gravity models, discrete choice models and the spatial search model, on the other hand, is much more general. With the proper assumption about the price distribution, the spatial search model can be transferred into a logit model, which in turn is structurally equivalent to a production constrained gravity model. This relationship is of particular relevance because it allows us to derive empirically applicable versions of the spatial search model. In section 8.5 we touch some of the related econometric questions.

Chapter 2

Economic Search Theory

In chapter 1 we have already talked loosely about search processes and the economic search problem. In this chapter we want to be more specific in laying out the basic structure of economic search theory. Because of the enormous amount of literature available in this area, we can provide only a cursory overview. In particular we will concentrate upon aspects that are important for our latter discussion of spatial search.

The development of an economic theory of search commenced with two seminal papers by George Stigler (1961, 1962). He formulates the problem in a way which is now known as "fixed sample size" (FSS) strategy. Given a set of alternatives the searcher decides about the size of the sample a-priorily, investigates the whole sample, and then chooses the alternative that provides the best (minimum or maximum) value. The criterion for the choice of an optimal sample size is the equating of the marginal cost of adding an alternative to the sample and the respective marginal expected return. The optimal sample size is the largest one where marginal returns exceed marginal cost.

It was soon realized (DeGroot, 1970; see also sections 2.1.3 and 2.2.1) that a sequential search strategy provides a higher expected return than the FSS strategy. Contrary to the FSS-search the individual decides after each alternative whether to continue searching or to accept the alternative. The optimal strategy is characterized by a sequence of critical values which delimit alternatives with acceptable values from those with unacceptable values. In the standard version of the search model (see the discussion below) the individual accepts the first alternative with an acceptable value.

2.1 Basic Search Models

We will start the more formal discussion by describing basic versions of the sequential search strategy and the FSS-strategy. In the third subsection we will compare the two strategies. Among the generalizations that we will discuss in section 2.2 there will be one that combines sequential and FSS-search into one strategy.

2.1.1 The Sequential Search Strategy

There are situations in which the individual searches for a high value of an alternative (e.g. a high wage in job search) as well as those where the aim is to find a low value (e.g. a low price in shopping). Formally the two problems are equivalent since we can always turn a minimization problem into a maximization problem by searching for the negative of the respective variable. Keeping this in mind we will lay out the basic argument in terms of a minimization problem. This corresponds to the decision we have made in chapter 1 about shopping being our basic reference activity.

As mentioned in section 1.3 a search process can be viewed as a series of (interrelated) decisions under uncertainty with one certain and one uncertain outcome. The certain outcome is the value observed at the specific alternative, whereas the uncertain outcome is the value of continuing the search process. The searcher can compute the expected minimum cost of continued search for each step of the search process. It represents a critical value that has to be compared with the value of the current alternative. If the value of the current alternative is above this threshold it is better for the individual to continue searching. Otherwise he/she better accepts the current alternative. Since this comparison has to be made at each step, the searcher has to derive a whole sequence of critical values based upon the expected minimum cost of continued search.

The Basic Model

Denote by X_i the value of the i-th alternative. This is a random variable distributed with probability density function f_i. We restrict X_i to non-negative values[1]. Thus $f_i(X) = 0$ for all $X < 0$. Moreover, we assume f_i to be bounded and continuous such that $\int_0^B f_i(x)\,dx = 1$, with B being the upper bound. The marginal cost of observing alternative i is c_i. The searcher cannot recall previously rejected offers; once an offer is rejected it is lost forever. There is a maximum number of n alternatives and the alternatives are observed in sequence $1,\ldots,n$. Practically all the economic search literature relies on the assumption of a given sequence[2] in which

---

[1]This is not a critical assumption. We make it simply for mathematical convenience. In chapter 8 we will have to remove this assumption.

[2]Often this assumption remains implicit or is hidden behind other assumptions that guarantee that any sequence of alternatives will yield the same result.

2.1. Basic Search Models

the alternatives are to be searched. In the spatial case we will have to drop this assumption. This will turn out to be of crucial importance for the structure and complexity of the model. Besides that, this set of assumptions describes a rather general search problem. Some of its special cases will be discussed in the sequel.

When the individual has observed the value of alternative $n-1$ the only valid option besides accepting this alternative is to pay cost c_n and accept alternative n, whatever its value is. Therefore, the expected minimum cost at this level, denoted y_{n-1}, is

$$y_{n-1} = c_n + E(X_n) = c_n + \int_0^B x f_n(x)\,dx\ .$$

Since we are dealing with a minimization problem, if the value of alternative $n-1$ (denoted X_{n-1}) is below the threshold y_{n-1} it is optimal for the individual to accept it; otherwise it should be rejected. Therefore, the expected minimum cost at level $n-2$ equals

$$\begin{aligned}
y_{n-2} &= c_{n-1} + E[\min(X_{n-1}, y_{n-1})] \\
&= c_{n-1} + \int_0^{y_{n-1}} x f_{n-1}(x)\,dx + \int_{y_{n-1}}^B y_{n-1} f_{n-1}(x)\,dx \\
&= c_{n-1} + \int_0^{y_{n-1}} x f_{n-1}(x)\,dx + y_{n-1}\left[1 - F_{n-1}(y_{n-1})\right]\ . \quad (2.1)
\end{aligned}$$

F_{n-1} denotes the cumulative density function of X_{n-1}. So, once the individual has derived y_{n-1} the value of y_{n-2} can be computed according to equation (2.1). Along the same line of reasoning one can then derive y_{n-3}, and so on.

In general, the sequence of critical values y_i is defined by the recursive relationship

$$\begin{aligned}
y_{i-1} &= c_i + \int_0^{y_i} x f_i(x)\,dx + \int_{y_i}^B y_i f_i(x)\,dx \\
&= c_i + \int_0^{y_i} x f_i(x)\,dx + y_i\left[1 - F_i(y_i)\right]\ . \quad (2.2)
\end{aligned}$$

Together with $y_n = B$, a formal version of the assumption that search is limited to n alternatives, this defines the whole sequence of critical values. Since there is no cost of stopping search, the critical values coincide with the expected cost of continued search. When turning to the spatial search problem in section 4 we will see that this is not necessarily the case.

Each one of these critical values represents the expected cost of continued search. Intuitively, the individual will continue searching only when

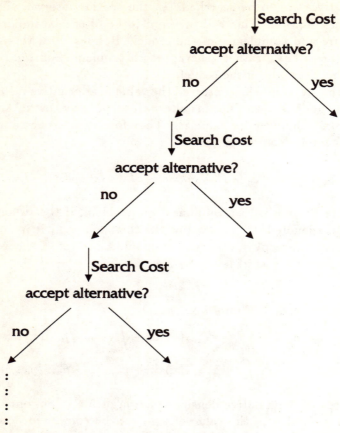

Figure 2.1: The Standard Search Process

the value he/she has in hand is higher than the expected cost of continuing. So, the cost the individual has to expect from the search sequence as a whole is just y_0. By following the optimal search strategy the individual can expect cost of y_0. This cost consists of the price of the alternative the individual finally chooses plus the cost it took to get to this alternative.

Graphically the search process can be presented as in figure 2.1. At each node of this tree the individual decides whether to accept the alternative observed or to continue searching. In the first case the decision tree is followed to the right, and the search process is stopped. In the other case the decision tree is followed to the left, the next alternative is investigated and the same decision made again. The optimal strategy through this process is characterized by the sequence of critical values, which guide the individual's decision at each fork.

An Alternative Formulation

This leads us to an alternative interpretation of the expected cost of search (y_0). At each point the individual compares the price of the alternative to the respective critical value. If the price is below the threshold the individual accepts this alternative. The probability of a specific alternative to be accepted can be derived therefrom. For the first alternative it is simply

$$P_1 = F_1(y_1) \ .$$

For alternative 2 to be accepted requires not only that the value of alternative 2 be lower than the threshold, but also that the individual searches beyond alternative 1. The choice probability is

$$P_2 = F_2(y_2)\left[1 - F_1(y_1)\right] \ .$$

The same argument leads to the conclusion that the choice probability for alternative i can be written as

$$P_i = F_i(y_i) \prod_{j=1}^{i-1} \left[1 - F_j(y_j)\right] \ .$$

In some cases it is preferable to look at the probability that the searcher will stop at a specific alternative provided he/she has reached this point in the search sequence. At alternative i this *conditional* choice probability is equal to the probability that the value of that alternative is below the corresponding threshold:

$$p_i = F_i(y_i) \ .$$

Based on the definition of choice probability, we can now derive the expected cost of a search sequence as the weighted average of the expected costs of all the possible stopping points (see figure 2.1). The expected cost at each stopping point is equal to the expected price of this alternative (provided the price does not exceed the threshold) plus the cost the individual has accumulated up to this point. The expected cost of the whole search sequence is therefore

$$\begin{aligned} y_0 &= P_1\left[c_1 + E(X_1|X_1 \leq y_1)\right] \\ &\quad + P_2\left[c_1 + c_2 + E(X_2|X_2 \leq y_2)\right] \\ &\quad + \ldots + P_n\left[c_1 + \ldots + c_n + E(X_n|X_n \leq y_n)\right] \\ &= \sum_{i=1}^{n}\left[c_i\left(\sum_{j=i}^{n} P_j\right) + P_i E(X_i|X_i \leq y_i)\right] \ . \end{aligned} \qquad (2.3)$$

As can be seen clearly from equation (2.3), the value of y_0 depends upon all the alternatives, because of the recursive structure of (2.2). Note that y_0 also depends upon the other critical values, which can be written in a similar way:

$$y_k = \sum_{i=k+1}^{n} \left[c_i \left(\sum_{j=i}^{n} P_j \right) + P_i E(X_i | X_i \leq y_i) \right] .$$

As the expected minimal cost of search (y_0) these values depend upon the whole remaining search sequence as well. The part which has already been passed, however, has no impact upon the critical values. In this sense, the searcher always looks forward, never back.

Marginal Changes

It is worthwhile to investigate the recursive relationship (2.2) a little further. There are two elements directly influencing y_{i-1}, namely the marginal cost c_i and the expected cost of continued search, the critical value y_i.

It is trivial to see from (2.2) that

$$\frac{\partial y_{i-1}}{\partial c_i} = 1 .$$

If the cost of proceeding from alternative $i-1$ to alternative i increases, the expected cost of continuing search at alternative $i-1$ increases by the same amount.

For the second relationship we find by taking the partial derivative of (2.2) with respect to y_i that

$$\frac{\partial y_{i-1}}{\partial y_i} = y_i f_i(y_i) + 1 - y_i f_i(y_i) - F_i(y_i) = 1 - F_i(y_i) . \quad (2.4)$$

So, if for some reason y_i increases marginally, the expected cost at alternative $i-1$ increases by $1 - F_i(y_i)$ times this amount. The same relationship holds for alternatives $i-1$ and $i-2$. Therefore, y_{i-2} increases by $[1 - F_{i-1}(y_{i-1})][1 - F_i(y_i)]$ times the increase in y_i. More generally, the expected costs are related by

$$\frac{\partial y_{i-k}}{\partial y_i} = \prod_{j=0}^{k-1} [1 - F_{i-j}(y_{i-j})] \quad (2.5)$$

Since F_i is a cumulative distribution function, relationship (2.5) has two immediate implications:

2.1. Basic Search Models

1. An increase in the expected cost of one alternative can never lead to a decrease in the expected cost of one of the alternatives preceding it. That is

$$\frac{\partial y_{i-k}}{\partial y_i} \geq 0 \quad \forall \ 0 \leq k < i$$

   and follows immediately from the fact that a cumulative distribution function cannot be negative. The equality holds when for one of the alternatives between i and $i-k$ we have $F_j(y_i) = 1$. This, however, implies that its choice probability is 1 and the individual will never proceed beyond this alternative.

2. An increase in the expected minimum cost of one alternative can never lead to a larger increase in the expected minimum cost of one of its preceding alternatives.

$$\frac{\partial y_{i-k}}{\partial y_i} \leq 1 \quad \forall \ 0 \leq k < i$$

   This follows from the fact that a cumulative distribution function cannot exceed 1. Again, the equality holds only in an extreme case, namely when all alternatives between i and $i-k$ have choice probability 0.

In the more realistic case of $0 < F_j(y_j) < 1$ a change in one of the expected cost changes all preceding expected costs in the same direction. The effect, however, fades out the further the two alternatives are apart in the search sequence.

The "Standard Search Model" of Economics

Our treatment of the sequential search strategy differs from what is known as the "standard search model" in the economic literature[3]. The reason is that we will need our more general formulation in chapter 4 in order to focus on the spatial aspect. The standard version of the model has been extended in numerous ways in the economic literature. A few of these generalizations will be discussed in section 2.2. However, the specific assumptions that we will discuss here, are applied in the extended versions of the model as well.

---

[3] In Operations Research the problem underlying this model is known as the unconstrained optimal stopping problem (see, e.g., Chow et al., 1971; Shiriaev, 1977). For a discussion of constrained versions of the optimal stopping problem see Müller-Funk, 1993.

In economics one usually assumes identical marginal costs and distributions, i.e., $f_i(x) = f(x)$, $c_i = c$ (see e.g., Diamond and Rothschild, 1989, p. 450-454). Therefore, the economic literature does not have to worry about the sequence in which the alternatives are investigated. In addition, the standard search model of economics assumes that there is an unlimited number of alternatives, i.e. $n = \infty$.

This model represents a limiting case of the model we have formulated above. It yields a famous formulation which despite of its prominence holds only in this special case.

In the fundamental recursive formula (2.2) there were two reasons for indexing the critical values: (1) that marginal costs and distributions were allowed to vary over the alternatives, and (2) the fact that with each rejected alternative the individual reduces the number of alternatives left for investigation. In the standard search model both effects are eliminated by assumption. Therefore, we can drop the index i in (2.2) and rewrite it as

$$y = c + y\left[1 - F(y)\right] + \int_0^y x f(x)\,dx \ .$$

The critical value, the *reservation price*, is constant throughout the search sequence. It is easy to see that it is determined by the following implicit equation:

$$c = \int_0^y (y - x) f(x)\,dx \ . \qquad (2.6)$$

So, under the above mentioned assumptions, when n goes to infinity the search problem simplifies considerably. In the limiting case of the standard search model the individual must compute only one critical value according to (2.6) rather than a whole vector of critical values as in our more general model. The reason is that with an infinite number of identical alternatives rejecting one alternative does not change the individual's situation at all. There is still an infinite number of identical alternatives left.

When only one of the three assumptions is dropped the individual has to compute the whole sequence of critical values by backward induction. To do so, the individual gets the alternatives in order and then computes all the critical values by working his/her way from the end of the sequence to the beginning just like we have done above.

2.1.2 The FSS-Search Strategy

The FSS-search strategy introduced by Stigler (1961, 1962) starts off by assuming an unlimited number of alternatives ($i = 1, \ldots, \infty$), each generating a random value (X_i) from the same probability distribution

2.1. Basic Search Models

($f_i(X_i) = f(X_i)$). The values are independent and the marginal costs of going from one alternative to the next are identical ($c_i = c$). This set of assumptions parallels the one we have made in the subsection above.

The FSS-strategy differs from a sequential strategy in the sense that the individual decides about the number of alternatives to investigate a-priorily and chooses the best one from this sample. Therefore, the individual has to determine the gain associated with adding an alternative to the sample and compare it with the cost. The expected minimum value of sampling n alternatives is equal to the expected minimum value in this sample. Since the values are independently and identically distributed, the probability that the minimum of n values is above a value ξ is:

$$\text{Prob}[\min(X_1,\ldots,X_n) > \xi] = [1 - F(\xi)]^n \ .$$

The cumulative density function, $G(\xi; n)$, of the minimum value of n alternatives is therefore

$$G(\xi; n) = \text{Prob}[\min(X_1,\ldots,X_n) \leq \xi] = 1 - [1 - F(\xi)]^n \ .$$

The probability density, $g(\xi; n)$, of the minimum value of n alternatives is obtained by taking the first derivative with respect to ξ:

$$g(\xi; n) = \frac{\partial 1 - [1 - F(\xi)]^n}{\partial \xi} = nf(\xi)[1 - F(\xi)]^{n-1} \ . \tag{2.7}$$

The expected minimum value of a sample of size n can be derived as

$$\begin{aligned}
E[\min(X_1,\ldots,X_n)] &= \int_0^B xg(x; n)\, dx \\
&= \int_0^B xnf(x)[1 - F(x)]^{n-1} \ . \tag{2.8}
\end{aligned}$$

The marginal expected price of increasing sample size can be determined by taking the derivative of (2.8) with respect to n (see McKenna, 1987a, p. 94). This yields

$$R(n) = \int_0^B xf(x)[1 - F(x)]^{n-1}[1 + n\ln(1 - F(x))]\, dx \ . \tag{2.9}$$

This is a concave, non-positive function strictly increasing in n. It converges to zero as n approaches infinity. This means that the searcher can expect to find better prices when he/she investigates a larger number of alternatives; the benefit (in absolute terms) of an extra alternative declines, however, when the sample size increases, and it practically vanishes when the sample size grows very large.

For each additional alternative the searcher has to pay search cost c which are constant and independent of the sample size. Therefore, as long as $c > 0$ the benefit of an extra alternative can compensate the cost only up to a certain sample size. The point where the benefit of the next alternative just compensates the cost of adding it to the sample determines the optimal sample size N in the FSS-search strategy. Since N has to be an integer it is defined by

$$R(N) + c \geq 0 \quad \text{and} \quad R(N+1) + c < 0 \;. \qquad (2.10)$$

2.1.3 Sequential and FSS-Strategy Compared

We can think of the sequential and the FSS-strategy as two alternatives approaches to the search problem, from which the searcher can choose. When neither the values of the alternatives nor the cost of search are influenced by the choice of strategy, the two strategies can be compared directly. As it turns out, in this case the sequential strategy is always superior to the FSS-strategy.

Before we discuss the relationship between the two strategies let us note a basic property of search strategies. Since the aim of any search strategy is to find the *best* alternative, in a minimization problem the total cost – the sum of search cost and the price paid – of any unrestricted search strategy (denote it by S) applied to a specific instance of the search problem cannot be lower than the return of the same search strategy applied to the same instance subject to some restriction R. This is

$$S(\mathbf{x}) \leq S(\mathbf{x}|R) \qquad (2.11)$$

where $\mathbf{x}$ denotes a vector of realizations of X.

The basic argument why the sequential strategy is superior to the FSS-strategy is as follows. We will use the framework of the basic search model that we have discussed above.

When comparing the sequential and the FSS-strategy we may experience three possible constellations:

1. The sequential search strategy stops at alternative N, the last alternative in the FSS-strategy sample. If we denote the length of the sequential search strategy by m, this case is characterized by $m = N$.
2. The sequential search strategy continues beyond alternative N; i.e. $m > N$.
3. The sequential search strategy stops before alternative N; i.e. $m < N$.

2.1. Basic Search Models

In the first case the two strategies obviously give the same result. They both imply search cost of Nc and a price of x_N. Because of the stopping condition of the sequential search strategy x_N is the first alternative falling below the critical value y.

In the second case the FSS-strategy stops before the sequential strategy. None of the alternatives in the sample of FSS-strategy meets the stopping criterion of the sequential strategy. Therefore, we can view the FSS-strategy as a sequential strategy which is restricted to the first N alternatives. We know from equation (2.11) that the return of the restricted strategy cannot exceed that of the unrestricted strategy. Since the sequential strategy continues at least to alternative $N+1$, the sequential strategy is superior to the FSS-strategy in this case.

The most complicated case is the third one. There we have to distinguish two subcases, namely

3.1 alternative m, the one that stops the sequential search strategy, gives the minimum value of all N alternatives in the FSS-search sample.

3.2 there is at least one alternative between $m + 1$ and N providing a lower price than alternative m.

In the first subcase the price paid is the same in both strategies, since in both cases alternative m is selected. However, the search cost of FSS-search is Nc as compared to mc in the sequential strategy. The FSS-strategy search cost exceeds the search cost of the sequential strategy by $(N - m)c$. The second subcase is the only one where the FSS-strategy possibly has lower total cost. The question arises whether it is worthwhile to give up alternative m for the alternative (say m') that provides a lower price, and, if it is, how likely this case is. In a sequential strategy of the standard search model the answer is easy. The expected cost of an unlimited search strategy starting at alternative $m + 1$ is y. Since the price of alternative m is below this threshold – otherwise sequential search would not stop – it is clearly suboptimal to start an unlimited sequential search strategy at this point. Since the actual strategy is limited to $N-m$ alternatives, the threshold is even higher. The probability for such a low price is too low to justify the extra search cost.

Suppose we know that there is an alternative between $m + 1$ and N which provides a lower price. We can then iterate the argument above. If there is only one such alternative, it would be better for the individual to search sequentially until this alternative is found, than to search all $N - m$ alternatives in a FSS-way. This would save the cost for all the alternatives between $m' + 1$ and N. If there is another alternative between $m' + 1$ and N which provides an even lower price, the same argument applies. We can continue in this way until all the alternatives are exhausted. In this last iteration we face a situation like case 1 above, where alternative N provides the maximum value.

So, in the end we cannot reach any final point where the FSS-search strategy is superior to the respective sequential strategy. However, since there are possible situations where the sequential strategy yields lower total cost than the FSS-strategy, we can conclude that the sequential search strategy is superior to the FSS-search strategy.

This argument depends heavily upon the assumption that neither the price of the alternatives nor the search cost are influenced by the choice of strategy. Technically this assumption ensures that the two strategies are comparable. The searcher cannot change the situation by choosing one or the other search strategy. However, in reality this is not always the case. As pointed out by Morgan and Manning (1985) search cost are made up of various components, one of which is the cost of the time it takes to investigate one alternative. If the individual can save on these costs by looking at more than one alternative at a time, it can easily be preferable to pick a bundle of alternatives in a FSS-way, investigate them at once and then decide (in a sequential way) whether to accept the best one of the investigated alternatives or to pick another bundle. The size of the bundle is determined as in the FSS-strategy.

This argument has been used by McKenna (1987a) to formulate a general search model. Since his model combines a number of extensions to the basic search model, we will discuss it in more detail in the next section.

2.2 Extensions of the Basic Search Models

The basic search model that we have discussed in section 2.1 leaves out a number of important aspects.

- In the basic model offers are lost as soon as they are rejected by the searcher. The searcher cannot go back to an earlier investigated alternative and accept it. In the search literature this is known as *recall*. We have ruled it out by assumption.
- We have not taken into account that search takes time and that when the searcher accepts an early alternative in the search sequence he/she can enjoy the utility provided by the product earlier than when an alternative later in the search sequence is accepted. In order to take this into account we would need to discount price offers and search cost according to their position in the search sequence.
- We have neglected that the searcher buys the respective product because of the utility he/she derives from consuming it. Instead we

have assumed the searcher to look for the lowest overall cost. To overcome this deficit we would need to define a utility function and base the searcher's decisions upon utility maximization.
- Besides the choice of a search strategy the searcher may also be able to invest extra resources and choose a higher search intensity. This may lead to more draws per period of time and a better chance of terminating search in a particular interval.
- In a similar way, chances to investigate offers may occur irregularly rather than in regular intervals. This is of particular importance in job-search. The searcher will have to take this uncertainty about arrivals of offers into account in his/her search strategy.
- As pointed out in section 1.3, the assumption of perfect knowledge about the price distribution is difficult to justify on theoretical grounds. A search model where the searcher has limited knowledge about the distribution and improves this knowledge during the search process (*adaptive search*) is theoretically more appealing. As pointed out in section 1.3 the assumption of imperfect information about the distribution introduces a number of interesting elements to the model.

We have omitted these aspects in our discussion of economic search models thus far, because it allowed us to make the fundamental mechanism of search processes more transparent; particularly that part which is most relevant for our discussion of spatial search. Most of the extensions mentioned above add to the complexity of the formulations but do not alter the basic mechanism of the search process.

Nevertheless, we will turn now to discussing the implications of these additional aspects. We will first discuss a search model proposed by McKenna (1987a), which incorporates some of the missing components and also combines sequential and FSS-search aspects. Then we will briefly discuss those aspects that have not been covered until then.

2.2.1 McKenna's General Search Model: Discounting, Utility, and Search Intensity

McKenna (1987a) integrates a considerable number of theoretical developments in the economic search literature in his general model. In particular he takes into account (1) a utility function, (2) discounting, (3) search intensity, and (4) to some extent bridges the gap between sequential and FSS-search. McKenna (1987a) does not allow for imperfect information about the distribution in his model, although he briefly discusses adaptive search. From this discussion he concludes: "By and large the additional complexity of adaptive search models has not been justified by the additional insights they offer" (McKenna, 1987a, p. 104). Taking into account our discussion in section 1.3 and the developments in the economics of information, this statement in this general form seems exaggerated to us. In a context like ours, however, the complexity of adaptive search would make the more general problem of spatial search practically unmanageable.

Drawing heavily from Morgan and Manning (1985), McKenna starts by dividing the searcher's time horizon into a number of time periods $t = (0, \ldots, T)$. In each period, the searcher may draw n_t observations at cost $c(n_t)$ from the distribution. When the first acceptable offer is observed, the searcher accepts it and terminates search. The searcher's problem is to define the optimal sample size, n_t^*, and the set of acceptable offers, $\mathcal{A}_t$, for each time period.

Price offers are independent identically distributed random variables, X, with density function f and cumulative density function F perfectly known to the searcher. Implicitly it is assumed that the decisions about accepting a price offer or continuing search are made at the end of the periods. Suppose that during period t the searcher has drawn n_t^* price offers, the smallest one of which is $\hat{x}_t$. When the searcher buys the product at this price and optimizes his/her expenditures, he/she reaches a utility level of $U_t(\hat{x}_t)$. The utility the searcher can expect from continuing search past period t is written $S_{t+1}(n_{t+1}^*)$. Therefore, the maximum utility the searcher can derive at this point in the search process is

$$V_t(\hat{x}_t) = \max\{U_t(\hat{x}_t), S_{t+1}(n_{t+1}^*)\} \ . \tag{2.12}$$

Since $\hat{x}_t$ is a price, U_t is actually an indirect utility function. It is derived from the direct utility function by substituting the demand functions for the quantities of goods (see e.g., Deaton and Muellbauer, 1980; Maier and Weiss, 1990). In this way the indirect utility function describes which utility can be achieved with a given level of income and price vector. To be precise we would need to write the indirect utility function as $U_t(\hat{x}_t; y, \boldsymbol{p})$ to express its dependence upon income (y) and all the other prices ($\boldsymbol{p}$). Since income and the other prices are assumed to be given and are beyond the scope of the discussion, we follow McKenna (1987a) in using the abbreviated notation.

The fact that U_t is an indirect utility function and $\hat{x}_t$ is a price immediately leads to

$$\frac{\partial U_t}{\partial \hat{x}_t} < 0 \ . \tag{2.13}$$

Since the searcher would prefer getting the respective good free rather than having to search for it, i.e. $U_t(0) > S_{t+1}(n_{t+1}^*)$ and the utility of

2.2. Extensions of the Basic Search Models

continued search does not depend upon $\hat{x}_t$ there must exist a price $\hat{x}_t^*$ for which the searcher is indifferent between continuing search and accepting the price:

$$U_t(\hat{x}_t^*) = S_{t+1}(n_{t+1}^*) \; . \tag{2.14}$$

The price $\hat{x}_t^*$ represents the reservation price in this model. It separates the acceptable from the unacceptable prices. The set of acceptable prices at time period t is therefore

$$\mathcal{A}_t = \{\hat{x}_t | \hat{x}_t \leq \hat{x}_t^*\} \; . \tag{2.15}$$

Consequently, at the end of each period the searcher will accept $\hat{x}_t$ and terminate search if $\hat{x}_t \in \mathcal{A}_t$, and reject $\hat{x}_t$ and search again if $\hat{x}_t \notin \mathcal{A}_t$. In this way the searcher determines whether to search for another period or not.

This determines the searcher's decision between periods. It parallels the situation of a sequential search process. The problem of how many observations the searcher will investigate during one period, is structurally equivalent to the FSS-search. We will turn to this point now.

During the period the searcher is assumed to sample the observations, select the best one from the sample, and proceed in an optimal way by either accepting it or rejecting it. We have determined the maximum utility the searcher can obtain from a specific observation in (2.12). The probability for drawing an observation with a specific value depends upon the number of times the searcher draws. McKenna (1987a, p. 93) therefore defines $S_t(n_t)$, the utility the searcher can expect from searching in the next period, as

$$S_t(n_t) = \bar{u} - c(n_t) + \beta \int_0^B V_t(x) \phi(x|n_t) \, dx \; , \tag{2.16}$$

where $\bar{u}$ is a 'fall-back' utility which the searcher incurs from searching, $c(n_t)$ is search cost measured in utility units[4], and $\beta = 1/(1+r)$ is the discount factor with r being an interest rate or discount rate. ϕ is the probability density function of the minimum price that can be found in a sample of size n_t. It depends upon the distribution of price offers through (see also (2.7))

$$\phi(x|n) = n f(x)[1 - F(x)]^{n-1} \; . \tag{2.17}$$

---

[4]Underlying this formulation is the assumption that the utility function is separable in search cost and price. In a more general formulation search cost would need to be included as an argument into the utility function (see, e.g., Hall et al., 1979).

We can determine the optimal sample size, n_t^*, as before by setting the partial derivative of $S_t(n_t)$ with respect to n_t equal to zero. This yields

$$c'(\hat{n}_t) = \beta \int_0^B V_t(x) f(x) [1 - F(x)]^{\hat{n}_t - 1} [1 + \hat{n}_t \ln(1 - F(x))] \, dx \, , \qquad (2.18)$$

with $c'(\hat{n}_t)$ being the partial derivative of $c(n_t)$ with respect to n_t evaluated at $\hat{n}_t$.

The optimal sample size in period t is just the integer part of $\hat{n}_t$. It represents the intensity with which the searcher will search during the time period. As shown by Gal et al. (1981) the search intensity increases from period to period when the number of search periods is limited. Conditions (2.18) and (2.15) together determine the searcher's optimal behavior in McKenna's general search model.

We can use equations (2.12), (2.14), and (2.16) defined for the optimal sample size to derive a very familiar expression about the utility in the different stages of the search process[5] (Φ represents the cumulative density function corresponding to ϕ):

$$U_{t-1}(\hat{x}_{t-1}^*) = \bar{u} - c(n_t^*) + \beta \int_0^{\hat{x}_t^*} U_t(Y) \phi(Y|n_t^*) \, dY + \beta U(\hat{x}_t^*)[1 - \Phi(\hat{x}_t^*|n_t^*)] \, . \qquad (2.19)$$

This equation is quite similar to (2.2). The major difference arises from the fact that now we are maximizing utility while (2.2) was based on minimizing cost. The introduction of a fallback utility and a more general cost function results in a slightly more complex cost component. Because of discounting the utility expectations are weighted by the discount factor β. The most important difference lies in the fact that the price offer distribution depends upon n_t^*, the number of offers the searcher decides to draw in this period. Behaviorally, the searcher has some control over the price offer distribution in McKenna's model. By choosing the sample size the searcher adjusts the price offer distribution according to his/her preferences. However, once n_t^* is determined, (2.19) does not differ fundamentally from the much simpler equation (2.2).

Morgan and Manning (1985) argue that this general model which combines interperiod sequential search and intraperiod FSS-search, is superior to both the sequential and the FSS-search strategy. Both can be viewed as constrained versions of the general model. The sequential search model is equivalent to the general model where the searcher is allowed to search

---

[5] We substitute (2.14) into (2.12). The resulting equation and (2.14) are substituted into (2.16) with the indices adjusted properly. After simplifying the integral we get (2.19).

only one alternative per period. The FSS-search model, on the other hand, can be derived from the general model by restricting the searcher to only one time period.

The crucial element in this argument and in the formulation of the general model as a whole lies in the idea of search periods. Since FSS-search occurs only within the search periods, when we make them shorter and shorter the FSS-search component will finally disappear. Only when there are scale effects, entry barriers etc. in the search cost[6], the concept of search periods makes sense theoretically. When the search cost, i.e. $\bar{u} - c(n_t^*)$, are linear homogenous in sample size, the searcher would be better off to search each alternative sequentially than to apply the two-step decision of the McKenna model.

The model of McKenna (1987a) introduced a number of the elements that we have identified to be missing from the basic search model of section 2.1: discounting, utility maximization, search intensity. However, as we have seen above, while these additions add parameters to the model, the basic structure of a search process is captured by the basic search model as we have described it in section 2.1. We feel confident that by basing our discussion of spatial search on the basic search model of section 2.1 we do not leave out any essential elements as far as the components taken into account by McKenna (1987a) are concerned.

2.2.2 Other Extensions of the Standard Economic Search Model

Recall

When the searcher can go back in the search sequence and accept an offer that he/she has rejected before, we say that the search process allows for *recall*. When all rejected alternatives remain available throughout the search process, there is *full recall*; with *partial recall* alternatives might not be available any more when the searcher returns to them.

The implications of allowing for recall in a search model depend very much on the original structure of the model. In the standard search model of economics as we have discussed it above – identical distributions and search cost, infinite number of alternatives – allowing for recall does not

---

[6]Morgan and Manning (1985) use a Ph.D. graduate seeking an academic post, and three sisters trying to get a house built in a limited period of time for illustrating their model. In both cases the choice process is characterized by a considerable time lag between the searcher's initiative to investigate an alternative and when they receive the offer (for details see Manning and Morgan, 1985, p. 923-925).

change the model at all. The optimizing searcher will never return to a previously rejected alternative. The reason for this is simple: The searcher will recall a previously rejected alternative only when its value is better than what he/she can expect from continued search. The expected value of continued search, however, is constant throughout the search process under the assumptions of the standard search model. This means that the searcher does not alter his/her level of aspiration. Therefore, an alternative which was unacceptable when it was investigated must remain unacceptable throughout the search process and will never be recalled.

Under less restrictive assumptions, however, the recall option proves to be of great importance. It provides a fallback option for the searcher which limits his/her risk. Unfortunately, this makes the formal structure of the search process considerably more complicated. Mainly because the searcher now also looks back at the alternatives he/she has investigated thus far.

Let us use the standard search model with a restricted number of alternatives[7] to illustrate this point. At each decision point the searcher now has three option: (1) accept the alternative just drawn, (2) reject the alternative and continue searching, (3) reject the alternative, quit searching, and recall the best one of the earlier alternatives. Define by λ_i the best one of the first i alternatives the searcher has investigated. In the case of a minimization problem λ_i is defined as

$$\lambda_i = \min(x_1, x_2, \ldots, x_{i-1}) \ . \qquad (2.20)$$

After having rejected alternative $i-1$ the searcher expects continued search to cost

$$\begin{aligned} y_{i-1} &= c_i + E[\min(X_i, y_i, \lambda_i)] \\ &= c_i + \int_0^{\min(y_i,\lambda_i)} x f(x)\, dx + \int_{\min(y_i,\lambda i)}^{B} \min(y_i, \lambda_i) f(x)\, dx \\ &= c_i + \int_0^{\min(y_i,\lambda_i)} x f(x)\, dx + \min(y_i, \lambda_i)\left[1 - F(\min(y_i, \lambda_i))\right] \ . \end{aligned}$$
$$(2.21)$$

Note that λ_i represents the lowest one of all the prices observed thus far. These prices are *realizations* of the random variable X. Since in the case of recall all y depend upon the respective λ, the searcher's search strategy depends upon the previously observed prices. When the searcher has observed only high prices thus far, he/she will be less selective in the following step of the search procedure than when he/she has observed at

---

[7]Alternatives $i = 1, \ldots, n$ with $F_i = F$ and $c_i = c$.

least one almost acceptable price. A specific price observed at i may be acceptable in the first case and unacceptable in the second.

In order to determine the optimal search strategy, i.e., to set the sequence of reservation prices, the searcher not only has to work his/her way through the search sequence by backward induction. He/she also has to anticipate all the possible sequences of price observations, how they affect λ, and what their impact is upon the reservation prices. This makes the search problem with recall also much more cumbersome for the optimizing decision maker. Analytically it is the dependence upon realizations of random variables that complicates the task.

Adaptive Search

Adaptive search causes similar conceptual problems than recall. When the searcher has only imperfect information about the price distribution, he/she will use the observations drawn to improve the knowledge about the price distribution. The searcher's prior understanding of the price distribution has to be combined with the evidence from the observations to form a posterior distribution. DeGroot (1970) discusses this information updating procedure in detail.

The aspect that leads to similar problems than with recall is that the searcher's knowledge during the search process depends upon the values of the alternatives he/she has investigated so far. Again, this makes the reservation prices dependent upon the realizations of X. In some circumstances it might even be that no reservation price[8] exists at all (for an example see Rothschild, 1974).

We have already discussed some important aspects of adaptive search in chapter 1. We have noted that adaptive search allows for a richer set of strategies than search with perfect information about the distribution. The searcher may employ different information activities in order to improve his/her knowledge about the distribution before investing into search. Differences in prior believes between searchers, due to their different experience, social background, education etc., will carry over into information gathering and search activities.

Although both, recall and imperfect information about the distribution, are of great importance in many types of search processes, we will not pursue these directions any further. The reason is the conceptual complications that go along with both types of extensions. Both lead to a dependence of the optimal search strategy upon the values of previous observations. In the spatial context, where search cost may change when

---

[8]In the sense that all prices lower or equal are acceptable, all prices higher unacceptable.

the searcher moves through space (see section 4), this causes particular problems for the recall option. The searcher will not only have to keep track of the best previously observed alternatives, he/she will also have to reevaluate these alternatives after each step because with the changing search cost their ranking may change. In any case, in order to be able to derive any meaningful results in our modeling effort, we feel that this simplification is justified. We are ready to admit, however, that restricting recall and assuming the searcher has perfect knowledge of the price offer distribution are the two most limiting assumption for our treatment of spatial search.

2.3 Search Based Markets

The search model as we have discussed it until now takes into account only one side of the market. The agents on either the supply side (e.g., job search) or the demand side (e.g., shopping) of the market engages in this fairly sophisticated procedure for identifying an acceptable offer for a market transaction. As has been shown before, this behavior can be derived from the standard assumptions about the motives of economic agents.

The respective other side of the market appears to be quite unsophisticated by comparison. According to the basic model structure firms looking for workers or shop owners trying to sell their products just generate one wage or price offer after another at random. They appear to act just like random number generators. There seems to be no economic incentive behind their behavior.

However, not all price offers[9] really make sense for the supplier. When we assume that the customer knows the supplier's wage offer distribution perfectly, the supplier should have at least the same level of knowledge. But when he does and also knows search cost, he/she can calculate the consumer's reservation price, and knows that asking any price above that will not lead to a market transaction. At the same time, when demand is perfectly inelastic below the reservation price as it usually is assumed to be in search models, the supplier must realize that any price below the reservation price will reduce his/her profits, since the consumer is willing to buy the respective product at the reservation price. The supplier would avoid any price offer below the reservation price, and the price offer distribution would collapse to a point (see also Rothschild, 1973, p. 1288f;

---

[9]We will again argue in terms of price offers and a minimization problem at the side of the searcher. The basic arguments hold for maximization problems (e.g., job search) with the appropriate adaptions.

2.3. Search Based Markets

Fisher, 1970; Diamond, 1971; Hey, 1974). In the light of this argument, a price offer distribution appears to be only a temporary phenomenon that would be eliminated by the search process it generates.

"The short answer to the question of what is required to sustain price dispersion appears to be some form of heterogeneity" (McKenna, 1987b, p. 115). Reinganum (1979), for example, assumes that firms differ in their constant marginal cost, which follow a specific continuous and differentiable distribution. Consumers, on the other hand, are homogeneous and cannot distinguish firms according to their marginal cost. Each firm derives its optimal price from maximizing its expected profits, taking into account that consumers will not buy above their reservation price. This leads to a search based equilibrium which is characterized by a non-degenerate price distribution. This distribution generates no price offers above the consumers' reservation price. The distribution below the reservation price originates from the heterogeneity of the firms and the elasticity of the consumers' demand: Since consumers buy more when the price is lower, those firms whose marginal cost are low enough can raise their profits by charging lower prices. Their profit maximizing price will be below the consumers' reservation price.

Axell (1977) develops a model with heterogeneous consumers. "Briefly, it is shown that a distribution of search costs induces a distribution of reservation prices which in turn generates a distribution of price offers" (McKenna, 1987b, p. 118). Carlson and McAfee (1983) and MacMinn (1980) combine heterogeneity on both sides of the market to derive an equilibrium with price dispersion.

All these contributions assume heterogeneity between the different agents of at least one size of the market. Salop (1977) shows that it may even be advantageous for the single firm to generate a price dispersion when consumers are heterogenous. He calls this the "noisy monopolist". "The very presence of dispersion both splits the market and charges a higher purchase price to the submarket of inefficient searchers" (Salop, 1977, p. 393).

2.4 Summary

In this chapter we have reviewed the main aspects of the standard search theory of Economics. Since search theory is well developed in Economics and has been applied to a number of economic questions, in this chapter we wanted to relate our discussion of spatial search to this extensive body of literature. Its main distinction with respect to our topic in this book is that economic search theory does not take into account the spatial distribution of alternatives. Spatial search can be viewed as an economic search model with this spatial component added.

In section 2.1 we present the basic search models developed in Economics. The focus is on the sequential search model, where the searcher draws one offer after another and decides after each draw whether to accept or reject this offer. Our presentation of the sequential search model is more general than what is often found in Economics in the sense that we allow for differences in search costs and in the distribution function. The model with identical search costs and distribution functions we call "standard search model". It is discussed as a special case. In our discussion of the sequential search model in section 2.1 we present different formulations of the model and discuss marginal changes of model parameters. The results we derive here will prove useful in later chapters.

An interesting variation of the economic search model is fixed sample size search. In this model version the searcher decides about how many alternatives to investigate and later selects the best one therefrom. The fixed sample size search model is of less relevance for our discussion of spatial search because its underlying strategy proves to be suboptimal under our usual set of assumptions. This is demonstrated in subsection 2.1.3 where we compare the two search strategies.

Section 2.2 is devoted to discussing extensions of the basic search models. First, we present a search model by McKenna which incorporates discounting, allows for a utility function, and lets the searcher adjust search intensity. Other possible extensions of the basic search model – recall and adaptive search – are discussed in subsection 2.2.2.

Section 2.3 provides a brief overview of models of search based markets. Because of the complexity introduced by the spatial component we will not be able to derive results for spatial search based market processes in the later chapters. Therefore, we have kept this discussion here quite brief.

Chapter 3

Prerequisites: Graphs, Routes, and Computational Complexity

Since the spatial search problem explicitly deals with alternatives distributed in two-dimensional space, we need a way to characterize the spatial layout of the problem. This links our problem to graph theory and the related theories of optimal routing and computational complexity. In this chapter we do not intend to provide a comprehensive introduction to any of these theories (for such an introduction see e.g. Gibbons, 1985; Parker and Rardin, 1988; Bondy and Murty, 1976). We will discuss only those aspects of these theories that are essential for our discussion of the spatial search problem.

3.1 Graphs

The alternatives of the spatial search problem and the links connecting them can be interpreted as *vertices* and *edges* of a *graph*. Since we allow the searcher to search each alternative only once, we can restrict our discussion to *finite, simple graphs*, i.e. graphs with a finite number of vertices and edges and without loops and multiple edges (see sections 4.3 and 4.4). For the spatial structure underlying the spatial search problem we will usually consider only undirected graphs. In this way, we generally exclude "one-way-streets". At few points of our discussion we will also need directed graphs, so-called *digraphs*. The connections between their vertices are directed and called *arcs*.

We will denote the vertices in the graph by the small letter v and a subscript (v_1, v_2, v_3, ...). In the context of the spatial search problem the vertices of the graph are the points where the searcher draws from the

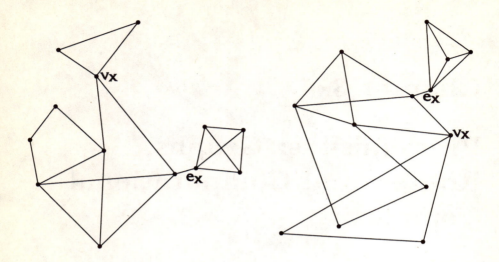

Figure 3.1: Example of a Graph

distribution and decides about stopping or continuing the search. The edges of the graph are indicated by e and a subscript (e_1, e_2, e_3, ...), the arcs of a digraph by a and a subscript (a_1, a_2, a_3, ...). In our case edges and arcs are important only because of the costs involved in traveling them. Therefore, we usually refer directly to the costs rather than to the edges. In graph theory, what constitutes the costs in our case is usually referred to as *weights* of the graph. According to the standard practice of graph theory we denote a graph by the capital letter G with reference to its vertices and edges, i.e. $G(V, E)$. Similarly, a digraph is denoted by $D(V, A)$.

A graph[1] is defined by its set of vertices and its set of edges. It is not a geometrical concept. Therefore, we may draw the same graph in many different ways. Whatever geometrical figures we get, whenever V and E are identical, they represent the same graph. Such geometrical figures are said to be *isomorphic*.

Figure 3.1 illustrates this point. Although they look quite differently, the two shapes in figure 3.1 represent the same graph, because they contain

---

[1]Because of the limited relevance digraphs have in our case, the following definitions and discussions concentrate only on graphs. Most definitions apply to digraphs as well (for more details see, e.g. Wilson and Watkins, 1990). We will refer to only those aspects of digraphs that are of particular importance for our discussion.

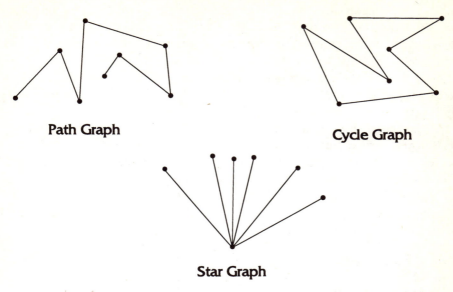

Figure 3.2: Special Graphs

the same vertices and the same connections between them (edges). Vertex v_x and edge e_x are of a type which is of particular importance for our problem. They are characterized by the fact, that if we remove any of them we will disconnect the graph. We refer to such a vertex as an *articulation point*. An edge, the removal of which will disconnect the graph, is called a *cut edge*. A graph with one or more articulation points (the endpoints of a cut-edge are articulation points) is called a *separable graph*. As we will see in chapter 5 separability has implications for the complexity of a spatial search problem.

Since our main concern is the search process we only need to consider *connected* graphs, i.e. graphs where each vertex is directly or indirectly connected to every other vertex. An important special case is that of a *complete graph*. In such a graph each vertex is directly connected to every other vertex. In a *complete digraph* every vertex is connected to every other vertex by a pair of arcs with opposite directions.

Special Graphs

The following graphs will be of particular importance in our discussion of the spatial search problem:

A *path graph* is defined as a connected graph whose vertices are connected to at most two other vertices, and where two of the vertices are connected to only one other vertex. Because of this definition, a path graph is isomorphic to a straight line on which the vertices are lined up, just like pearls on a string. Because we require two of the vertices to be connected to only one other vertex, the string has two clearly defined endpoints.

A *cycle graph* is a graph whose vertices are connected to exactly two other vertices. The cycle graph is isomorphic to a circle. We can get from a path graph to a circle graph by connecting its endpoints.

A *star graph* is a graph that has one vertex which is connected to every other vertex, but none of the other vertices are connected among each other. The star graph is isomorphic to a star-like figure, where all other vertices are surrounding a central vertex.

Figure 3.2 shows a path graph, a cycle graph, and a star graph. Note, that the graphs are only *isomorphic* to the shapes mentioned above.

3.2 Routes

We define a *route* as an ordered sequence of connected vertices in the graph defining the spatial search problem[2]. In this way a route defines a sequence of alternatives through which the searcher may proceed. In graph theory this is usually called a *path*, or, if closed, a *cycle*. Because of the close relationship of the spatial search problem to *routing problems* we prefer to use the term route.

We denote routes by capital letters $(A, B, C, \ldots)$. The *size* of a route – written $|A|$ – is defined by the number of alternatives in the route. The *length* of a route is defined as the sum of edge-weights. We write the length of route R as $l(R)$. Besides the absolute reference described above we will also refer to vertices according to their relative position in a route. This position is indicated by numbers in square brackets. So, $A[1]$ refers to the first alternative in route A, $A[2]$ to the second, and so on. Consider the following two routes, both consisting of the same five alternatives:

$$A = (v_1, v_2, v_3, v_4, v_5) \qquad B = (v_3, v_1, v_2, v_4, v_5)$$

Alternative v_1 is the first alternative in route A, but the second alternative in route B. So, we can refer to it as $A[1]$ or $B[2]$.

A route which connects all available alternatives is called a *complete route*. If the end-point is identical to the starting point we call it a *closed route*. Closed complete routes will play a prominent role in our discussion. When we perform all the permutations of alternatives in a given graph we

---

[2]Because we can restrict ourselves to simple graphs we do not need to specify the edges of a route.

3.2. Routes

derive the *set of all complete closed routes* through this graph. We refer to this set as $\mathcal{R}$.

When a closed complete route visits each vertex exactly once, it is called a *Hamiltonian route*. We refer to a graph $G(V, E)$ for which a Hamiltonian route exists as a *Hamiltonian graph*. The problem of determining whether or not a particular graph is Hamiltonian is known to be particularly complex. We will return to this point in the following section.

To each route we usually have a number of *partial routes* and *subroutes*. A partial route of a route is one, where one or more alternatives of the original route are skipped. For example, route $C = (v_1, v_3)$ is a partial route of route A. A subroute of a route is one, where alternatives are discarded from the beginning and/or the end of the route but not from within the sequence forming the subroute. So, each subroute is always a partial route, but not vice versa. For example, route C is not a subroute of A, whereas route $A_1 = (v_2, v_3, v_4, v_5)$ is both a subroute and a partial route of A.

Because of our focus on search problems, route A_1 is an important special case of a subroute. It is the subroute we get when discarding the first alternative from route A. We will always indicate such subroutes by a subscript. More generally, R_n is the route we get when we discard the first n alternatives from route R. To each such route there exists a *complementary subroute*, $\bar{R}_n$, which is just the first n alternatives of route R. We will write the relationship between R, R_n and $\bar{R}_n$ as

$$\bar{R}_n = R - R_n \qquad \text{and} \qquad R = R_n + \bar{R}_n .$$

As a convention, a subroute always ends with a vertex. So, if we cut a route R between vertex $R[i]$ and $R[i+1]$, the edge connecting the two vertices belongs to route R_i, not to $\bar{R}_i$. The reason for this convention is that the individual will travel to an alternative (and bear the respective costs) only when he/she plans to search this alternative. Therefore, it is most meaningful to keep an edge and the vertex it leads to together and break up a route immediately after the vertex. In our discussion of the spatial search problem we usually require the searcher to return to the home location after terminating search. In this case he/she follows a subroute and then returns home. We will call such a route a *closed subroute*. It can be thought of as a subroute concatenated with the trip home.

Occasionally we will also need *inverse routes*, written R^{-1}. An inverse route is the original route in inverse sequence. For example, $A^{-1} = (v_5, v_4, v_3, v_2, v_1)$.

3.3 Computational Complexity

The problem of finding routes with specific characteristics through a graph has been an important stimulus for the development of complexity theory. It is the aim of complexity theory to categorize problems according to their computational complexity, which means according to their general tractability. Routing problems like the "Traveling Salesman Problem", the "Postman's Problem" or the "Shortest Path Problem" have played an important role, often because of their unexpected level of complexity. While the "Shortest Path Problem", the problem of finding the shortest route between any two vertices in a graph, is fairly easy and well solved, for example, the "Traveling Salesman Problem", the problem of finding the shortest complete, closed route through a graph, belongs to a group of problems which "continue to frustrate researchers after two centuries of attention" (Parker and Rardin, 1988, p. 3). We will introduce those fundamental aspects of complexity theory which are of relevance for our discussion of the spatial search problem.

As written by Parker and Rardin (1988, p. 12) "complexity theory seeks to classify problems in terms of the mathematical order of the computational resources required to solve the problem via digital computer algorithms." As every programmer knows, solving a problem with a computer program requires computer time as well as computer memory, where there is often a tradeoff between the two. Since we are only concerned with the fundamentals of complexity theory we will consider time requirements only. So, when we write about complexity we always mean *time-complexity*.

The complexity of an algorithm is simply defined as "the number of computational steps that is takes to transform the input data to the result of the computation" (Gibbons, 1985, p. 8f). The computing time for solving a problem is usually some function of the size of that problem, in a routing problem of the size of the graph. Of course, computer time requirements may also depend upon the structure of a specific problem, i.e. the structure of the input data. Because of its structural properties one instance of a problem may require much less computer time than another instance of the same problem even if it is of exactly the same size. For example, the performance of some sorting algorithms depends heavily on whether the input data come randomly or are already in some order. Complexity theory is usually interested in the worst-case behavior of an algorithm. Thus it tries to find an upper bound for the time requirements of an algorithm.

We can write the time requirement – complexity – of an algorithm as a function of problem size. If we denote the problem size as n, the complexity-function of an algorithm may be

$$C(n) = 15 + 0.2n + 0.001n^2 \ . \tag{3.1}$$

The computer program for this algorithm may contain two nested loops, each running from 1 to n.

The *order* of the complexity function is an important element in complexity theory. We say that two functions F and G whose domain is the natural numbers are of the same order if

$$F(n) \leq JG(n) \tag{3.2}$$

for all $n > n_0$, where J and n_0 are two positive constants, and also

$$G(n) \leq KF(n)$$

for all $n > m_0$, where K and m_0 are again two positive constants. If only (3.2) holds, F is of lower order than G.

If the function consists of a sum of terms, like equation (3.1), low order terms can be ignored in determining the overall order. It is convenient to describe the order of a function in terms of the simplest representative function. So, (3.1) is of order n^2, the order of its highest order term. Formally we write this as: $15 + 0.2n + 0.001n^2$ is $O(n^2)$.

The order of the complexity-function provides an ordering of the complexity of different algorithms. Quite clearly

$$O(n) < O(n^2) < O(n^3) < \ldots \ .$$

More interestingly, it can be shown (see, e.g. Gibbons, 1985, p. 10) that a term like m^n, with m being any positive constant, is always of higher order than *any* polynomial. Thus, we have

$$O(n^k) < O(m^n) \tag{3.3}$$

with k and m being any positive constants. Similarly, we can show that

$$O(m^n) < O(n!) \ . \tag{3.4}$$

Figure 3.3 graphs the relationship between problem size and computer-time for problems of different order. As we see, for very small numbers of n the computational requirements are quite similar. From a certain point on, the graph of $n!$ grows much more than any other graph. We had to truncate this graph at $n = 7$ in order to keep the graph at a scale where we can still see the other graphs. At $n = 11$ the graph of $n!$ reaches a value of almost 40 million whereas 11^3 is only 1331. The above

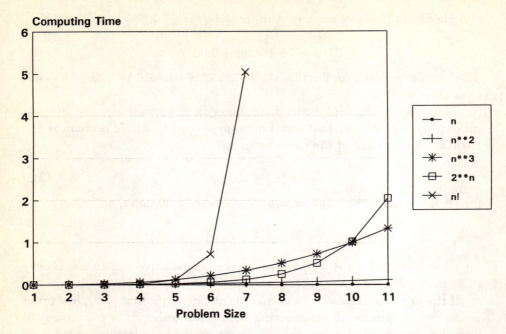

Figure 3.3: Time Complexity for Problems of Different Order and Size

mentioned definition of time complexity tells us that this gap will become even more pronounced as n increases. A similar argument can be made for the relationship between 2^n and n^3.

Relationships (3.3) and (3.4) show that from a certain problem size on, problems that are of $O(m^n)$ or $O(n!)$ become much more complex than any problem of any polynomial order. Moreover, this difference in complexity increases at an increasing rate as problem size grows. This notion has led to a fundamental distinction in complexity theory and to a classification of problems we will discuss in the sequel. An algorithm is said to be *efficient* when its complexity function is of $O(n^k)$ (polynomial order), where k is *any* positive constant.

3.3.1 Types of Problems

While our main focus is on *optimization problem*, complexity theory usually deals with *decision problems*. In an optimization problem we are searching for some optimum strategy, optimum route, etc. In a decision problem, on the other hand, we are always expecting an answer of *yes* or *no*. However, the two types are closely related and to each optimization problem we can formulate an analogous decision problem. We will illustrate this point by use of the Traveling Salesman Problem (see Parker and Rardin, 1988, p. 23f). Formulated as an optimization problem the Traveling Salesman Problem is:

> Given a graph $G(V, E)$ with weights w_{ij} for each vertex pair v_i and v_j find the complete closed route in G with minimum length (sum of weights).

The analogous decision problem to the Traveling Salesman Problem is:

> Given a graph $G(V, E)$ with weights w_{ij} for each vertex pair v_i and v_j and W, does there exist a complete closed route in G with length no greater than W?

"In general, we convert optimization problems to their decision problem counterpart by posing the question of whether there is a feasible solution to a given problem having objective function value equal or superior to a specifies threshold" (Parker and Rardin, 1988, p. 24).

The order of the complexity-function is an important criterion for classifying decision problems. Problems admitting algorithms of polynomial time complexity are said to belong to the class P. It is the class of problems that can be solved by an efficient algorithm even in the worst case. Another class, which contains the class P as a sub-class, is the class of *non-deterministic polynomial* problems; class *NP* for short. Problems of this class can be solved by total enumeration of all possible solutions, where for each possible solution we can determine in polynomial time whether it solves the decision problem or not. Looping over all possible solutions, however, may not be possible in polynomial time. So, these problems are easy to verify, but not necessarily easy to solve. Figure 3.4 illustrates this situation in a Pascal-like algorithm. The algorithm consists of a loop over All-Possible-Solutions which passes each possible solution on to the function (Check). This function determines *in polynomial time* whether the candidate solution really solves the decision problem or not. If it does, the algorithm terminates and passes the answer (*yes* in this case) on to the calling program. If no solution exists the algorithm exhausts all possible solutions and terminates with the answer *no*.

The potential problem with decision problems in class *NP* lies in the loop over All-Possible-Solutions. Only when the number of possible solutions increases polynomially with problem size, the whole algorithm is of polynomial order. In this case, the problem belongs to the class P. If the number of possible solutions increases with $n!$, for example, the algorithm in figure 3.4 is *not* of polynomial order, i.e. the problem cannot be solved efficiently with this algorithm (although there might be another algorithm for this problem that is efficient).

```
Function Solution-to-NP-Problem-Exists : exists;
begin
  for Possible-Solution over All-Possible-Solutions do
    begin
      Problem-solved := Check(Possible-Solution);
      if Problem-solved goto Solved
    end; {endfor}
  Solved:
  exists := Problem-solved;
end;
```

Figure 3.4: An Algorithm Solving Problems from Class *NP*

Whether $P = NP$ is an unresolved question. However, the theory has been able to identify another class of problems, which is of particular importance in our context. They are called *NP-complete* and "form an equivalence class of what might be considered the most difficult problems in *NP*" (Gibbons, 1985, p. 223). A problem is *NP-complete* if

1. it belongs to the class *NP*, and
2. every problem in *NP* polynomially reduces to this problem.

Parker and Rardin (1988, p. 19) define polynomial reduction in the following way: "Problem (P) *polynomially reduces* to problem (P') if a polynomial time algorithm for (P') would imply a polynomial time algorithm for (P)". Or, formulated in more practical terms, there exists an efficiently computable function which relates problem (P) to problem (P') in such a way that the answer to problem (P) is *yes* if and only if the answer to problem (P') is *yes*.

The class of *NP-complete* problems is very important. Because of the fact that every problem in *NP* polynomially reduces to any of its members, if we were able to find an efficient algorithm for just one *NP-complete* problem we had derived efficient algorithms for *all* problems in the class *NP*. At the same time we had demonstrated that P actually equals NP.

Once we know a fair number of *NP-complete* problems, as we do now, it becomes fairly easy to add problems to the class. We only need to prove (1) that the new problem belongs to *NP* and (2) that *one* of the problems known to be *NP-complete* polynomially reduces to the new problem. This second step is sufficient since we already know that every problem in *NP* polynomially reduces to this known *NP-complete* problem.

This fascinating set of properties of the class of *NP-complete* problems has a disturbing implication. Taking into account that Garey and Johnson (1979), for example, list over 300 *NP-complete* problems chances are low that efficient algorithms exist for *NP-complete* problems. Although until now nobody has been able to prove the non-existence of such an algorithm, complexity theory strongly supports the conjecture that efficient algorithms for solving *NP-complete* problems do not exist.

It is important to note, however, that this theoretical "result" in its full severity applies only to the general case. It means that *NP-complete* problems are too complex to allow for an algorithm which solves every instance of the problem with an acceptable time horizon. However, small problems may be tractable even with an inefficient algorithm simply because of their small scale. If we accept to stay with small scale problems, even *NP-complete* problems can be quite tractable. Secondly, it might be possible to impose some restrictions upon the general problem which simplify it such that this special case can be solved by an efficient algorithm. Thirdly, we may try to come up with approximate solutions. This strategy is of particular importance in the context of economic optimization problems since it allows us to derive "acceptable" results. If we can derive such a result efficiently and can be sure that it is not too far from the optimum, this strategy might be economically optimal in the sense that the gain of moving from the acceptable to the optimal result is small in comparison with the resources it requires. In the context of the spatial search problem we will come back to these arguments in chapter 5.

3.3.2 The Traveling Salesman Problem

The Traveling Salesman Problem (TSP) which we have already mentioned a few times above and defined on page 51 is probably the most prominent unsolved problem in mathematics and computer sciences. Its history goes back to work by Euler and by Vandermonde in the 18th century (for an overview of the history of the TSP see Hoffman and Wolfe, 1985). The importance of the TSP in our context stems from its close relationship with the spatial search problem. We will discuss this relationship in chapter 4.

The TSP derives its attractivity mainly from the gap between its "simplicity of statement and difficulty of solution" (Garfinkel, 1985, p. 17). The problem is easy to understand and quite realistic. It does not require a weird mathematical mind to come up with the problem of finding the shortest route through a given number of points in space. Postmen, garbage collectors, the transport industry are dealing with problems of this type on an everyday basis. Robots and computer-aided machinery usually combine a number of operations and can work more efficiently when they do them with minimum movements. In structural terms the TSP is equivalent to a large number of other practical problems. Many examples

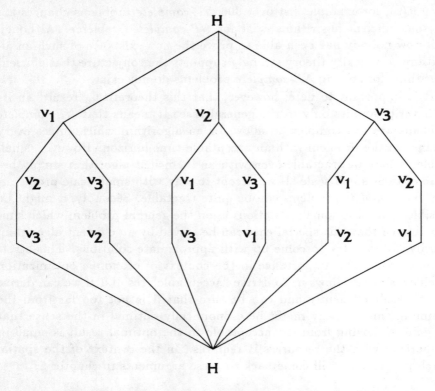

Figure 3.5: The Structure of the Traveling Salesman Problem

can be found in the literature, some of which seem quite unrelated to the TSP at first sight (see e.g. Garfinkel, 1985).

As proved by Garey and Johnson (1979) the TSP belongs to the class of *NP-complete* problems. This implies that until today no efficient algorithm exists for solving the TSP in its general form (for a discussion of well-solved special cases see Gilmore et al., 1985). The complexity of the TSP derives from the necessity to check every possible solution (full enumeration, see figure 3.4). In the worst case the number of possible solutions increases with the factorial of problem size. We will illustrate this point by use of a complete graph of size 3 (see figure 3.5). In trying to find the shortest complete closed route through the graph – we refer to this solution of the TSP as a *traveling salesman route* – the traveling salesman can turn from his home location to any of three alternatives (v_1, v_2, v_3). Once he has chosen the first alternative on the route, say v_1, in the next step he has two alternatives remaining to choose from (v_2, v_3). After he has chosen the second one there is only one remaining. The traveling salesman will visit this last alternative and return home. In this example there are 6

($= 3 * 2 * 1$) routes through the graph. In general, in a complete graph the traveling salesman has n alternatives to choose from in the first step, $n-1$ in the second, and so on, until there is only one alternative left. Therefore, the number of possible routes in a complete graph is $n!$ and any algorithm that tries to find a traveling salesman route by checking every possible route has a complexity function of $O(n!)$ (see also figure 3.3).

We want to underline two properties of a traveling salesman route which will be of interest in our later discussion. These properties will allow us to see whether a specific route is a valid candidate for being a traveling salesman route or not. The first property is:

> In an undirected graph the inverse of a traveling salesman route is also a traveling salesman route.

This is actually a property of a route in an undirected graph rather than of a traveling salesman route. Since the length of a route is defined as the sum of the edge-weights (costs) of the route and in an undirected graph edge-weights are symmetric (i.e. $c_{ij} = c_{ji}$) it follows for each route that it has the same length as its inverse route. Since this holds for all routes it applies to traveling salesman routes as well.

The second property can be stated as:

> In a complete undirected graph with weights proportional to Euclidian distance a traveling salesman route has no intersections.

It derives from a much more general argument which we will state by using figure 3.6. Suppose we have a graph where vertices $v_1, \ldots, v_4$ and edges $e_1, \ldots, e_4$ are arranged as in figure 3.6. Edges e_3 and e_4 intersect at point M thus forming sub-edges e'_3, e''_3 and e'_4, e''_4. Suppose that the costs associated with these edges and sub-edges confirm to the triangle inequality[3]. Given these assumptions, can a route that intersects at M be a traveling salesman route? Let us denote this route as T. Its length is

$$\begin{aligned} l(T) &= C(v_2, v_3) + c_{31} + C(v_1, v_4) + c_{42} \\ &= C(v_2, v_3) + c_{3M} + c_{M1} + C(v_1, v_4) + c_{4M} + c_{M2} \end{aligned} \quad (3.5)$$

where $C(v_i, v_j)$ denotes the total costs of going from v_i to v_j along this route. Because of the triangle inequality we have

---

[3]The triangle inequality states that when three (sub-)edges form a triangle the sum of the weights of any two (sub-)edges is larger than the weight of the third edge.

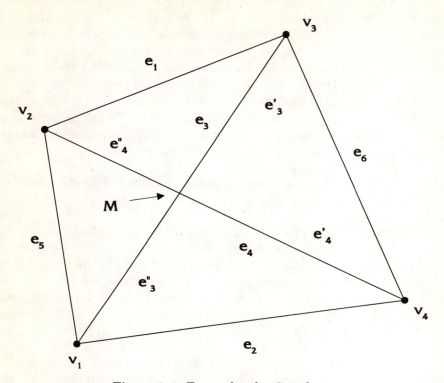

Figure 3.6: Example of a Graph

$$c_{12} < c_{1M} + c_{M2} \quad \text{and} \quad c_{34} < c_{3M} + c_{M4} \:. \tag{3.6}$$

Since we are dealing with an undirected graph $c_{ij} = c_{ji}$ and we get from (3.5) and (3.6)

$$\begin{aligned} l(T) &= C(v_2, v_3) + c_{3M} + c_{M4} + C(v_4, v_1) + c_{1M} + c_{M2} \\ &> C(v_2, v_3) + c_{34} + C(v_4, v_1) + c_{12} \:. \end{aligned}$$

Thus, under the above set of assumptions, i.e. when edges like those in figure 3.6 exist, costs are symmetric and conform with the triangle inequality, to each route with an intersection there exists a *shorter* route without an intersection. Therefore, our original route cannot be a traveling salesman route.

The propositions of our second property guarantee that these assumptions hold. The completeness of the graph guarantees that the respective edges exist. Since edge-weights are assumed to be proportional to euclidian distance also the triangle inequality holds.

3.4 Summary

In this chapter we have discussed some important concepts that will be needed in later chapters. We concentrate on those aspects that are of major relevance for the following discussion of spatial search and do not attempt to provide a complete overview of the respective theories. The focus is on three related subjects: graphs, routes, and computational complexity.

Section 3.1 discusses some important aspects of graph theory. This is important in our context, because graphs are a flexible tool for characterizing the spatial structure of a spatial search problem. We discuss the fundamental elements of graphs and some basic results of graph theory. Also, we mention special types of graphs that will provide special cases in later chapters.

In section 3.2 we develop a terminology and notation for describing how a searcher proceeds through a graph. The order in which alternatives (vertices of the graph) are visited defines a route. We define different types of routes (e.g., complete routes, partial routes, subroutes) that will be useful in later chapters.

The final section 3.3 is devoted to a brief introduction to complexity theory. The concepts discussed here will be of particular importance in our discussion of the complexity of the spatial search problem (section 4.2). We define what is meant by computational complexity and how problems can be classified into various types according to their complexity. In particular we discuss problems that can always be solved in polynomial time (class *P*) and non-deterministic polynomial problems (class *NP*). Of specific relevance for our discussion will be *NP-complete* problems, a class of particularly complicated problems. We review some characteristics of these problem classes and discuss, how it can be determined that a problem is *NP-complete*. This technique will be applied in section 4.2. We close this chapter by discussing the traveling salesman problem, a famous example of an *NP-complete* problem.

Chapter 4

The General Spatial Search Problem

In this chapter we want to focus on search problems in space. Explicitly taking into account space in the search problem leads to some major modifications of the basic models as they were discussed in section 2. In particular, some of the assumptions that simplified the problem considerably in section 2 are not applicable or at least extremely questionable in a spatial search context.

In this chapter we want to analyze the spatial search problem in its most general form. It is the main purpose of this chapter to conceptualize this problem, look into its major components and to investigate its complexity. As it will turn out, the spatial search problem in this general form is practically intractable. In the next chapter (chapter 5) we will be discussing possible ways to avoid this complexity. In section 5.1 we will investigate additional assumptions that might simplify the problem. In section 5.2 our focus will be on heuristic approaches to the spatial search problem and approximations to the (generally unobtainable) exact result.

Practically all search activities take place in space and are shaped by their spatial context. Even when an individual investigates shopping alternatives by phone, the spatial pattern of telephone zones influences the cost borne for search activities.

The spatial search problem differs from the basic search problem discussed in chapter 2 by the fact that the alternatives are distributed in space. The individual starts from a residential location (we call it *home*) and visits the locations of the alternatives to search their values. Depending on the type of problem we are looking at the individual either stays at the alternative chosen or returns home. Because it is the more general case, in our discussion we will generally deal with the second case, i.e. assume that the individual has to return home after terminating search.

The other version – the individual stays at the chosen alternative – can be derived therefrom by setting the cost of returning home equal to zero.

Contrary to the standard search problem, in the spatial search problem the individual has to make two interrelated decisions. He/she has to decide about

1. the sequence in which to investigate the alternatives, and
2. whether to accept an alternative or to continue searching.

As we will see, it is the combination of these two decisions that makes the spatial search problem so complicated. To our knowledge, the spatial search problem has not been approached systematically before[1]. Only some special cases of the spatial search problem have been discussed in the literature. We will turn to some of them in the latter chapters.

4.1 Definition of the Spatial Search Problem

4.1.1 Basic Assumptions

To be more specific about what we mean by the spatial search problem, we will use the following set of assumptions[2] throughout our presentation (general assumptions):

G.1 Each individual – searcher – has a specific home location and faces a finite number of outlets at discrete locations in two-dimensional space where a homogeneous good can be bought. We also call these outlets *alternatives*. They form a connected graph $G(V, E)$.

G.2 The searcher attempts to maximize expected utility. As long as we are considering only one good this implies that he/she wants to buy this good at lowest expected total costs.

G.3 The searcher either buys exactly one unit of the respective product or determines demand based on the expected costs before starting the search process. During search the searcher's demand is fixed, i.e. the quantity he/she plans to buy is never altered in reaction to the search procedure.

---

[1] An exception is Maier (1991), an earlier version of this chapter.

[2] We will always present our argument in terms of a minimization problem. As mentioned in chapter 2, however, this does not restrict the general value of our argument.

4.1. Definition of the Spatial Search Problem

G.4 All the suppliers carry a sufficient supply of the respective product (no capacity restrictions). The price they charge is the realization of a random variable (X), the distribution function $(F_i(x))$ of which is known to the searchers[3]. Since x is a price, $F_i(x) = 0$ for all $x < 0$. From the searchers point of view, these random variables are independent.

G.5 The costs of going from one alternative to searching another are given and a-priorily known to the searcher for all possible combinations of alternatives (including home).

G.6 The searcher may search each alternative only once.

This set of assumptions defines the spatial search problem. Assumption G.1 together with assumption G.5 defines the spatial structure of the individual's search problem. Because the alternatives are arranged in a graph there is no "natural" sequencing of alternatives. The individual has to find the optimal sequence of alternatives, i.e. he/she is facing a *routing problem*. Assumption G.2 defines a decision criterion. Assumption G.3 separates decisions about the search process from those about demanded quantities. This assumption is quite common in the search literature although it often remains implicit. Nevertheless, it is quite restrictive. It rules out that the searcher adjusts consumption plans during search as a consequence of the income spent on search costs. The assumption rules out, for example, that at some point in the search process the searcher terminates the search process *without* buying the product. Assumption G.4 rules out capacity restrictions on the supplier's side and the need for adaptive search behavior. The last sentence rules out that the supplier discriminates searchers according to the behavior they showed at other locations. So, when he/she starts searching, the searcher is assumed to know from which distribution each supplier will draw the offer. This assumption, however, does not prevent the supplier from adjusting the distribution, e.g. in reaction to adjustments made by other suppliers. The supplier has to make these adjustments between search activities.

Because of its direct relationship to the spatial structure assumption G.5 needs some elaboration. We basically assume that there exists a matrix which specifies the costs of moving between home and all alternatives and that this matrix is known by the individual. This matrix is called the *cost matrix* and symbolized by C. The second part of the assumption parallels the assumption of a known price distribution in G.4.

The cost matrix is an essential parameter of the spatial search problem. It is closely, although not immediately, related to the graph $G(V, E)$. In

---
[3]The index i represents the alternatives.

assumption G.5 we have stated that the cost are known for *all possible combinations of alternatives (including home)*. Consequently, the cost matrix is of dimension $(n + 1) \times (n + 1)$. Since we have not imposed any restrictions upon the graph G, however, not all the alternatives are necessarily connected by edges. So, what do the respective elements of the cost matrix represent?

In contrast to graph theory, our interest here is on searching the price distributions at alternatives rather than on connecting to them. Note that in assumption G.6 we prevent the searcher from *searching* an alternative more than once. This does not restrict the searcher in going to an alternative without searching it on the way to another yet unsearched alternative. This is a major distinction to standard graph theory, and has be to kept in mind in the latter discussion. However, we can restructure the spatial search problem in such a way that it is in line with graph theory. This also answers the question about the cost matrix.

In addition to the original graph $G(V, E)$ describing the spatial structure of the spatial search problem we can define a digraph $G'(V', A')$ with the same set of vertices as G, i.e. $V = V'$. In G' we connect every alternative to all the other alternatives that the searcher may search[4] immediately before or after the respective alternative, irrespectively of whether they are directly connected or not. Since we have not imposed any restrictions upon the sequencing of alternatives in the spatial search process, G' must be a complete digraph, i.e. one where each vertex is connected to every other vertex by a pair of arcs of opposite directions. We can define the arc weights for this digraph as the lowest cost the searcher has to bear between searching one alternative (vertex) and searching another. These arc weights are equal to the off-diagonal elements of the cost matrix. Because of assumption G.6 the diagonal elements of the cost matrix are irrelevant.

The cost matrix as defined in assumption G.5 may actually contain any type of costs the searcher has to bear between searching at one location and searching at another. Some may be space related, others not. For example, the matrix may contain the time costs of interrogating the price, which may be alternative specific but are usually unrelated to spatial aspects. Also the space related costs may be quite different. They may be related to any distance measure, to travel time in a road network, may take into account road conditions, congestion, etc. The only limitation we face from assumption G.5 is that the costs are known and cannot be changed by the searcher through search behavior (e.g. by skipping alternatives in order to avoid the rush hour on a specific link).

---

[4] For the sake of simplifying the language, let us treat the home location as a searchable alternative as well.

4.1. Definition of the Spatial Search Problem

In particular, we may define the elements in the cost matrix in the following way:

$$c_{ij} = \bar{c}_{ij} + \tau_j \quad \text{with} \quad \bar{c}_{ij} \geq 0 \ . \tag{4.1}$$

The term $\bar{c}_{ij}$ refers to the space related costs, whereas τ_j is that part of costs that is associated with alternative j (alternative related costs). Note that we have assumed non-negativity only for space related costs. The alternative related costs may as well be negative. In this case they represent a gratification the searcher receives for visiting alternative j. We will come back to this aspect of the distance matrix later in this chapter.

Assumptions G.1 to G.6 are general in the sense that we will obey them throughout the remaining presentation.

When dealing with the spatial search problem in this general form, the searcher has to decide about the sequence in which to visit the alternatives and about the critical values at the various alternatives. These two elements – we will refer to them as the *routing problem* and as the *stopping problem* – are interrelated and in the general model one cannot be solved independently from the other.

4.1.2 An Algorithm for Solving the General Spatial Search Problem

However, we can nest the routing and the stopping problem and solve them sequentially. This procedure is similar to conditional optimization (Maier, Weiss, 1990). It consists of the following three steps:

Algorithm 4.1 Optimal Solution for the Spatial Search Problem

1. *Enumerate all possible routes through the graph describing the spatial layout of the problem.*

2. *For each route, compute the optimal search strategy (conditional on the route) and derive the expected costs for this particular route therefrom.*

3. *Compare the – conditional – expected returns of all possible routes to find the one with the minimum expected costs.*

By enumerating the routes in the first step we also define different sequences in which to investigate the alternatives. In the second step we use one sequence after another to derive the expected costs of a search strategy conditional on each sequence. In the third step we select the sequence which – when employing an optimal search strategy – gives the lowest expected costs. In a complete graph with n alternatives (vertices) there are $n!$ possible sequences of alternatives. In an incomplete graph the number might be lower, particularly when we take into account some of the structures and results we will be discussing in chapter 5.

The second step is performed *conditional on a particular route*. We will now formulate this procedure in a general form which holds for any number of alternatives and any possible price distribution. Later on we will illustrate this procedure with an example that will yield additional insights.

Suppose we have a graph with n vertices and want to compute the expected costs of a search strategy along route R through this graph ($y(R)$). As in chapter 2, we employ the technique of backward induction. When the searcher has rejected the first $n-1$ alternatives he/she will accept alternative n at any price because of assumption G.2. This can again be formalized by $y(R_n) = \infty$. Therefore

$$\begin{aligned} y(R_{n-1}) &= C(R[n-1], R[n]) + C(R[n], H) + E(X) \\ &= C(R[n-1], R[n]) + C(R[n], H) + \int_0^\infty x f_n(x)\, dx \quad, (4.2) \end{aligned}$$

where $C(R[n-1], R[n])$ represents the element $R[n-1], R[n]$ of the cost matrix, i.e. the costs of going from the $n-1$-st alternative in route R to the n-th alternative. In the same way, $C(R[n], H)$ is the costs of going home from alternative $R[n]$. We use the index n also in conjunction with the probability density function f. This is not a precise formulation, since n refers to the relative position within a specific route. To be precise we would need to define another index, say k, whose value is such that $v_k = R[n]$ (see Maier, 1993a). This notation turns out to be quite complicated. Since the focus of our discussion will be on the cost component and in many cases we will assume identical price distributions, we feel that the simplified notation is worth the small loss in precision.

In all steps ahead the searcher has to decide about accepting or rejecting the particular price offer. It is optimal for him/her to accept a price offer which is lower than the expected costs of continued search minus the costs of going home from this specific location. The latter term enters the formulation because of the assumption that the searcher returns home after searching. Contrary to the search model of chapter 2 the reservation price now differs from the expected costs of continued search. Since after accepting a price offer the searcher still has to go home, in the spatial search model the reservation price at alternative i in route R ($\bar{x}(R_i)$) is

$$\bar{x}(R_i) = y(R_i) - C(R[i], H) \ . \qquad (4.3)$$

Therefore, the expected costs at alternative $i-1$ can be derived as

4.1. Definition of the Spatial Search Problem

$$\begin{aligned} y(R_{i-1}) &= C(R[i-1], R[i]) + \int_0^{\bar{x}(R_i)} (x + C(R[i], H)) f_i(x)\, dx + \\ & \quad \int_{\bar{x}(R_i)}^{\infty} y(R_i) f_i(x)\, dx \ . \end{aligned} \qquad (4.4)$$

By substituting (4.4) into the right hand side of (4.3) we can express the reservation price in the usual recursive form:

$$\begin{aligned} \bar{x}(R_{i-1}) &= C(R[i-1], R[i]) + (C(R[i], H) - C(R[i-1], H)) + \\ & \quad \int_0^{\bar{x}(R_i)} x f_i(x)\, dx + \bar{x}(R_i)[1 - F_i(\bar{x}(R_i))] \ . \end{aligned} \qquad (4.5)$$

Note that all the reservation prices are conditional on route R and that since $y(R_n) = \infty$ we also get $\bar{x}(R_n) = \infty$ from (4.3).

Iterative application of (4.5) yields the sequence of threshold values (reservation prices) that characterizes the optimal search strategy for the sequence of alternatives given by route R. As we will see in our example, the search strategy will differ for another route.

As in chapter 2 we can derive choice probabilities and expected total costs for a search sequence along route R. We only need to distinguish carefully between the expected costs of continued search and the reservation price. The choice probabilities are:

$$\begin{aligned} P(R[1]) &= F_1(\bar{x}(R_1)) \ , \\ P(R[i]) &= F_i(\bar{x}(R_i)) \prod_{j=1}^{i-1} [1 - F_j(\bar{x}(R_j))] \qquad \forall \ i = 2 \ldots n \ . \end{aligned} \qquad (4.6)$$

Again we can define a conditional choice probability for each alternative:

$$p_i = F_i(\bar{x}(R_i)) \ . \qquad (4.7)$$

The expected total costs can basically be derived in the same way as in chapter 2. Only the notation becomes more difficult because of the need to refer to a specific route and to make sure each subroute starts and ends at home.

$$\begin{aligned} y(R) &= \sum_{i=1}^n \Bigg\{ C(R[i-1, i]) \left(\sum_{j=i}^n P(R[j]) \right) + \\ & \quad P(R[i])\, [C(R[i], H) + E(X_i | X_i \le \bar{x}(R_i))] \Bigg\} \\ & \quad \text{with } R[0] = H \ . \end{aligned} \qquad (4.8)$$

With this formulation we can split the total expected costs into "expected travel costs" ($y^T(R)$) and "expected costs of purchase" ($y^P(R)$).

$$y^T(R) = \sum_{i=1}^{n}\left\{C(R[i-1,i])\left(\sum_{j=i}^{n}P(R[j])\right) + P(R[i])C(R[i],H)\right\} \text{ with } R[0] = H$$

$$y^P(R) = \sum_{i=1}^{n}\{P(R[i])E(X_i|X_i \leq \bar{x}(R_i))\} \text{ with } R[0] = H$$

Note that not only $y^T(R)$ but also $y^P(R)$ depends upon the route. This dependence is indirect via the impact of the route on the choice probabilities and the reservation prices.

The third step in our algorithm for solving the general spatial search problem is simply a matter of keeping track of the lowest expected return found so far and the corresponding sequence of reservation prices. While (4.8) describes the minimum expected total costs of searching along route R, the minimum expected total costs for the whole search problem are

$$y = \min_{R \in \mathcal{R}}(y(R)) \ . \tag{4.9}$$

The optimal route through the search problem, R^*, is therefore defined by

$$R^* = \{S|y(S) = \min_{R \in \mathcal{R}}(y(R))\} \ .$$

The whole algorithm can be implemented by the two procedures[5] displayed in figure 4.1. Procedure SEARCH performs the computations of step 2 in our discussion. Procedure GENERAL-SPATIAL generates the routes, calls procedure SEARCH and keeps track of the best route found so far.

Let us look into these procedures in more detail. The algorithm assumes that there is a data matrix Cost that contains the costs of going from one alternative to another. Home is encoded as alternative 0. Also, the algorithm assumes that the functions INTEGRAL and F are available, where INTEGRAL receives a lower and upper bound as parameters and returns the conditional expected value of the price distribution between these two bounds. Function F receives only one parameter and returns the value of the cumulative distribution of the price distribution at this value. Implicitly we assume that the price offer distribution is identical at all alternatives. If this is not the case we need more complicated calls to

---

[5] We use a Pascal-type programming language.

```
Procedure GENERAL-SPATIAL;
type
  route = array[0..n] of Integer;
var
  optimal-route : route;
  minimum-costs : real
  R             : route;
  costs-R       : real;
  i             : longint;

Function SEARCH (R : route) : real;
var
  res-price : real;
  i         : integer;
begin {function SEARCH}
  res-price := Cost[R[n],0] + Cost[R[n-1],R[n]]
             - Cost[R[n-1],0] + INTEGRAL(0,infinity);
  for i := n-1 downto 1 do
      res-price := Cost[R[i-1],R[i]] + Cost[R[i],0]
                 - Cost[R[i-1],0] + INTEGRAL(0,res-price)
                 + res-price*(1-F(res-price));
  SEARCH := res-price + Cost[0,0];
end; {function SEARCH}

begin {proc. GENERAL-SPATIAL}
  minimum-costs := infinity;
  for i := 1 to n! do
    begin
      R := PERMUTATION(i);
      costs-R := SEARCH(R);
      if costs-R < minimum-costs then
        begin
          minimum-costs := costs-R;
          optimal-route := R;
        end; {endif}
    end; {endfor}
end; {proc. GENERAL-SPATIAL}
```

Figure 4.1: An Algorithm Solving the General Search Problem

INTEGRAL and F. The basic structure of the algorithm, however, remains the same. A third function, PERMUTATION, returns a specific permutation of the alternatives in a variable of type route.

Procedure SEARCH is local to procedure GENERAL-SPATIAL and therefore imbedded into it. Procedure GENERAL-SPATIAL starts with defining data type route as an array of n integer values. In this array-type we store the sequence of alternatives that defines a route. The procedure uses five variables: optimal-route is used to store the currently best route, minimum-costs is used to store the costs of the currently best route, R is used to store the actual route, costs-R is used to temporarily store the costs of this route, and i is an index-variable of a for-loop over all possible routes. Since the maximum value of this index-variable is $n!$ we define it be of type longint.

The executable statements of procedure GENERAL-SPATIAL start with begin {proc. GENERAL-SPATIAL}. In the first statement minimum-costs is set to a very high constant. The main part of procedure GENERAL-SPATIAL is a for-loop over the *number of all possible routes*. In this loop we get the respective sequence of alternatives from function PERMUTATION, get the respective costs from function SEARCH and then check whether the costs of the actual route are lower than the currently minimum costs. If they are, we store the current route and its costs in the variables optimal-route and minimum-costs. At the end of procedure GENERAL-SPATIAL, after it has looped over all possible routes, optimal-route and minimum-costs contain the optimal route and the corresponding costs.

Function SEARCH is called once for each route. It receives the variable R of type route from the calling procedure and returns a real-type variable. Locally, the function uses a real-type variable res-price for storing the reservation price at the different stages of the search process and again an index-variable i which is now of type integer.

The executable statements of function SEARCH implement the recursive definition of the reservation price (4.5). In the first line we compute the reservation price of alternative $n-1$ (see (4.2) and (4.3)). Then index i loops from $n-1$ down to 1 to recursively compute all the reservation prices according to (4.5). In the last statement we add Cost[0,0], which should be zero anyway, to the final reservation price in order to get the expected costs. Via SEARCH this value is returned to the calling procedure.

In a later subsection this algorithm will help us to prove that the general spatial search problem is *NP-complete*.

4.1. Definition of the Spatial Search Problem

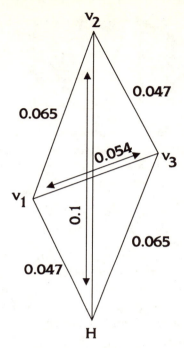

Figure 4.2: The General Spatial Search Problem: Example

4.1.3 An Illustrating Example

We now want to illustrate the spatial search problem and the above algorithm for solving it with a simple example (this example follows Maier, 1991). With this example we can also illustrate some important aspects of the spatial search problem. Suppose an individual's home and three alternatives are arranged as in figure 4.2. We mark home by H and the alternatives by v_1, v_2 and v_3. The costs are as indicated in figure 4.2. For simplicity and illustrative reasons we set them proportional to distance. The prices at all alternatives be independently and uniformly distributed between 0 and 1, i.e. there is no systematic difference between the suppliers. Moreover, we assume that the individual has to return home after searching.

Since the individual starts from home and ends at home there are 3! different complete routes through the system[6].

---

[6]For the moment we will restrict ourselves to complete routes. As we will see later, in some situations it might be optimal to skip alternatives, i.e. consider partial routes. However, allowing for partial routes does not change the fundamental structure of the model (see section 4.3).

A: $H \to v_1 \to v_2 \to v_3 \to H$
B: $H \to v_1 \to v_3 \to v_2 \to H$
C: $H \to v_2 \to v_1 \to v_3 \to H$
D: $H \to v_2 \to v_3 \to v_1 \to H$
E: $H \to v_3 \to v_1 \to v_2 \to H$
F: $H \to v_3 \to v_2 \to v_1 \to H$

For each complete route there are subroutes when the individual decides to stop before exhausting the alternatives. In our example, for each route in the list above there are two subroutes. For the route A, for example, there are the following subroutes

$\bar{A}_1$: $H \to v_1 \to H$
$\bar{A}_2$: $H \to v_1 \to v_2 \to H$

Now, let us compute the expected cost of route A. We will compute this measure by backward induction as in Section 2. Suppose the individual has reached alternative v_2 and decided against accepting it. The only option he/she has available is to go to alternative v_3, accept it and return home. Therefore, the expected cost at alternative v_2 with alternative v_3 available, i.e. subroute A_2, is

$$y(A_2) = c_{23} + E(x) + c_{3H} = 0.612 \qquad (4.10)$$

where c_{23} is the cost of going from alternative v_2 to v_3 and c_{3H} that of returning home from v_3.

The searcher will accept the price offered at alternative v_2 only if he/she can pay for the trip home and is still better off than proceeding to alternative v_3. So, the reservation price ($\bar{x}(A_2)$) is 0.512. The expected cost of going to alternative v_2 from immediately after rejecting a price offer at location v_1 (subroute A_1) is therefore

$$y(A_1) = c_{12} + c_{2H} + E[\min(X, \bar{x}(A_2))] = 0.5460 \ . \qquad (4.11)$$

Pushing the same argument one step further reveals that the expected return of the whole search sequence along route A is

$$y(A) = c_{H1} + c_{1H} + E[\min(X, \bar{x}(A_1))] = 0.4688 \ . \qquad (4.12)$$

We can do these computations for all six possible route and will get the results displayed in Table 4.1. As it turns out, route B has the lowest expected costs and is therefore the optimal route. This route is displayed in figure 4.3.

Not all the routes follow the same roads through the system. Some of them use the diagonals between alternatives v_1 and v_3, or H and v_2,

4.1. Definition of the Spatial Search Problem

Route	Sequence	Expected Costs
A:	$H \to v_1 \to v_2 \to v_3 \to H$	0.4688
B:	$H \to v_1 \to v_3 \to v_2 \to H$	0.4614
C:	$H \to v_2 \to v_1 \to v_3 \to H$	0.5321
D:	$H \to v_2 \to v_3 \to v_1 \to H$	0.5227
E:	$H \to v_3 \to v_1 \to v_2 \to H$	0.4858
F:	$H \to v_3 \to v_2 \to v_1 \to H$	0.4859

Table 4.1: Expected Costs for all Possible Routes

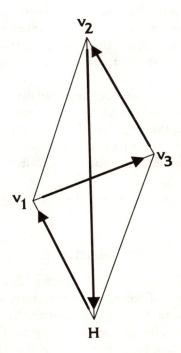

Figure 4.3: The General Spatial Search Problem: Optimal Route through Example

Route	Choice Probabilities		
	P_1	P_2	P_3
A:	0.499	0.257	0.244
B:	0.485	0.300	0.215
C:	0.420	0.332	0.248
D:	0.405	0.319	0.276
E:	0.463	0.332	0.205
F:	0.463	0.275	0.262

Table 4.2: Choice Probabilities for all Possible Routes

others do not. This, however, is not the primary reason for the differences in the expected returns. If we compare route B to route D they use the same roads, just in different order (route D is the inverse route of B). Nevertheless, the expected costs are quite different. The reason is that route D starts with alternative v_2, which is more than twice as far from home than alternative v_1. Since there is a positive probability that the individual stops at the first alternative investigated, the expected costs differ.

That the individual's stopping behavior in turn depends upon the route taken can be seen when we compare routes A and B. Both start with alternative v_1 but differ in the way the other two alternatives are sequenced. Therefore, the expected costs of search past the first alternative, i.e. sub-routes A_1 and B_1, differs for the two routes. For route A we get

$$y(A_1) = 0.5460 \ , \qquad (4.13)$$

and for route B

$$y(B_1) = 0.5316 \ . \qquad (4.14)$$

So, if the individual observes a value between $y(B_1) - c_{1H}$ and $y(A_1) - c_{1H}$ at alternative v_1, he/she will accept it if searching along route A but will reject it if following route B. This, of course, has an impact upon the probabilities with which alternatives are chosen. From our assumptions it is easy to see that when following route A the individual stops at alternative v_1 with probability 0.499, when following route B he stops with probability 0.485.

We can draw a number of conclusions from this example.

1. The expected costs of the spatial search strategy depend upon the chosen route.

4.1. Definition of the Spatial Search Problem

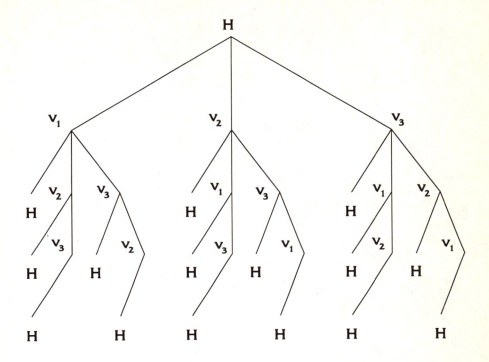

Figure 4.4: The Decision Tree for the General Spatial Search Problem

2. The choice probabilities of the alternatives depend upon the chosen route.
3. In a spatial search context a route and its inverse usually have different expected costs.
4. Even in a complete undirected graph with weights conforming the triangle inequality the optimal route of the spatial search problem may intersect.

Since the last two points do not conform with the fundamental properties of traveling salesman routes that we have mentioned in chapter 3 we can conclude that although the alternatives are identical in terms of their stochastic properties

- a traveling salesman route is not necessarily an optimal spatial search route, and
- the optimal spatial search route is not necessarily a traveling salesman route.

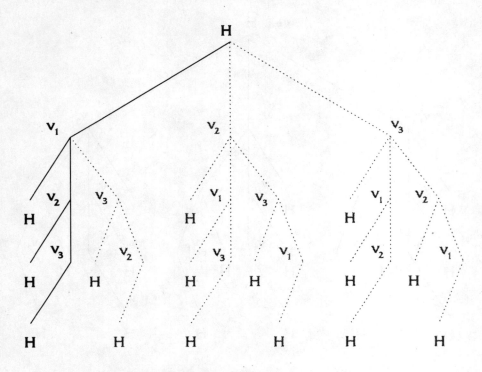

Figure 4.5: The Decision Tree for the Optimal Path

Despite this result, there is a close relationship between the traveling salesman problem and the spatial search problem. Later on we will use this relationship for demonstrating that the spatial search problem is *NP-complete*.

Figure 4.4 represents the whole decision problem of our example. At home the individual can choose between alternatives 1, 2 and 3. If he/she proceeds to alternative 1, he/she may accept the value observed there and return home. Or, the individual may decide to proceed to another alternative and has to choose then between alternatives 2 and 3. Suppose the individual decides to go to alternative 2 at this step. Again, he/she may accept the alternative and return home or proceed to another alternative. The only one left at this point is alternative 3. After that, the searcher must return home.

If we do the same for all other routes we end up with figure 4.4. It differs from the decision tree of chapter 3 (figure 3.5) in the sense that the branches in figure 4.4 differ in length. They do so because of the search component of the decision problem. By cutting out the optimal route $H123$ (see figure 4.5) we see that it is actually an optimal subtree, which closely resembles the graphic representation of the search problem in chapter 2 (figure 2.1).

Once the decision about the route through the system is made, the problem reduces to a standard sequential search problem as we have discussed it in chapter 2 (see also section 4.6). So, the search process and its expected outcome depend upon the routing decision. However, as we have seen above, the routing decision in turn depends upon the expected return of the search process so that in the general spatial search problem we cannot solve one separately from the other. Both parts of the problem have to be solved simultaneously.

4.2 The Complexity of the General Spatial Search Problem

In this section we want to prove the following theorem about the computational complexity of the general spatial search problem (see also Maier, 1993a).

> **Theorem 4.1** *The General Spatial Search Problem as defined by assumptions G.1 - G.6 is* NP-complete.

As mentioned in chapter 3 in order to prove that a specific problem is *NP-complete* we have to show that (see, e.g. Garey and Johnson, 1979)

1. it belongs to the class *NP*, and
2. every problem in *NP* polynomially reduces to this problem.

The first step is equivalent to showing that for a candidate solution we can determine in polynomial time whether the result of a candidate solution is below (or above) a given threshold. Since every *NP-complete* problem has the property that every problem in *NP* polynomially reduces to it, for step two it is sufficient to show that *one* from the class of *NP-complete* problems polynomially reduces to the spatial search problem. We will use the traveling salesman problem.

Proving the first step is rather simple. For a specific route we can compute the expected costs by backward induction. In figure 4.1 this was done in function **SEARCH**. For a route of length n this step may require the numerical evaluation of $2n-1$ integrals (one for each call of **INTEGRAL** and **F**). Since the price distributions are assumed to be independent (assumption G.4) the integrals can be evaluated in sequence. Although numerically computing integrals may be cumbersome and time consuming, since its time requirement is independent of n it does not add to the computational complexity of the function. Therefore, the complexity function of function **SEARCH** in figure 4.1 is of order $O(n)$. This proves that the general spatial search problem belongs to the class *NP*.

The second step is more cumbersome to prove. We need to find a specific formulation of the spatial search problem, the solution of which is directly related to the solution of the traveling salesman problem. Moreover, the transitions from the traveling salesman problem to the spatial search problem and from the solution of the spatial search problem back to the traveling salesman solution need to be computable in polynomial time.

Recall the definition of search costs in equation (4.1). We mentioned the possibility of negative values of τ, representing a gratification for the visiting searcher. Suppose that $-\bar{\tau}$ is the level of gratification the searcher receives at each alternative. So, we add to equation (4.1)

$$\tau_j = -\bar{\tau} \ . \tag{4.15}$$

Moreover, we assume that the price distribution is the same at each alternative, i.e.,

$$F_i(X) = F(X) \ . \tag{4.16}$$

When $\bar{\tau}$ is large enough, the searcher will receive a net-benefit from each alternative and consequently he/she will have no incentive for terminating the search before exhausting all the alternatives. In this case, the searcher will always travel through the whole graph, just like the traveling salesman. He/she will buy the respective good – the basic aim of the search effort – at the last alternative visited.

Whatever route the searcher takes, he/she will always visit all n alternatives. Therefore, he/she will always accumulate a total amount of $-n\bar{\tau}$ in gratification and pay the price $E(x)$ for the good he/she is searching for. So, the only cost element which the searcher has to watch is the space related part of the search costs, $\bar{c}_{ij}$ (see (4.1)). Depending on the route he/she takes through the graph the searcher will accumulate different elements $\bar{c}_{ij}$ from the cost matrix. This sum of route related cost elements, however, is just the *length of the route* (see section 3.2).

Summarizing all these elements, the expected costs of the searcher are

$$y(R) = -n\bar{\tau} + E(x) + l(R) \ . \tag{4.17}$$

To minimize these expected costs the searcher has to find the route with minimum length. This route, however, is nothing but the traveling salesman route. When knowing $y(R)$ the length of the traveling salesman route can directly be derived from (4.17) as

$$l(R) = y(R) - E(x) + n\bar{\tau} .$$

This argument shows that we can structure the spatial search problem in such a way that it yields the solution to the corresponding traveling salesman problem. The crucial element of this argument is a sufficiently large value of $\bar{\tau}$. What is left to be shown is that for any spatial search problem we can derive a suitable value for $\bar{\tau}$ in polynomial time.

The only purpose of $\bar{\tau}$ in our proof is to ensure that the searcher will not stop searching before he/she has exhausted all possible alternatives. Therefore, we have to set $\bar{\tau}$ large enough to compensate the searcher for the highest costs he/she may encounter when going from one alternative to another. As we know from section 4.1, there are three cost elements involved:

1. the space related costs of going to another alternative,
2. the expected price of the good at the new alternative, and
3. the change in the costs of going home.

Because of our assumptions, the second item is $E(x)$ at all alternatives. The other two items are directly related to the terms $\bar{c}_{ij}$ in the cost matrix. Since the cost matrix contains the costs of going from one alternative to another irrespective of whether they are adjacent in the graph or not, the maximum value for both items is the maximum $\bar{c}_{ij}$ in the cost matrix. We can therefore derive a suggestion for a *sufficiently large* $\bar{\tau}$ quite easily as

$$\bar{\tau} = E(x) + 2\max(\bar{c}_{ij}) . \qquad (4.18)$$

Finding this value requires at most two nested loops of size n over the cost matrix. This task is therefore of $O(n^2)$. So, there is a polynomial time algorithm for deriving $\bar{\tau}$ as is necessary for the second step of our proof. So, the traveling salesman problem, and with it every other problem in *NP* polynomially reduces to the spatial search problem as we have defined it.

This completes our proof of theorem 4.1. In two steps we have been able to show that the spatial search problem belongs to the class *NP* and that every problem in *NP* polynomially reduces to it.

The second step of the proof crucially depends upon equation (4.1). The idea of a gratification may be disturbing for the reader. Two remarks are in order here:

1. The restructured spatial search model that we have used in our proof is only needed for linking the two concepts and for the *formal* aspects of the proof. We do not claim that a situation with such a high level of gratification has any practical relevance. Nor do we consider this a practically useful version of a spatial search model. It is just one special case of our much more general model.
2. When read correctly, the proof says that because our spatial search model *allows* for cost structure (4.1) it is *NP*-complete. A more restrictive cost structure may lead to a less complex problem. The proof does not apply to any special case of our model.

Theorem 4.1 is of central importance to our argument. It shows that attempting to find a general solution to the spatial search problem (as defined by assumptions G.1 to G.6) is an unwarranted endeavor. However, it does not mean that we should terminate our discussion of spatial search models right now. The reasons are at least threefold:

1. The result of theorem 4.1 applies to the general solution, i.e., for a model with any number of alternatives. If we restrict ourselves to a small number of alternatives the problem might be fairly manageable. Despite the small number of alternatives, these special cases may yield interesting insights into spatial relationships which go beyond the results derivable from more restrictive but less complex model versions. Some of these arguments will be picked up in chapters 6 - 8.
2. The theorem also applies to a rather general version of the spatial search problem. Imposing additional restrictions on the spatial search problem may yield less complex variants. We will concentrate on this aspect in chapter 5.
3. Despite its complexity the spatial search model represents a problem that is encountered quite frequently in reality. This suggests that people apply heuristic approaches to the spatial search problem, the quality of which poses an interesting research question. Again, this argument will be picked up in chapter 5.

4.3 Incomplete Routes

In section 4.1 we have explicitly restricted ourselves to complete routes. In this section we want to remove this restriction and discuss the implication of allowing partial routes. We will allow the searcher to investigate a subset of the available alternatives rather than the full set. As it turns out, allowing for partial routes does not really change the search problem.

4.3. Incomplete Routes

This more general case can easily be integrated into the framework of section 4.1.

Suppose we are looking at one of the possible routes through a given graph, say route A, being the optimal complete route through the graph for the respective spatial search problem. The size of the route, $|A|$, be n. The question we are interested in now is, whether the expected cost of search can be lowered by leaving out one of the alternatives in route A. In more general terms, the question is: In a given spatial search problem, does there exist a partial route which yields lower search costs than the optimal complete route?

To answer this question we will use the following theorem:

Theorem 4.2 *Every partial route through a graph is equivalent to a complementary subroute of at least one other complete route through the graph.*

Let us denote the partial route that we get by skipping the ith alternative in route A as A'. Using the definition of subroutes and complementary subroutes given in section 3.2 we can write the relationship between A and A' in the following way:

$$A' = \bar{A}_{i-1} + A_i \ . \qquad (4.19)$$

Route A' is a partial route of route A. The theorem argues that it is also a complementary subroute of another complete route. Suppose, route B can be described as

$$B = \bar{A}_{i-1} + A_i + A[i] \ . \qquad (4.20)$$

Since A' contains all vertices from the complete route A except vertex $A[i]$, route B is clearly a complete route through the graph. It contains exactly the same vertices as route A, only in different order. If we drop the last vertex from route B, i.e. form the complementary subroute $\bar{B}_{n-1}$, we see from (4.20) that it can be written as

$$\bar{B}_{n-1} = \bar{A}_{i-1} + A_i \ . \qquad (4.21)$$

From (4.19) and (4.21) we get

$$A' = \bar{B}_{n-1} \ .$$

A similar relationship can be found in the case when we are skipping two or more alternatives. The resulting partial route is again equivalent to a (complementary) subroute of another complete route. It does not make any difference in a spatial search problem whether we leave out alternatives from within the route or from its end.

The implication of this theorem is that in the current discussion we only need to consider complementary subroutes. So, we can rephrase the above mentioned question as: In a given spatial search problem, does there exist a complementary subroute to any complete route which yields lower search costs than the optimal complete route. Since in the spatial search problem we always have to investigate all complete routes, this question can be answered quite easily. Actually, as we will see below, we have implicitly answered this question already in section 4.1.

Since A is by definition the optimal complete route, i.e. the complete route with minimum expected costs, a necessary condition for the existence of a complementary subroute $\bar{B}_{n-1}$ with lower expected costs of search is

$$y(\bar{B}_{n-1}) < y(B) \ .$$

Can this condition be met? When would the expected costs of a complementary subroute be lower than the expected costs of the respective complete route? We will answer this question by use of the following theorem.

Theorem 4.3 *Suppose we have two routes, R and S, through the graph of a spatial search problem, for which $\bar{R}_i = \bar{S}_i$ ($i \leq |R|, i \leq |S|$). Then*

$$y(R) \geq y(S) \quad \text{iff} \quad y(R_i) \geq y(S_i) \ .$$

The proof for this theorem follows from the our discussion of marginal changes in chapter 2 (equations (2.4) and (2.5)). There, we have seen that whenever the expected costs increase at some point of the search process, the expected costs of the whole search process cannot decrease. Because of the condition of the theorem we can write the two routes as

$$R = \bar{R}_i + R_i \qquad (4.22)$$
$$S = \bar{R}_i + S_i \ , \qquad (4.23)$$

and since they are identical for the first i alternatives, the ordering of minimum expected costs that result from R_i and S_i cannot be reversed through the first i alternatives.

Since $B = \bar{B}_{n-1} + B_{n-1}$, routes B and $\bar{B}_{n-1}$ are related in exactly the same way as routes R and S. While in route B there is one alternative left after $B[n-1]$, in route $\bar{B}_{n-1}$ all available alternatives are exhausted at

4.3. Incomplete Routes

this point. If we denote the empty route as $\hat{B}_{n-1}$, the respective minimum expected costs can be written as:

$$y(B_{n-1}) = C(B[n-1], B[n]) + c(B[n], H) + E(x) ,$$
$$y(\hat{B}_{n-1}) = \infty .$$

In combination with theorem 4.3 we get therefrom

$$y(\bar{B}_{n-1}) \geq y(B) .$$

This shows that the necessary condition for the existence of a complementary subroute with lower minimum expected costs of search cannot be met. Therefore, the answer to the question we have raised in this beginning of this section is negative. It is summarized in the following theorem.

> **Theorem 4.4** *In a given spatial search problem, there can never exist a partial route which yields lower minimum expected costs than the optimal complete route.*

As a consequence, when trying to solve the spatial search problem we only need to investigate complete closed routes, i.e. the routes in set $\mathcal{R}$. Therefore, the results we have derived above where we have restricted ourselves to complete routes hold in general.

One has to be careful interpreting this result, however. It does not imply that the searcher will always consider visiting all the alternatives available. It might well be that some alternatives are so isolated from the others that it is optimal for the searcher never to visit them. The choice probabilities for these alternatives will be zero and the searcher will always stop searching before getting to this set of alternatives.

Let us be more specific about this. Because of theorem 4.2 we can always treat the unused alternatives as being located at the end of the search sequence. Suppose, that the choice probabilities are zero for all alternatives starting with $k + 1$. This implies that the marginal choice probability is 1 for alternative k

$$p(R[k]) = F_k(\bar{x}(R_k)) = 1 . \tag{4.24}$$

At a finite value of $\bar{x}(R_k)$ this can only be the case when the distribution for alternative k has a finite upper bound (see theorem 4.6 below). Otherwise, there will always be a (small) non-zero probability for finding an acceptable alternative after alternative k and consequently a marginal choice probability below 1 for alternative k.

From (4.6) we know that for all alternatives from $k+1$ to n the product term contains $1 - F_k(\bar{x}(R_k))$ which becomes zero when substituting (4.24). Consequently, (4.24) is sufficient to make all the choice probabilities for alternatives $k+1\ldots n$ become zero.

What is the implication of these results for minimum expected total costs? Equation (4.8) which gives the minimum expected total costs is formulated in terms of the contributions of each alternative (from 1 to n) to total expected costs. Each contribution consists of two elements, namely

$$C(R[i-1,i])\left(\sum_{j=i}^{n} P(R[j])\right)$$

and

$$P(R[i])[C(R[i],H) + E(X_i|X_i \leq \bar{x}(R_i))] \quad \text{with } R[0] = H \;.$$

For $i = k+1\ldots n$ all the probabilities in the summation in the first element are zero, which makes the first element equal zero for all these alternatives. In the second element, the term in square brackets is multiplied by the respective choice probability, which for alternatives from $k+1$ to n is zero, so that the second element is zero as well. Consequently, the contributions to the minimum expected total costs of alternatives $k+1$ to n are all zero and the searcher obtains the same minimum expected total costs irrespective of whether he/she takes these alternatives into account or not. Note, however, that the mimimum expected total costs of the complementary subroute can never be *lower* than those of the complete route. This is in accordance with theorem 4.4.

The property described in theorem 4.4 is actually a special case of a more general result about the spatial search problem. The statement we have made for the optimal route in theorem 4.4 actually holds for *every* route:

> **Theorem 4.5** *For any route R in a given spatial search problem, none of the partial route that can be derived from R can have lower minimum expected cost than route R.*

This follows from the fact that the searcher is optimizing his/her search (stopping) behavior according to the route chosen. We can proof this theorem simply by applying the recursive equations (4.4) and (4.5).

Let us look at any three neighboring alternatives in route R, say $R[i-1]$, $R[i]$, and $R[i+1]$, and consider deleting $R[i]$ to form a partial route R'. The minimum expected cost $y(R_{i+1})$ are clearly not influenced by what

4.3. Incomplete Routes

we do at $R[i]$. Therefore, we can derive the following minimum expected cost for subroutes:

$$\begin{aligned}
y(R_i) &= C(R[i], R[i+1]) + \int_0^{\bar{x}(R_{i+1})} (x + C(R[i+1], H)) f_{i+1}(x)\, dx \\
&\quad + \int_{\bar{x}(R_{i+1})}^{\infty} y(R_{i+1}) f_{i+1}(x)\, dx & (4.25) \\
y(R_{i-1}) &= C(R[i-1], R[i]) + \int_0^{\bar{x}(R_i)} (x + C(R[i], H)) f_i(x)\, dx \\
&\quad + \int_{\bar{x}(R_i)}^{\infty} y(R_i) f_i(x)\, dx & (4.26) \\
y(R'_{i-1}) &= C(R[i], R[i+1]) + C(R[i-1], R[i]) \\
&\quad + \int_0^{\bar{x}(R_{i+1})} (x + C(R[i+1], H)) f_{i+1}(x)\, dx \\
&\quad + \int_{\bar{x}(R_{i+1})}^{\infty} y(R_{i+1}) f_{i+1}(x)\, dx\ . & (4.27)
\end{aligned}$$

By use of these equations and (4.3) we can derive the following result for the difference between the minimum expected return of route R and the respective partial route R':

$$y(R_{i-1}) - y(R'_{i-1}) = \int_0^{\bar{x}(R_i)} (x - \bar{x}(R_i)) f_i(x)\, dx\ . \qquad (4.28)$$

Since we are subtracting the upper limit of integration from x, (4.28) has to be non-positive. This proofs theorem 4.5. Note that the theorem does not require R to be a complete route. It might well be a partial route itself. Again, route R' may yield the same minimum expected cost as route R. It is easy to see that this is the case if and only if alternative $R[i]$ has a choice probability of zero.

As we have said above, theorem 4.5 results from the fact that the searcher is assumed to optimize search behavior along any route. When we move from R to R' we impose the constraint upon the searcher, not to investigate alternative $R[i]$. Imposing an additional constraint upon an optimizer, however, can never lead to a better outcome.

Theorem 4.5 has the following important corollary:

Corollary 4.1 *When one or more alternatives are added to a given graph, minimum expected cost will never increase.*

Since we can view the optimal route through the original graph as a partial route of a complete route through the new graph (not necessarily the optimal one) the proof follows immediately from theorem 4.5.

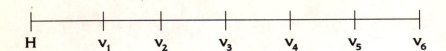

Figure 4.6: Determining the Relevant Alternatives: Example

4.4 The Relevant Alternatives in a Spatial Search Problem

Our discussion about incomplete routes in section 4.3 is closely related to the question of how many and which alternatives are of relevance for a given spatial search problem. Until now we have "solved" this problem simply by assuming n given alternatives. In the most general, i.e. global, context for most search problems there is a huge number of alternatives distributed over different countries and continents. But for a customer looking for some piece of furniture in, say, Vienna, Austria, is it really relevant to know about furniture stores in Los Angeles and Shanghai?

In practical terms not, of course. But are there any theoretical results that can tell us which alternatives we have to consider and which ones can be ignored? Since solving the spatial search problem is computationally far too complicated for a large number of alternatives (see section 4.2), we are looking for some features of the parameters of the spatial search problem that allow us to distinguish between the relevant and the irrelevant alternatives. Therefore, at the heart of the above mentioned question lies the problem whether we can determine the set of relevant alternatives from the structure of the distance matrix and the parameters of the price distribution.

Intuitively we would argue that only the alternatives in the vicinity of the searcher's home location will be of relevance in the search problem, and that we can ignore alternatives located further away. But what is the relevant distance; is it the distance from home or the distance between two adjacent alternatives? Can we derive a "critical distance", such that alternatives located further away than this distance are irrelevant? If yes, how can we determine this distance?

Let us introduce these questions by looking at a few simple examples. Suppose we have 6 alternatives and the home location forming a path graph (see chapter 3) with the home location being located at one of the

4.4. The Relevant Alternatives in a Spatial Search Problem

endpoints (see figure 4.6). As we will show in chapter 5, the optimal route through this graph is to visit the alternatives in sequence. Price offers at all alternatives are again generated according to a 0-1 uniform distribution.

Relevant for a specific search problem are those alternatives the elimination of which will change the optimal search strategy for the search problem. All the other alternatives, i.e. those that can be eliminated without any implications for the optimal search strategy, are irrelevant. Because of the recursive structure of the basic equations that describe the optimal strategy, a change at one point of the problem usually carries over to the preceding parts. Only when an alternative has a choice probability of zero, it can be eliminated without any implications for the optimal search strategy. Consequently, for any specific search problem we can determine the irrelevant alternatives by looking at the choice probabilities. When an alternative has choice probability zero, we can drop it from the search problem without altering the search problem or don't have to consider this alternative in the first place.

Let us begin by looking at the case where the distance between any two adjacent alternatives (including home) is 0.1. In this case we can compute the expected cost to be 0.6328. All the alternatives are part of the spatial search problem; the choice probabilities are:

$P_1 = 0.6335$	$P_4 = 0.0315$
$P_2 = 0.2328$	$P_5 = 0.0116$
$P_3 = 0.0856$	$P_6 = 0.0050$

Now, let us change the distances to $c_{1,2} = c_{2,3} = c_{4,5} = c_{5,6} = 0.04$, $c_{3,4} = 0.34$. The distance from home to the first alternative remains at 0.1.

What we did is to keep alternatives v_1 and v_6 at their respective locations and to move v_2 and v_3 closer to v_1, and v_4 and v_5 closer to v_6. The overall distance between v_1 and v_6 remains the same as before (0.5).

With this change the expected costs fall to 0.5709, and only the first three alternatives are relevant for the spatial search problem; the choice probabilities are:

$P_1 = 0.4918$	$P_4 = 0.0000$
$P_2 = 0.2948$	$P_5 = 0.0000$
$P_3 = 0.2134$	$P_6 = 0.0000$

We note that although alternative v_6 is as far from the home location as it was before, it does not belong to the set of relevant alternatives any more. Obviously, the distance from the home location is not sufficient for distinguishing between relevant and irrelevant alternatives.

To see whether the distance between two adjacent alternatives allows us to differentiate between those relevant for the spatial search problem and those that are not, let us use the first 4 alternatives of the last example. Since alternatives v_5 and v_6 are irrelevant in this case (as is v_4), we can eliminate them without changing the problem. Expected cost and choice probabilities remain the same as in the case of 6 alternatives. The distance between alternatives 3 and 4 (0.34) is too big that the searcher will ever visit v_4.

Let us add to this problem with 4 alternatives two additional alternatives outside v_4 to form a path graph again. The new alternative v_5 be 0.005 units from v_4, v_6 the same distance from v_5. When solving this problem we see that the expected costs decline marginally, the choice probabilities, however, become:

$P_1 = 0.4918$	$P_4 = 0.0005$
$P_2 = 0.2948$	$P_5 = 0.0004$
$P_3 = 0.2122$	$P_6 = 0.0003$

Although we have not changed anything between home and v_4, alternative v_4 becomes relevant again for the spatial search model. Also, v_5 and v_6 have non-zero choice probabilities.

We conclude from these examples that neither an alternative's distance to home nor its distance to adjacent alternatives provides sufficient information for determining whether the alternative is relevant for the spatial search problem or not. There must be a more complex relationship at work.

The mechanism becomes apparent when we look at our basic equations (4.5) and (4.6) again. The choice probability for any alternative can only be zero when either the conditional choice probability for this particular alternative is zero, or when the conditional choice probability is one for one of the alternative preceding it. In either case, equation (4.6) becomes zero. In the first case the alternative is so unattractive relative to others that it will never be chosen in the particular situation. In the second case, an earlier alternative is so attractive relative to others that the searcher will always choose it when he/she gets to it. Because of theorem 4.2 the two cases are actually identical. When there is an irrelevant alternative within our search sequence, we actually skip it and look at the corresponding partial route. From theorem 4.2 we know, however, that each partial route is equivalent to a complementary subroute of at least one other complete route. In other words, we can always move one or more irrelevant alternatives to the end of our search sequence, in which case they are always preceded by one alternative with a conditional choice probability of one.

4.4. The Relevant Alternatives in a Spatial Search Problem

From (4.7) we know that the conditional choice probability is determined by the level of the reservation price of the continued search sequence. Only when the reservation price $\bar{x}(R_i)$ is so high that there is no chance that the random price offer at the i-th alternative can be higher, the searcher will quit there with certainty. In order for this condition to hold the price distribution for this alternative must have an upper bound; there must be a price level X^u for which

$$f_i(X) = 0 \quad \forall \quad X \geq X^u .$$

This is an important property of any search problem. Because of its complexity property it is of particular relevance for the spatial search problem. Therefore, we will summarize it in the following theorem:

Theorem 4.6 *A search problem can have irrelevant alternatives only when its price distribution is bound from above.*

It is a direct consequence of this theorem that when a price distribution is unbound from above *always all alternatives in the world* have to be considered in a spatial search problem. In this case we can never eliminate any alternatives as being irrelevant.

But even when the price distribution is bound from above, it is difficult to identify any irrelevant alternatives a-priorily. The reservation price, which has to exceed the upper bound for an alternative to have a conditional choice probability of one, is determined by the characteristics of those alternatives not yet searched. As we have seen above in our examples, an additional – or a particularly attractive – alternative in the later parts of the search sequence may lower the reservation price at the i-th alternative enough so that the searcher is willing to continue to search.

In order to see the role search costs play, let us look at equation (4.5). Suppose that the searcher can be certain to get the respective product at alternative R_i for free. In (4.5) this means that $\bar{x}(R_i) = 0$. Substituting into (4.5) we see that the reservation price $\bar{x}(R_{i-1})$ will exceed X^u even under this strategy as long as

$$X^u \leq C(R[i-1], R[i]) + (C(R[i], H) - C(R[i-1], H)) .$$

This result has a very straightforward interpretation: As long as the costs to go to the next alternative plus the additional costs for returning home from there are greater or equal to the highest price that can be charged the searcher will not go to the next alternative, even when he/she can get the product there free.

In this formulation – as well as in (4.5) and all our previous discussion – we have implicitly used zero as the lower bound of the price distribution. However, there might be another price level X^l for which

$$f_i(X) = 0 \quad \forall \quad X \leq X_i^l \ .$$

If such a lower bound exists, it is the best option for the searcher to get the product for this lowest price with certainty. In this case the price distribution at alternative R_{i-1} collapses and (4.5) becomes

$$\begin{aligned}\bar{x}(R_{i-1}) &= C(R[i-1], R[i]) + (C(R[i], H) - C(R[i-1], H)) + \\ &\quad \int_{X^l}^{X^l} x f_i(x)\, dx + X^l[1 - F_i(X^l)] \\ &= C(R[i-1], R[i]) + (C(R[i], H) - C(R[i-1], H)) + \\ &\quad X^l \ .\end{aligned}$$

This yields the following condition for the level of search costs beyond which alternatives have to be irrelevant:

$$X^u - X^l \leq C(R[i-1], R[i]) + (C(R[i], H) - C(R[i-1], H)) \quad (4.29)$$

Whenever this condition holds for two alternatives $R[i]$ and $R[i-1]$ in the optimal search sequence, the conditional choice probability for alternative $R[i]$ is one, and alternative $R[i-1]$, $R[i-2]$, etc. all have choice probability zero.

A few points are important to note here:

- Condition (4.29) is sufficient for identification of irrelevant alternatives, but not necessary. When the searcher will not get X^l with certainty at $R[i-1]$ but is facing a price distribution in the usual way, he/she will have to expect some higher costs from continued search. In this case, alternatives beyond $R[i]$ may be irrelevant, even when condition (4.29) does not hold. As we know from our previous discussion, the expected costs of continued search depend upon the searcher's routing and stopping behavior through the remaining alternatives. Therefore, all the complexity results apply to the problem of determining the expected costs of continued search, and it is impractical to base (4.29) upon this more stringent figure.
- Condition (4.29) is of practical value only when the price distribution has a lower bound (in addition to the upper bound required by theorem 4.6). When it does not have a lower bound, we can set X^l to $-\infty$ and condition (4.29) can never be met by any finite costs.

- Condition (4.29) illustrates the relationship between the price distribution and search costs. The left hand side gives the spread of the price distribution as difference between upper and lower bound. The right hand side gives the costs incurred in going to the next alternative which consist of the costs of going there and the increase or decrease of the costs of going home. Note that the price level has no effect on condition (4.29). It is just the relationship between costs and spread of the distribution which determines whether an alternative is relevant or not.

This result is particularly important when we are dealing with separable graphs (see section 3.1). When condition (4.29) holds for the two endpoints of a cut edge we know that all the alternatives in the subgraph containing $R[i-1]$ are irrelevant and can be ignored. As a practical example, consider a shopping problem. Will it be sufficient to analyze the alternatives in the searcher's home city or do we also have to take into account those in neighboring cities? From condition (4.29) we know that the answer to this question depends not only on search costs but also on the spread of the price distribution of the product we are taking into account.

4.5 Parameter Changes in the Search Problem

In this section we want to analyze what happens to a given spatial search problem when its parameters change. Parameters of the spatial search problem are the elements of the cost matrix C and the cumulative distribution functions F_i at the various alternatives.

4.5.1 Shifting and Scaling the Search Problem

As a first step, let us look at changes that are uniformly applied to a whole set of parameters. More specifically, we will analyze what happens to the spatial search problem when

- all the prices and/or all costs increase by a certain amount
- all the prices and/or all costs are changed by a certain factor.

Let us define a new random variable, Z, that in the first case is related to X by[7]

---

[7]Because we have explicitly excluded negative prices, α has to be restricted to such values that Z is non-negative. This has no implications for the general argument.

$$Z = X + \alpha \ . \tag{4.30}$$

When we use the new random variable Z instead of X in equations (4.2) – (4.7) we find[8]

$$\begin{aligned} y_z(R_{n-1}) &= C(R[n-1], R[n]) + C(R[n], H) + E(x) + \alpha \\ &= y_x(R_{n-1}) + \alpha \ . \end{aligned} \tag{4.31}$$

Therefore, the reservation price $\bar{z}(R_n)$ based on Z is

$$\bar{z}(R_i) = y_z(R_i) - C(R[i], H) = \bar{x}(R_i) + \alpha \ . \tag{4.32}$$

When we compute $y_z(R_{n-2})$ based on (4.4), (4.31) and (4.32) we realize that expected costs and reservation prices for X and Z are related in the following way:

$$\begin{aligned} y_z(R_i) &= y_x(R_i) + \alpha \\ \bar{z}(R_i) &= \bar{x}(R_i) + \alpha \ . \end{aligned} \tag{4.33}$$

Since the shift of the reservation price just compensates that of the distribution[9], we see from (4.6) that the choice probabilities remain unchanged.

Because all expected costs are affected in the same way, their relative positions remain unchanged. Therefore, the optimal route must be identical for Z and X.

We can apply the same line of argument to the case of a rescaling of the spatial search problem. We do this by multiplying both the price variable and all cost elements by a factor $\alpha (> 0)$.

$$Z' = \alpha X \qquad C_{z'} = \alpha C \tag{4.34}$$

Some simple algebraic operations yield

$$\begin{aligned} y_{z'}(R_i) &= \alpha y_x(R_i) \\ \bar{z}'(R_i) &= \alpha \bar{x}(R_i) \ . \end{aligned} \tag{4.35}$$

Again, the transformation of the price distribution is compensated by that of the reservation price. Choice probabilities and optimal route remain unchanged.

---

[8] We indicate figures referring to X and Z by a subscript x and z, respectively.
[9] $F_z(\bar{z}) = F_x(\bar{z} - \alpha) = F_x(\bar{x})$.

It is easy to see from (4.4) that when we multiply only the random variable or the cost matrix, we do not get a similarly simple relationship. The same holds, when we add a constant to the cost matrix. In both cases choice probabilities change and also the optimal route may be altered. The reason is that in both cases we change the internal structure of the spatial search problem. We will discuss such changes in the section below.

Equations (4.33) and (4.35) show that we can shift the price distribution or rescale all cost components of the spatial search problem without fundamentally changing its solution. Choice probabilities and optimal routes remain unchanged, expected costs and reservation prices for the altered problem can be easily derived from those of the original one.

4.5.2 Changes in the Structure of the Search Problem: Stopping Effects vs. Routing Effects

Since they are easier to handle mathematically and nevertheless provide the essential insights, in this subsection we will concentrate on changes in the cost matrix. Such changes may result from some changes on one of the edges of the graph, e.g. an improvement in road conditions, congestion etc., or from the relocation of one of the vertices. Both types of changes usually have an impact upon various elements of the cost matrix, not just one.

At a general level we can argue that such changes alter the original graph of the spatial search problem so that after the change the searcher faces a new graph. Let us denote the two graphs by G_0 and G_1, where G_0 represents the graph before the change, G_1 that after it.

Before we can look into the effects a change in the cost matrix may have upon the search strategy, we have to expand our notation. Since we are now comparing the consumer's behavior in two different spatial settings – represented by the two graphs – we add reference to the respective graph in minimum expected costs and choice probabilities as well as in the indicator for the optimal route. $R^*(G_0)$ represents the optimal route through graph G_0, $R^*(G_1)$ that through graph G_1. Note that the two routes may be identical but are not necessarily so. By $y(R^*(G_0)|G_1)$, for example, we denote the costs the consumer has to expect when following the optimal route through graph G_0, i.e. $R^*(G_0)$, through graph G_1. The minimum expected cost of searching through graph G_0 would now be written $y(R^*(G_0)|G_0)$ in our extended notation. Similar modifications need to be made for the choice probabilities. $P(R[i]|R^*(G_0), G_1)$ represents the choice probability for the i-th alternative in route $R^*(G_0)$ when the actual graph is G_1. The choice probability (4.6) would now be written $P(R[i]|R^*(G_0), G_0)$.

When the underlying graph changes from G_0 to G_1 the utility maximizing searcher will adapt routing as well as search behavior in order to reach the new minimum expected cost $y(R^*(G_1)|G_1)$. Therefore, the impact the change from G_0 to G_1 has upon the searcher's minimum expected cost is $y(R^*(G_1)|G_1) - y(R^*(G_0)|G_0)$. We call this the *total effect*. It can partly be attributed to changes in the searcher's stopping behavior, partly to changes in the routing behavior. Accordingly, we may say that the total effect of a change from G_0 to G_1 on minimum expected cost is made up of a *stopping effect* and a *routing effect*.

With the notation developed above we can define the total effect, routing effect, and stopping effect on minimum expected cost as:

$$\underbrace{y(R^*(G_1)|G_1) - y(R^*(G_0)|G_0)}_{\text{total effect}} = \\ \underbrace{y(R^*(G_0)|G_1) - y(R^*(G_0)|G_0)}_{\text{stopping effect}} + \\ \underbrace{y(R^*(G_1)|G_1) - y(R^*(G_0)|G_1)}_{\text{routing effect}} \quad . \quad (4.36)$$

As can be seen from this definition, the stopping effect is that part of the total effect that results from the adaptation of the stopping behavior when the original optimal route, $R^*(G_0)$, is retained. The routing effect is the additional effect that results from an adaptation of the optimal route. So, when the optimal route through G_1 is the same as that through G_0 ($R^*(G_1) = R^*(G_0)$) the routing effect is zero and we can observe only a stopping effect.

The two effects relate directly to the elements of the above algorithm for solving the spatial search problem. This allows us to derive some properties of the two effects. The stopping effect is determined by (4.4) and (4.5), the routing effect by (4.9). From (4.4) and (4.3) we see that as long as the route remains unchanged the stopping effect on minimum expected cost is a continuous function of the underlying change in the cost matrix. The routing effect, on the other hand, is discontinuous. It is non-zero only when the optimal route changes. Because $y(R)$ is the objective of the spatial search problem, for small changes in the cost matrix the routing effect on minimum expected cost is usually small. The routing effect leads to a continuous but non-differentiable relationship between minimum expected cost and changes in the cost matrix. Because the searcher will switch from route G_0 to G_1 only when the minimum expected cost along G_1 is below that of G_0, in a minimization problem the routing effect must always be non-positive, irrespective of whether the respective cost component is increasing or decreasing.

4.5. Parameter Changes in the Search Problem 93

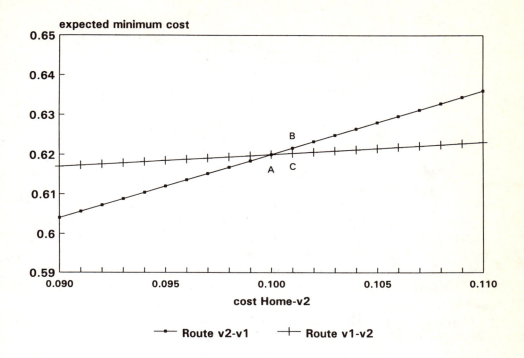

Figure 4.7: Stopping and Routing Effects for Minimum Expected Cost

The sign of the stopping effect, on the other hand, is determined by the slopes of the functions relating the minimum expected cost of the various routes to the respective cost element. We know from chapter 2 that a marginal increase in cost can never lead to a decrease in minimum expected cost. The minimum expected cost function for each route is monotonically increasing in all elements of the cost matrix. Therefore, the stopping effect always has the same sign as the underlying cost change.

A similar argument can be made concerning the total effect of a cost increase. In the case of a change in the optimal route, it can be viewed as the result of two moves along monotonically increasing functions; the first one up to the point where the two curves intersect, the second afterward. Therefore, the total effect must have the same sign as the stopping effect. It follows therefrom that a positive stopping effect can never be overcompensated by the negative routing effect.

Similarly to (4.36) we can define total effect, stopping effect and routing effect for choice probabilities as well and write the relationship between them as:

$$\underbrace{P(R[i]|R^*(G_1),G_1) - P(R[i]|R^*(G_0),G_0)}_{\text{total effect}} =$$
$$\underbrace{P(R[i]|R^*(G_0),G_1) - P(R[i]|R^*(G_0),G_0)}_{\text{stopping effect}} +$$
$$\underbrace{P(R[i]|R^*(G_1),G_1) - P(R[i]|R^*(G_0),G_1)}_{\text{routing effect}} .$$

Because of the definition of choice probabilities in (4.6) the stopping effect is again a continuous function of the underlying change in the cost matrix as long as the route remains unchanged. The routing effect, however, is discontinuous and may now lead to dramatic changes in the choice probabilities. When the optimal route changes, alternatives may move to the front or to the back of the search sequence. Depending upon the parameters of the search problem, the implications for the choice probabilities may be dramatic. As we will see below, the stopping effect may be positive as well as negative and far exceeded by a routing effect.

Let us illustrate these points with the following small example. Consider a graph with three vertices – one home location and two alternatives (v_1, v_2) – and edges connecting between all of them. At each alternative the searcher can draw from a 0-1 uniform distribution. Cost of going from home to v_1 as well as cost of going from v_1 to v_2 are 0.1 each. The cost of going between home and v_2 are altered in increments of 0.001 between 0.09 and 0.11. Quite clearly, as long as c_{2H} is below 0.1 it is optimal for the searcher to go to v_2 first and possibly v_1 second. When c_{2H} is larger than 0.1, the searcher will go to alternative v_1 first and possibly v_2 second. At $c_{2H} = 0.1$ the searcher is indifferent between the two routes and will choose one of them at random. As we can see from figure 4.7 this is the point where the two curves, representing the minimum expected costs for the two routes, intersect. At this point, A, a routing effect can be observed. When we move to $c_{2H} = 0.101$, the minimum expected cost of the optimal route, C, are only slightly smaller than those of route (v_2, v_1), B. The total effect of a parameter change from $c_{2H} = 0.1$ to $c_{2H} = 0.101$ is represented by the vertical distance between points A and C. The stopping effect corresponds to the vertical distance between A and B, the routing effect to that between B and C. We see that the routing effect is negative, and partly compensates the positive stopping effect. This corresponds to the theoretical results derived above.

When we draw the corresponding graphs for choice probabilities (figure 4.8), we see that the picture differs markedly. For values of c_{2H} below 0.1 alternative v_2 is the first one to be visited and it will be chosen with

4.5. Parameter Changes in the Search Problem

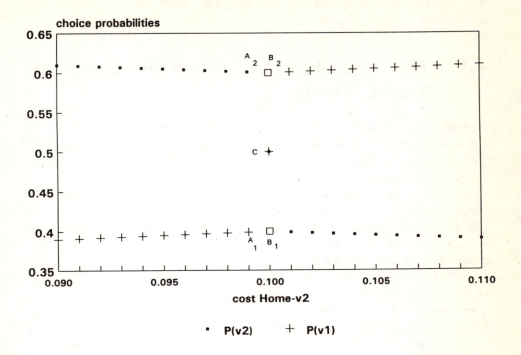

Figure 4.8: Stopping and Routing Effects for Choice Probabilities

a probability greater than 0.6. Accordingly, the choice probability for alternative v_1 is below 0.4 in this case. When we move from 0.099 to 0.1 for c_{2H} the searcher finds that the two routes offer the same minimum expected cost and is therefore indifferent between them. When following route (v_2, v_1) the searcher will select alternative v_2 with probability 0.6, and alternative v_1 with probability 0.4. He/she will select this route only with a chance of 0.5, however, with the same probability he/she may choose route (v_1, v_2) which offers the same minimum expected cost. The choice probabilities for route (v_1, v_2) are 0.6 and 0.4 for alternative v_1 and v_2, respectively. So, the searcher will choose each one of the two alternatives with probability 0.5.

We can calculate total effect, stopping, and routing effect for the choice probability of each of the alternatives. For alternative 1 the total effect of changing c_{2H} from 0.099 to 0.1 is represented by the vertical distance between A_1 and C. The stopping effect corresponds to the vertical distance between A_1 and B_1, the routing effect to that between B_1 and C. As we can see, the routing effect by far exceeds the stopping effect. Both are positive in this case, for alternative v_1 they are both negative. As we will see later, stopping and routing effect for choice probabilities do not necessarily carry the same sign.

4.6 The Spatial Search Model and Economic Search Theory

In section 4.2 we have established a direct relationship between the spatial search problem and the traveling salesman problem. We have used this relationship in our proof of theorem 4.1. We can establish a similar relationship between the spatial search problem and the "standard (sequential) search model" of economic search theory (see chapter 2). The implications of this relationship are far less important. It does not provide any additional insight into the complexity of the spatial search model. It mainly shows that the spatial search problem contains the standard search model as a special case as well.

When comparing figures 4.4, 4.5, 2.1, and 3.5 we get an intuitive idea of the relationships between the spatial search model, the traveling salesman model and the standard search model. In section 4.2 we have established the relationship to the traveling salesman problem by forcing each search route to use all the available alternatives. This eliminated the side branches from figure 4.4 and left us with the graph in figure 3.5. Similarly, in establishing the relationship to the standard search model we restructure the spatial search model in such a way that the routing part becomes irrelevant, i.e. whatever route the searcher follows the search problem remains unaltered.

We can do this by eliminating all the space related cost components from the spatial search problem. More precisely, we assume that in equation (4.1) the additional conditions

$$\bar{c}_{ij} = 0, \qquad \tau_j = \tau \qquad \forall \ i,j > 0 \qquad (4.37)$$
$$c_{i0} = 0 \qquad \qquad \forall \ i$$

hold. These conditions eliminate any cost differences between the alternatives and allow the individual to return home at no extra cost. In addition, as in section 4.2, let us assume that all the price distributions are identical:

$$F_i(X) = F(X) \qquad \forall \ i \ . \qquad (4.38)$$

So, we have a search problem with n alternatives where each one can be accessed at cost τ and generates a price according to the price distribution $F(X)$. This, however, is the standard search model with a limited number of alternatives as we have discussed it in chapter 2.

In order to show that assumptions (4.37) and (4.38) indeed do transform the spatial search problem into the standard search model, let us substitute our assumptions into equations (4.2) - (4.4). Equation (4.2) becomes

$$y(R_{n-1}) = y_{n-1} = \tau + \int_0^\infty x f(x)\, dx \; . \tag{4.39}$$

Since the right hand side of (4.39) does not depend upon the route, we can drop the reference to route R from the left hand side as well. Because of the assumption that the individual can return home from each alternative for free, the equation for the reservation price simplifies to

$$\bar{x}_i = y_i \; .$$

Substituted into (4.38) this yields

$$y_{i-1} = \tau + \int_0^{y_i} x f(x)\, dx + y_i(1 - F(y_i))$$

which matches exactly equation (2.2) in chapter 2. This shows that the standard search model of economics is a special case of the general spatial search model.

4.7 Summary

In this chapter we have discussed the spatial search problem in its most general form. Section 4.1 is devoted to defining the spatial search problem. We develop and discuss a list of assumptions that define the spatial search problem in its most general form. We investigate the structure of the problem, suggest an algorithm for solving it and illustrate it with a simple example. The obvious problem of the suggested algorithm is that it requires the full enumeration of all possible routes through the graph that characterizes the spatial structure of the spatial search problem.

Therefore, in section 4.2 we investigate the complexity of the general spatial search problem. We can show that the problem is *NP-complete*, which means that it falls into a class of very complex problems. Because of the need to enumerate all possible routes, the computational requirements increase tremendously when the number of alternatives increases. This result is central to our argument. It motivates the discussion in chapter 5 and simplifications we apply in later chapters.

In the rest of the chapter we investigate the structure of the spatial search problem as it was defined in section 4.1. In the first two sections of chapter 4 we have restricted our attention to complete routes. Therefore, section 4.3 analyzes the implications of allowing partial routes. The searcher may investigate a subset of the available alternatives rather than the full set. As it turns out, this does not change the search problem. We show that incomplete routes can easily be integrated into the framework of section 4.1. Consequently, the results we have derived there hold in the case of incomplete routes as well.

Section 4.4 asks the question whether there are any criteria available that let us distinguish relevant from irrelevant alternatives a-priorily. This is an important question because it may help us restrict the number of alternatives that we have to take into account in a spatial search problem. As we know from section 4.2 the computational requirements increase dramatically with larger numbers of alternatives. As it turns out, we can identify irrelevant alternatives only when the price distribution is bounded from above. When this is not the case, there will always be a positive chance that the observed price offer at the relevant alternative is higher than the reservation price, however high the latter one will be. For the case of a price distribution that is bounded from above we derive sufficient conditions for alternatives to be irrelevant.

In section 4.5 we discuss the effects of parameter changes on the spatial search problem. We find that the spatial search problem remains structurally unchanged when we either shift all price distributions by a certain amount or scale all prices and costs by some positive factor. More interesting are the reactions of the spatial search problem to marginal changes of one of the parameters. We can identify two types of effect: stopping effects and routing effects. The stopping effect results from the searcher's adjustment of stopping behavior, the routing effect results from the adjustment of routing behavior. Together they give the total effect. While the searcher adjusts his/her stopping behavior continuously, routing effects occur only at certain points in parameter space. We derive results for stopping and routing effects on expected costs and on choice probabilities.

Section 4.6 compares the general spatial search model as defined in section 4.1 to the search model of economics, as we have discussed it in chapter 2. We show that the standard search model of economics is a special case of the general spatial search model.

Chapter 5

Tractable Spatial Search Problems

In chapter 4 we have demonstrated that the spatial search problem as we have defined it there is highly complex. It belongs to a class of problems for which it seems a general solution does not exist. Although minimum expected cost and choice probabilities can be computed quite easily for a spatial search problem with few alternatives, when the number of alternatives increases, the resource requirements for solving the spatial search problem grow beyond bounds.

The reason for the complexity of the spatial search problem lies in its routing component. Since the alternatives are distributed in space, the searcher has to find the optimal route through the graph characterizing the spatial structure of the search problem in order to solve it. However, there are generally $n!$ complete closed routes through a graph of size n. Moreover, since the stopping problem and the routing problem are interrelated. The searcher has to solve them simultaneously to find the strategy that minimizes the expected cost.

In this chapter we shall discuss some possibilities to overcome the intrinsic complexity of the spatial search problem. The available strategies can be classified into two broad categories:

- We may impose additional constraints upon the general spatial search problem as defined in section 4 that simplify the routing problem and allow us to solve it efficiently and – preferably – separately from the stopping component of the spatial search problem. Some strategies of this type will be discussed in section 5.1.
- We may redefine the objective of the searcher so that he/she is trying to find a *good* solution to the spatial search problem rather than the optimal one. Such strategies that intend to approximate the optimal strategy are known as heuristics. We shall discuss some heuristics

for the spatial search problem in section 5.2. Given our results about the complexity of the spatial search problem, heuristic solutions can be motivated from an economic point of view as well in this context. It may be economically superior to go for a solution that is known to be fairly close to the optimum but can be derived at low cost, rather than investing a large amount of resources into finding the optimal solution.

It is interesting to note that the stopping component and the routing component of the spatial search problem react quite differently to increases in problem size. While routing problems are relatively simple to solve for a small number of alternatives – one only has to compare a small number of possible routes – and become more and more complex when the number of alternatives increases, the search problem is most easily solved for an infinite number of alternatives – given that some additional assumptions hold (see chapter 2).

5.1 Simplified Spatial Structures

Since the reason for the complexity of the general spatial search problem is the simultaneity of routing and search, the simplifying assumptions we are going to make in this chapter are targeted toward separating the two. This can be done by either

- making assumptions about the spatial structure of the problem and thus drastically simplifying the routing decision, or
- by assuming a search structure which does not depend upon the route through the systems.

In either case we need to be aware that we are dealing with simplifications. So, the results we derive may not be valid in the case of the general spatial search problem.

In section 5.1.1 we will deal with the case of linear space. We start the discussion by assuming that the alternatives are distributed along a line and that the searcher's home location is at one end of it. In the next step, we allow the home location to be anywhere on this line, and finally we connect the ends of the line and arrange the alternatives in a circle[1].

---

[1] We use the terms "line" and "circle" here to make our discussion compatible with the corresponding spatial literature (see chapters 6 - 8). We need to note, however, that because of the structure of the spatial search problem we are actually dealing with path graphs and cycle graphs, two structures that are only isomorphic to a line and a circle.

5.1.1 Linear Space

The assumption of linear space is very prominent in the spatial literature. It has been used by Hotelling in his 1929 seminal paper on "Stability in Competition" (see also chapter 7). More recent analyses based on the concept of linear space are, e.g. by Stahl (1982), Mai (1984). In this literature, linear space is conceptualized in two different ways, both of which we will use below: (1) as a straight line, and (2) as the perimeter of a circle. These simple geometrical structures are usually assumed to simplify the derivation of analytical results. In essence, however, linear space does not need to be a *straight* line or the perimeter of a *circle*. It is only necessary that the alternatives form a graph which is isomorphic to such a geometrical figure. The essential elements are that the graph must be connected, and that each vertex is connected to at most two other vertices. Nevertheless, in order to remain compatible with the respective spatial literature we will use straight lines and circles in the discussion below. We should keep in mind, however, that the results we derive hold for any graph which is isomorphic to the graphs underlying these geometric figures.

In our context, assuming the alternatives to be located on a straight line might actually be a rather realistic assumption for some types of problems. We can think of the line as a road that connects the alternatives (e.g. shopping centers lined up on a suburban highway); the individual follows this road in search for the best price offered. On the other hand, the endpoints of the line represent some special cases, which in some cases lead to analytical problems that dominate the problem in question (see Eaton, Lipsey, 1975). This can be avoided by assuming the linear space to be the perimeter of a circle.

As we will see later, the assumption of linear space alone is not sufficient to completely eliminate the computational complexity of the spatial search problem. When we impose some additional constraints, however, we strips the spatial search problem of some of its more interesting features.

Alternatives on a Line, H at Endpoint

The first simplification we want to look at is when the alternatives are distributed along a line. In graph theory this is usually called a *path graph*. To start off we assume that the individual's home (H) is located at one endpoint of the line. The alternatives labeled $v_1, \ldots, v_n$ are distributed at arbitrary points along the line (see figure 5.1).

Assuming this spatial structure may drastically simplify the routing part of the spatial search problem. Intuitively one may expect that the

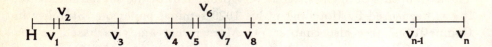

Figure 5.1: Simplified Spatial Structure: Alternatives Along a Line

searcher's optimal route is to investigate the alternatives in the same sequence as they appear on the line. In this case the optimal route can be determined independently from the stopping problem and without computational problems. Since at each point there is always only just one "next alternative on the line", the routing problem actually disappears. In order to draw these conclusions, however, we need to demonstrate that investigating the alternatives as they appear on the line is indeed the optimal strategy, irrespective of the price offer distributions.

To be more specific, let us define two alternative routes through the search problem:

$$R = (\ldots, v_1, v_2, v_3, v_4, \ldots)$$
$$S = (\ldots, v_1, v_3, v_2, v_4, \ldots)$$

which by assumption are identical before alternative v_1 as well as after alternative v_4. Route R is the one that we think is optimal (alternatives are searched in sequence), route S goes from alternative v_1 to v_3, skipping alternative v_2, then turns back to v_2, and finally proceeds to v_4.

Rather than by computing the minimum expected cost of the two routes directly, we will prove this property of a search problem in linear space in an indirect way. We will divide the transition from route R to route S into two steps, and show that neither of these steps can lead to lower minimum expected cost of the search process. The two steps of the transition from route R to route S are sketched in figure 5.2. In the first step, we move alternative v_2 from its current location to that of alternative v_3. In the second step we insert cost c_{23} between alternatives v_3 and v_2 as well as between v_2 and v_4. When the two alternatives occupy the same location, the searcher can go between them at no cost. He/she is clearly indifferent between investigating first v_2 or v_3. This point characterizes the transition from the ordering of alternatives in route R to that in route S; i.e. a routing effect.

5.1. Simplified Spatial Structures

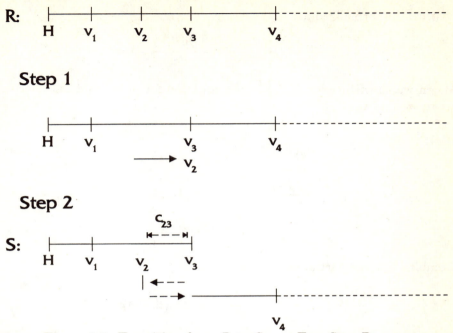

Figure 5.2: Transition from R to S as a Two Step Process

Since the route remains unchanged within the range of each step, we can use marginal calculus for drawing conclusions about each of the steps. Since the minimum expected costs are identical at the point where the routing effect occurs (see section 4.5), we can combine our arguments for the two steps in order to draw conclusions for the transition between R and S as a whole.

In order to prove that moving one alternative marginally down the road cannot decreases the minimum expected cost, we use alternatives v_1, v_2, and v_3 out of the spatial structure displayed in figure 5.1, and move alternative v_2 toward alternative v_3. More specifically, when we say that "v_2 is moved toward v_3" we mean that the cost of going from an alternative to the left of v_2 to v_2 ($c_{i2}, c_{2i}, \forall i < 2$ or $i = H$) are increased, the cost of going from v_2 to an alternative to the right of it ($c_{i2}, c_{2i}, \forall i > 2$) are decreased by the same marginal amount. The first type of change tends to increase the minimum expected cost of the search procedure, while the second type of change tends to decrease it. So, we actually want to show that the sum of the two effects cannot be negative. Since we are operating in linear space, there are only two elements of the cost matrix relevant for the first type of effect, namely c_{12} and c_{2H}. For the second type of effect, only c_{23} is relevant. So, our hypothesis that moving alternative v_2 marginally down the road toward v_3 cannot decrease minimum expected cost can be formalized as:

$$\frac{\partial y(R_1)}{\partial c_{12}} + \frac{\partial y(R_1)}{\partial c_{2H}} - \frac{\partial y R(_1)}{\partial c_{23}} \geq 0$$

When we substitute for $\bar{x}(R_2)$ in the equation for $y(R_1)$ and take derivatives, we find that

$$\frac{\partial y(R_1)}{\partial c_{12}} = 1 \;,$$
$$\frac{\partial y(R_1)}{\partial c_{2H}} = F_2(\bar{x}(R_2)) \;,$$
$$\frac{\partial y R(_1)}{\partial c_{23}} = 1 - F_2(\bar{x}(R_2)) \;.$$

Combining these partial derivatives yields

$$\frac{\partial y(R_1)}{\partial c_{12}} + \frac{\partial y(R_1)}{\partial c_{2H}} - \frac{\partial y(R_1)}{\partial c_{23}} = 2F_2(\bar{x}(R_2)) \quad \geq 0 \;. \tag{5.1}$$

This shows that the first one of the two steps that we have defined in order to get from R to S cannot reduce the minimum expected cost of the search process. Note that the effect is zero when the choice probability for $R[2]$ is zero. In this case the searcher will skip alternative v_2 and always proceed from v_1 directly to v_3 so that the cost changes cancel each other.

In the second step, we add cost between alternatives $S[2]$ and $S[3]$ as well as between $S[3]$ and $S[4]$. Since we are actually moving alternative v_2 back toward its original location, but now requiring the searcher to follow route S, we are reducing the cost of going home from v_2 by the same margin. From a very similar argument than the one above we can derive the total effect for a marginal change as

$$\frac{\partial y(S_2)}{\partial c_{23}} - \frac{\partial y(S_2)}{\partial c_{2H}} + \frac{\partial y(S_2)}{\partial c_{24}} = 2[1 - F_2(\bar{x}(R_2))] \quad \geq 0 \;. \tag{5.2}$$

Again, the total effect is non-negative. It is zero only when alternative v_2 is chosen with certainty.

When we compare the conditions under which the effect in (5.1) and (5.2) are zero we see that they are mutually exclusive. Therefore, as long as $c_{23} > 0$ the minimum expected cost of search along route S will always be higher than those of search along route S.

This line of reasoning actually proves the following, more general theorem:

Theorem 5.1 *Regardless of the price distributions at the various alternatives, whenever the searcher's current location, v_i, and two alternatives v_j and v_k are arranged such that $c_{ij}+c_{jk} = c_{ik}$, alternative v_j will be before alternative v_k in the optimal route through the remaining graph.*

This result has the following implication for our specific spatial search problem:

Corollary 5.1 *When all the alternatives of a spatial search model form a path graph and the searcher's home location is at one end of the path graph, the search problem can be solved efficiently by algorithm 4.1.*

Because of theorem 5.1, there is really no routing problem in the case when all alternatives are on a line and search starts at one end of the line. Before calculating the reservation prices, the searcher knows the optimal sequence in which the alternatives ought to be investigated. When using algorithm 4.1 the searcher only has to compute the n integrals in the recursive application of (4.4), each of which can be accomplished in constant time. The whole algorithm is therefore of complexity $O(n)$, i.e. it is efficient.

Alternatives on a Line, Unrestricted Location of H

The restrictions we imposed upon the spatial search problem so far in this chapter were really twofold:

1. we assumed all alternatives to be located on one line (linear space), and
2. we assumed the home location to be at one of the two ends of the line.

While it is obvious that moving from a connected graph G to linear space reduces the number of possible routes, what is the significance of the assumption about the home location of the searcher? Will relaxing this assumption lead to a more complex spatial search problem?

Consider, for example, the situation in figure 5.3 where there are alternatives $v_1,\ldots,v_5$, and home is located between v_2 and v_3. Now, there is more than one route that the searcher can follow without passing any yet unsearched alternative. For example, he/she may start with alternatives v_2 and v_1, and then search v_3, v_4, and v_5. Alternatively, the searcher may first search v_3, v_4 and v_5, and then turn to v_2 and v_1. Obviously, now there are two sides of the graph available for the searcher and as long as

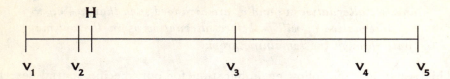

Figure 5.3: Linear Space with Interior Home Location

he/she has not exhausted all the alternatives on one of the two sides there are always *two* next alternatives available; one to the left, and one to the right.

In order to deal with this complication, we will now generalize the routing problem for linear space. This generalization will incorporate our previous version, where the home location was assumed to be at one end of the line, as a special case.

The searcher cannot choose alternatives freely from the two sides. Because we know that it is suboptimal to pass yet unsearched alternatives, at each time there is at most one alternative available for the searcher on either side. In our example, he/she can start searching alternative v_2 or v_3, but not v_1 or v_4 since this would require passing v_2 or v_3, respectively. This does not rule out the possibility that the searcher does not draw from the random distribution at alternative v_2. This case will occur when the distribution function at v_2 is such that there is no chance to draw a value below the reservation price at this point. Then, the choice probability for v_2 is zero and the searcher seemingly bypasses this alternative. However, it is still in the route at its appropriate place and the searcher still computes a reservation price for this alternative.

In order to show how many different routes the searcher can follow through the graph in this situation, we will look at the problem from a slightly different perspective. Rather than dealing with the alternatives, we will look at the route choices the searcher has on his/her way through the graph. As noted above, as long as none of the two sides is exhausted the searcher can always turn either left or right for the next alternative. With each such decision, the searcher removes one alternative from the respective side. So, in a situation with n alternatives, m to the left of the searcher's home location and $n - m$ to the right, the searcher will m-times select an alternative to his/her left, and $(n - m)$-times one to the right. Denote a decision of the first type by L and one of the second type by R. The searcher's routing decision is now one about sequencing the m Ls and

5.1. Simplified Spatial Structures

the $n - m$ Rs. The number of routes is therefore equal to the number of different ways in which one can order m units of one type and $n - m$ units of another. This, however, is nothing but the binomial coefficient. So, when there are m alternatives at one side of the searcher's home location in linear space, and $n - m$ at the other, there are $\binom{n}{m}$ different routes for the searcher to choose from.

When we apply this result to the specific constellation above, with the home location being at one end of the linear space, we get as a result

$$\binom{n}{0} = \binom{n}{n} = 1 ,$$

the one route that we have shown to be optimal in this situation.

Another feature that follows directly from the result about the number of routes is that the more centrally located the searcher's home, the greater the number of possible routes through the graph. For a given n the largest number is

$$\binom{n}{\text{int}(n/2)} , \qquad (5.3)$$

where int() yields the integer part of the number in parentheses.

As far as the number of routes through the graph and computational complexity is concerned, a central home location represents the worst case scenario. How is it related to the size of the graph?

To keep the notation simple let us just look at even values of n. In this case (5.3) can be written as

$$\binom{n}{n/2} = \prod_{i=0}^{n/2-1} \frac{n-i}{n/2-i} . \qquad (5.4)$$

In order to simplify the notation let us use

$$K_{n,i} = \frac{n-i}{n/2-i} .$$

It is easy to see from (5.4) that the following relationships hold for $K_{n,i}$:

$$K_{n,0} = 2 \quad \forall \ n ,$$
$$K_{n,i} > K_{n,i-1} \quad \forall \ 0 < i < \frac{n}{2} .$$

As a consequence, all the $n/2$ $K_{n,i}$ that are multiplied in (5.4) to get the maximum number of routes have to be equal to 2 or larger. Therefore, we see that

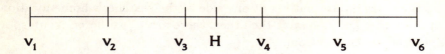

Figure 5.4: Search Along a Line: Example

$$\binom{n}{n/2} > 2^{n/2} .$$

This shows that the maximum number of routes through the graph in linear space increases faster than $2^{n/2}$ with increasing size of the graph. So, when we apply algorithm 4.1 to this simplified version of the spatial search problem, we see that it requires the enumeration of more than $2^{n/2}$ routes. The whole algorithm is therefore of complexity $O(n*2^{n/2})$. Quite clearly, the algorithm is inefficient.

The reason for the large number of routes is the fact that at each alternative the searcher has to decide whether to search an alternative from the left branch or from the right (as long as there are alternatives left on both). Intuitively one might argue that when the searcher has decided to investigate an alternative on one side of the graph, the trip to this alternative takes him/her closer to all the other alternatives in this branch and the searcher will therefore always continue in this direction until all the alternatives there are exhausted. That such a search strategy is not necessarily optimal can be demonstrated by a simple example.

Consider, for example, the graph in figure 5.4, where we have six alternatives equally spaced at locations $v_1 \ldots v_6$ (we will come back to this basic structure in chapter 6). Each supplier is assumed to generate price offers according to a $0-1$ uniform distribution and search costs set equal to distance. The distance between any two adjacent suppliers in figure 5.4 be 0.1. The searcher's home location, H, is between alternatives v_3 and v_4, 0.04 units from v_3.

If the searcher were located right in the middle between v_3 and v_4, the two sides of the graph would appear identical for the searcher and he/she would therefore be indifferent between going first to v_3 or to v_4. However, since the distance from H to v_3 is smaller than that to v_4, the searcher will decide to visit v_3 first. If the price offer at this location is not attractive

Table 5.1: Expected Cost for Selected Routes

route	expected cost
$(v_3, v_4, v_5, v_6, v_2, v_1)$	0.481689
$(v_3, v_2, v_1, v_4, v_5, v_6)$	0.508316
$(v_4, v_5, v_6, v_3, v_2, v_1)$	0.545464

enough the searcher may continue further to the left or to the right. In both directions the nearest alternative is a distance of 0.1 away. However, further to the left there are only two more alternatives to search while to the right there are three. This additional alternative makes it more attractive for the searcher to turn right and search alternatives v_4, v_5, and v_6. If no acceptable price offer can be found at any of these locations, the searcher continues to alternatives v_2, and v_1 (for a more elaborate discussion see chapter 6).

As we see, the optimal route through the search problem changes directions at v_3. Table 5.1 demonstrates that indeed route $(v_3, v_4, v_5, v_6, v_2, v_1)$ yields lower minimum expected cost than any route that follows one direction until all the alternatives there are exhausted.

Alternatives on a Circle

An interesting variation of linear space can be derived when we place the alternatives on a circle. We may think of getting from the line that we had above to the circle by connecting the two endpoints. In graph theory this structure is known as a *cycle graph*. In this constellation the searcher cannot exhaust all the alternatives on one side of the graph. Wherever he/she is on the graph, as long as there is at least one alternative left the searcher has to decide whether to go left or right. When there is only one alternative left, this decision is trivial. As a consequence, when there are n alternatives, the searcher has to decide $(n-1)$-times whether to choose the next alternative to the left or to the right. Following our argument above, this leads to a total number of 2^{n-1} different routes. Contrary to the case above, where the number of routes varied with the location of the searcher's home in the graph, now the searcher always has to deal with 2^{n-1} possible routes. Again, algorithm 4.1 from chapter 4 is clearly inefficient in this case. It is of complexity $O(n * 2^{n-1})$.

Moreover, whenever n is larger than 2, there are more possible routes around the circle than on a line. This follows from the following property of the binomial coefficient (see e.g. Mott et al., 1983, p. 165ff)

$$\sum_{i=0}^{n} \binom{n}{i} = 2^n \ . \tag{5.5}$$

When we arrange the binomial coefficients in the famous Pascal triangle, equation (5.5) describes the sum over its n-th row. Therefore, when n alternatives are arranged on a circle, the number of possible routes corresponds to the sum of all the elements of row $n-1$ of the Pascal triangle. When the same number of alternatives are distributed on an line, the maximum number of routes corresponds to one element of the n-th row of the Pascal triangle. At the same time, it corresponds to the sum of the two adjacent elements in row $n-1$ of the Pascal triangle. This sum, however, must be smaller than the sum over all the elements of row $n-1$, for all $n > 2$.

Again, the number of 2^{n-1} possible lines represents the worst possible case. In some situations going into one of the two possible directions may clearly be suboptimal, and the corresponding decision will therefore be trivial. As noted above this is the case when there is only one alternative left. In whatever direction the last alternative is nearer, the searcher will select this direction. Since by assumption the corresponding element in the distance matrix contains the shortest distance to this alternative, this choice or route is already anticipated in the distance matrix.

However, there is a more interesting constellation that reduces the number of routes the searcher has to consider. Whenever the searcher gets to a point, where the distance to the next alternative in one direction is larger than half the perimeter of the circle, it is suboptimal to choose this direction at this step and all the remaining steps. This is very easy to prove. Since the distance to this alternative, say v_i, in the one direction, say to the left, is larger than half of the perimeter, the distance to v_i to the right must be smaller. So, if v_i is the next alternative the searcher wants to investigate, he/she can save travel cost when turning to the right at the current location rather than to the left. However, since v_i is the next alternative to the left of the searcher's current location, when going to the right, the searcher must pass by all the other remaining alternatives before getting there. As we know from above, passing alternatives and going back to them later in the route cannot be an optimal strategy. Therefore, in the optimal route all these alternatives have to come in the sequence in which they are lined up on the circle, and v_i must be the last alternative in the optimal route.

The same argument holds for all the remaining alternatives, simply because the distance to the next alternative to the left, v_i, must increase when the searcher moves to the right. Therefore, the respective distance can never be smaller than half the perimeter for any one of the other

5.1. Simplified Spatial Structures 111

alternatives.

Whenever this situation occurs, the searcher is in exactly the same situation as if the alternatives were located on a line and the alternatives of one side were exhausted. It is as if the long arc of the circle were clipped away. From this point on, the routing problem is trivial.

However, whether and when this situation will occur in a given search problem along a circle depends upon the specific locations of the alternatives and of the searchers home, i.e. the structure of the cost matrix. It might well be, that the decision is trivial only for the last alternative. Therefore, as long as the cost matrix remains unspecified, we must be prepared to deal with the worst case, which is to enumerate 2^{n-1} routes.

5.1.2 Simplified Structures in Non-Linear Space

As we have seen above, linear space alone does not guarantee that the spatial search problem can be solved efficiently by algorithm 4.1. We need to impose the additional restrictions that the linear space is isomorphic to a path graph and also have to restrict the searcher's home location. When we do not impose these restrictions, the number of routes through the graph may increase exponentially with problem size. Although the computational complexity of the spatial search problem in linear space is lower than that for the general case, enumerating all the possible routes and finding the optimal one may turn out to be too large a job even in the case of linear space.

In many cases alternatives are distributed such that they can hardly be considered to be located along a line. This raises the question whether there are any structures in two dimensional space that might reduce the complexity of the general search problem.

Searching a Star Graph

In some cases it makes sense to assume that the searcher returns home after every alternative he/she investigates. A good example is job search. Since the searcher will have to commute from home to the location of the job in case it is accepted, the fact that the trip to one alternative may bring the searcher nearer to another alternative is much less important than the second alternative's distance from the searcher's home location. This makes the searcher's home location much more important than it was in the previous case.

We can introduce this increased importance of the home location into the spatial search model by assuming that the searcher always returns home after investigating one alternative. The resulting search pattern is

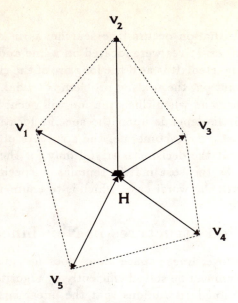

Figure 5.5: Star Graph

a *star graph* (see figure 5.5). This implies that the searcher always looks at the spatial search problem from the same perspective. Distances to remaining alternatives do not change during the search process as they did in the general case discussed in chapter 4. Whenever the searcher has returned to the home location, the distances to and the price distribution at any one of the remaining alternatives are the same as they were at the beginning of the search process.

Before we analyze the consequences this assumption has for the spatial search problem, let us use it in order to simplify our notation. Since the searcher always has to return home, irrespective of whether he/she accepts an alternative or not, we can add the cost of going to the alternative and the cost of returning home into just one cost figure:

$$c_i = c_{Hi} + c_{iH} \; . \tag{5.6}$$

Because the starting point is always the home location, we only need one index in order to characterize this cost element. This simplifies the formal structure of the spatial search problem to the structure we had in chapter 2. Using (5.6) the expected minimum cost at the $i-1$-st alternative simplifies to

$$y(R_{i-1}) = c_i + \int_0^{y(R_i)} x f_i(x) \, dx + y_i \left[1 - F_i(y(R_i))\right] \; , \tag{5.7}$$

which closely resembles equation (2.2). However, while we did not worry

5.1. Simplified Spatial Structures

about the sequence in which the alternatives are searched because of our a-spatial focus in chapter 2, we now realize that when the searcher has control over the sequence in which alternatives are investigated, the question of the optimal sequence remains unanswered in chapter 2. We have avoided this problem there by assuming that "the alternatives are observed in sequence $1, \ldots, n$". From our current perspective we realize that there might be a routing problem even in an a-spatial search model as the one we discussed in chapter 2. We will come back to this point later on.

Let us start the analysis of the implications a star graph has for the spatial search problem by imposing an additional simplifying assumption. Let us assume that all the price offers are generated according to the same cumulative probability function. With this assumption, the alternatives may differ only by the cost c_i defined in (5.6). When two of the alternatives differ in these cost, will this difference allow us to determine the sequence in which they ought to be searched?

Suppose we have two alternatives v_i and v_j, for which the relationship

$$c_i < c_j$$

holds. The optimal search sequence up to v_i and v_j as well as that after the two alternatives may be given. So, the problem of finding the optimal sequence reduces to whether v_i should be investigated first and then v_j, or the other way round.

In order to keep the notation consistent, suppose that there are $k-2$ alternatives in the first part of the search sequence. Therefore, we denote by $y(R_k)$ the minimum expected cost of search after v_i and v_j. Note that because we can incorporate the cost of returning home into transportation cost, y_k is equal to the reservation price at this stage. Let up write the two possible search sequences as

$$R = (\ldots, v_i, v_j, \ldots)$$
$$S = (\ldots, v_j, v_i, \ldots) \ .$$

Applying the recursive equation (5.7) and using our simplifying assumptions we get

$$y(R_{k-1}) = c_j + \int_0^{y(R_k)} x f(x)\, dx + y(R_k)\left[1 - F(y(R_k))\right] ,$$
$$y(R_{k-2}) = c_i + \int_0^{y(R_{k-1})} x f(x)\, dx + y(R_{k-1}\left[1 - F(y(R_{k-1}))\right] ,$$
$$y(S_{k-1}) = c_i + \int_0^{y(R_k)} x f(x)\, dx + y(R_k)\left[1 - F(y(R_k))\right] ,$$

$$y(S_{k-2}) \;=\; c_j + \int_0^{y(S_{k-1})} x f(x)\, dx + y(S_{k-1}[1 - F(y(S_{k-1}))] \;\;.$$

We can compute the difference between $y(R_{k-1})$ and $y(S_{k-1})$, as well as that between $y(R_{k-2})$ and $y(S_{k-2})$ therefrom as

$$\begin{aligned}
y(R_{k-1}) - y(S_{k-1}) &= c_j - c_i > 0 \\
y(R_{k-2}) - y(S_{k-2}) &= \int_{y(S_{k-1})}^{y(R_{k-1})} (x - y(R_{k-1})) f(x)\, dx + \\
&\quad (c_i - c_j) F(y(S_{k-1})) < 0 \;\;.
\end{aligned} \qquad (5.8)$$

Because the routes R and S do not differ for the first $k-2$ alternatives, the relationship between $y(R_{k-2})$ and $y(S_{k-2})$ cannot be reversed during this part of search. Therefore, the cost of following route R are lower than the cost of following route S.

We can apply this line of argument to every pair of alternatives in the search problem. This results in the following theorem:

Theorem 5.2 *In a star graph with identical price distributions at all alternatives, it is optimal to search the alternatives in increasing order of transportation costs.*

Since the cost matrix collapses to a vector, and the optimal route can be determined directly from it according to theorem 5.2, we get the following result about algorithm 4.1:

Corollary 5.2 *When the alternatives of a spatial search model form a star graph and prices at all alternatives are generated according to the same cumulative probability distribution, the search problem can be solved efficiently by algorithm 4.1.*

Will this result remain valid when we do not restrict the probability distributions? Obviously not. Because of the structure of (5.7), when there is no constraint upon the probability distribution we can generate whatever value desired for $y(R_{i-1})$ by choosing the appropriate probability distribution. At the same time, the minimum expected cost at one step also depend upon the minimum expected cost at the previous step, which in turn is a result of the transportation cost, probability distribution and search sequence of all the remaining alternatives. It seems that in this case, when the probability distributions may vary over the alternatives, the searcher has to investigate all the permutations for arranging the alternatives in a route. If this is indeed the case[2] the searcher faces a spatial search problem as complex as the most general one; despite the fact that the alternatives are arranged in a star graph.

---

[2]We cannot provide a proof at the moment. For every reasonable simplified

5.1. Simplified Spatial Structures

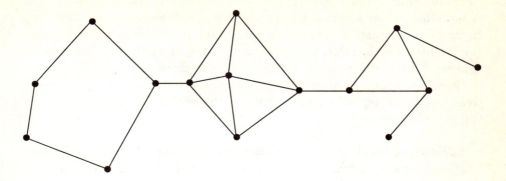

Figure 5.6: Separable Graph

Separable Graphs

In chapter 3 we have defined a connected graph to be separable when the graph contains at least one vertex, the removal of which will disconnect the graph. Such vertices are called articulation points. An edge connecting two articulation points is called cut-edge. Separable graphs consist of clusters of vertices which are closely connected among each other but connect to neighboring clusters via one particular vertex (and maybe a cut-edge). When we think of the clusters of vertices as cities, shopping centers etc., we see that separable graphs are of particular importance in a spatial context.

From the point of view of the spatial search problem, separability of the underlying graph may offer considerable computational advantages. If we can show that in the optimal search strategy the searcher will always investigate all the alternatives within one cluster before proceeding to another cluster, the routing problem reduces from one with n alternatives to a series of routing problems, each with a much smaller number of alternatives.

Consider a graph like the one in figure 5.6. It can be separated into three clusters, each consisting of five vertices. So, the graph has 15 vertices, implying that in the general case the searcher has to choose from 15! possible routes. However, when we try to find the optimal route through each cluster separately, for each one of these sub-problems there are only 5 vertices and therefore 5! possible routes.

We can derive a new graph from the one in figure 5.6 by collapsing

---

strategy, however, we could construct a numerical example that demonstrates that the respective strategy yields a suboptimal route. We will discuss some of these strategies later on in this chapter.

each cluster of vertices into one vertex of the new graph. Because of the separability of the original graph, the new graph forms a spanning tree. In the case of figure 5.6 it is even a path graph for which all the respective results that we have derived above apply. So, in figure 5.6 there are at maximum three different ways of ordering the three clusters.

Provided that it is optimal for the searcher to exhaust all the alternatives in one cluster before moving on to the next one, he/she can apply the following strategy:

1. Collapse the alternatives within the clusters into one vertex to generate a spanning tree and find all possible routes through this spanning tree.
2. For each route through the tree take the last cluster, treat the articulation point as home location and find the optimal spatial search strategy through the alternatives in this cluster.
3. Feed the resulting minimum expected cost into the respective vertex in the previous cluster.
4. Repeat steps 2 and 3 for all the clusters in the spanning tree.
5. Identify the route that yields the lowest expected cost.

If we count each subroute through one of the clusters separately, the searcher has to deal with $3 \times 5!$, i.e. 360 different routes for each path through the spanning tree. Since there are 3 of those higher level routes, in the example of 5.6 the searcher has to investigate 1080 routes at maximum[3]. Without this simplification, the number of routes the searcher has to compare is $15! \approx 1.308 \, 10^{12}$.

This argument, however, is based upon the hypothesis that in the optimal route the searcher should always exhaust all the alternatives in one cluster before moving on to the next cluster. Is this hypothesis valid in the most general case? Unfortunately not.

We can use graph of figure 5.4 in order to construct a counter example. The edge connecting v_3 and v_4 in this graph is clearly a cutting edge. When we remove it the graph becomes disconnected. Therefore, we can combine vertices v_1, v_2, v_3 into one cluster, and v_4, v_5, v_6 into another. However, as has been demonstrated in table 5.1 the optimal route for the searcher through this example is $(v_3, v_4, v_5, v_6, v_2, v_1)$. So, in the optimal route the searcher investigates one alternative from the first cluster, moves to the second cluster, and returns to the first cluster afterward. This violates the hypothesis on which the above argument was based. As a consequence, the

---

[3]Note that we do not correct for those orderings of clusters that repeat the optimization sub-problem of other orderings. So, this number includes some double counting.

simplification does not apply to separable graphs in general. The solution derived by applying this algorithm is not guaranteed to be the optimal one. However, it may be used as a heuristic procedure for "solving" the spatial search problem.

5.2 Heuristics and Approximations

As we have seen in the previous sections, the spatial search problem is difficult to solve even for some quite restrictive spatial structures. Frequently, people face decisions similar to that of the spatial search problem. Despite the complexity, in most cases they seem to make quite reasonable decisions.

This raises the question of whether one can construct decision rules for the spatial search problem which will yield a reasonably good, although not necessarily the optimal, result. Such decision rules are called *heuristics*, the analysis of which constitutes a significant part of the research on other NP-hard problems.

The use of heuristics in the context of the spatial search problem can also be motivated economically. Depending on the size of the problem, any attempt to finding the optimal routing and stopping strategy for a specific spatial search problem might be quite costly in terms of computing time. In comparison, the gain one may expect from moving from a heuristic to the optimal (full enumeration) solution may be fairly limited. In economic terms we would say that the marginal costs of moving from the heuristic to the optimal (full enumeration) solution exceed the marginal returns, and it is therefore not justified to invest the resources into this move. In this sense, a heuristic solution to the spatial search problem may really be the economically optimal one.

Conceptually we can motivate the use of a heuristic by extending the individual's objective function from "find the routing and stopping strategy with least expected cost" to "apply that strategy for solving the spatial search problem for which the sum of the expected costs of search and the costs of applying the algorithm are minimal". With this change we have extended the spatial search problem from one of finding the best route and search strategy through the graph to one of finding the best (heuristic or optimal) strategy.

In practice we have not gained much from redefining the searcher's objective function in such a way. In order to compute the exact values of this objective function, the searcher must derive the expected costs for the various heuristics – possibly including full enumeration. He/she would thus have to solve the spatial search problem in a number of ways in order to then select one of them. The choice of heuristic need therefore be made on some other grounds, like experience, intuition, or general performance characteristics of the various heuristics.

5.2.1 General Aspects of Spatial Search Heuristics

Performance Guarantees

When dealing with heuristics for the spatial search problem ideally we want to make statements about their performance in any instance of the spatial search problem, not just a specific one. We would like to be able to select the best heuristic, irrespective of the graph, cost matrix, and price distributions of the specific spatial search problem and to have the guarantee that the result of the heuristic will be within some acceptable range of the best solution.

Unfortunately, it is unlikely that one can derive at such a performance guarantee. As proved by Sahni and Gonzalez (1976), a polynomial-time heuristic for the traveling salesman problem which is guaranteed to be not more than a prespecified factor higher than the optimal solution can only exist, when $P = NP$, i.e. when the traveling salesman problem and all the other NP-complete problems can be solved by a polynomial-time algorithm. Although there is no proof that NP-complete problems cannot be solved by polynomial-time algorithms, it is rather unlikely that such an algorithm exists[4]

Because of the relationship between the traveling salesman problem and the spatial search problem that we have established in section 4.2, the argument of Sahni and Gonzalez carries directly over to the spatial search problem. Let $OPT(I)$ be the expected cost of the optimal solution of instance I of the spatial search problem, and $A(I)$ the expected cost of heuristic A. We can reformulate the theorem of Sahni and Gonzalez (see also Johnson and Papadimitriou, 1985) in the following way:

Theorem 5.3 *Suppose there is a polynomial-time heuristic A for the spatial search problem and a constant r, $1 \leq r < \infty$, such that for all instances I*

$$A(I) \leq r\,\mathrm{OPT}(I) \ .$$

Then P = NP.

The proof of this theorem (see Johnson and Papadimitriou, 1985, p. 147f) uses the fact that the problem of determining whether a specific

---

[4]Remember that we are looking into heuristics because of the non-availability of an efficient algorithm.

5.2. Heuristics and Approximations

graph has a Hamiltonian route[5] is known to be *NP*-complete. We will show that if such a heuristic existed, it could be used to solve the Hamiltonian route problem in polynomial time.

Suppose we are given a graph $G(V, E)$ with $n > 2$ vertices and we wish to know whether it has a Hamiltonian route. We can construct another, complete, graph, G', with the same set of vertices and a distance matrix defined as:

$$c_{ij} = \begin{cases} 1, & \text{if } \{v_i, v_j\} \in E, \\ rn, & \text{otherwise.} \end{cases}$$

Now define a (degenerate) cumulative probability distribution

$$F_i(x) = \begin{cases} 0, & \text{for } x < 0, \\ 1, & \text{for } x \geq 0. \end{cases}$$

for each vertex. Assuming a gratification τ as defined by (4.18) we can define the elements of a new cost matrix as:

$$\bar{c}_{ij} = c_{ij} + \tau.$$

We know from section 4.2 that because of the gratification the optimal search strategy always exhausts all the available alternatives (vertices), and investigates them in a sequence that yields the lowest travel cost. Therefore, when G has a Hamiltonian route, the searcher can reach all the vertices in G' via edges with cost 1. The expected cost of search through G' is $-n\tau + n$ in this case. Applying heuristic A in this case, we get

$$A(I) \leq rn(1 - \tau) \ .$$

Whenever G does not have a Hamiltonian route, the searcher must travel at least one edge with cost rn, and the expected cost must be

$$A(I) \geq rn + n - 1 - n\tau \geq rn + 1 - n\tau \geq rn(1 - \tau) + 1 \ ,$$

where the second inequality results from $n > 2$, the third one from $r \geq 1$ and $\tau > 0$.

So, when we apply heuristic A to G' and get expected cost of $rn(1-\tau)$ or less, G must be Hamiltonian. If it were not, expected cost would be at least $rn(1-\tau)+1$. Since we would have been able to determine this with a polynomial-time algorithm, we would have had assigned the Hamiltonian

---

[5] A Hamiltonian route (Hamiltonian cycle in graph theory language) is a closed complete route that visits each alternative exactly once (see chapter 3).

route problem and all other *NP*-complete problems (including the spatial search problem) to the class *P*. This proves theorem 5.3.

Theorem 5.3 shows that there is little chance for finding a heuristic that will perform well in *every* instance of the spatial search problem. The instances for which a given heuristic performs poorly, however, might be very rare, and usually the heuristic may give very good results. In this sense theorem 5.3 uses a very strict criterion for the performance of a heuristic and its content should not be viewed to pessimistically.

Heuristics and the Structure of the Spatial Search Problem

The logical structure of the spatial search problem actually justifies a much more optimistic perspective as far as heuristics are concerned. Because of the stopping component of the spatial search problem, deviations from the optimal strategy are weighted differently whether they occur early or late in the route. When the route derived from a heuristic coincides with the optimal route for the first 4 or 5 alternatives, chances are good that the searcher will have terminated searching before ever getting into the suboptimal part of the route. This does not imply that the heuristic-based spatial search strategy coincides with the optimal one for those short search sequences. Since the reservation prices are based on the suboptimal part of the route as well, in general they will deviate from the optimal vector of reservation prices. The searcher may therefore accept suboptimal or reject optimal price offers when basing the decisions upon a heuristic strategy.

Another argument in favor of spatial search problem heuristics is the fact that – at least theoretically – the searcher will determine an optimal stopping strategy, even for a suboptimal route. The stopping part of the spatial search problem can be solved easily (polynomially) for a given route. Our heuristic, therefore, always applies only to the routing component of the spatial search problem. When there is one part in a specific route, where search is more costly than in the optimal strategy, the searcher will adjust the reservation prices at earlier alternatives in such a way that the chance for reaching the suboptimal part of the route will be fairly low. Of course, the searcher can never overcome the penalty of a suboptimal route entirely, but by adjusting the stopping behavior he/she makes the best out of the suboptimal situation.

Approaches to the Analysis of Heuristics

Two approaches to analyzing the "average" performance of heuristics can be found in the literature. The probabilistic approach (Karp and Steele, 1985) makes assumptions about the distribution of instances for a specific

5.2. Heuristics and Approximations

problem in the event space and derives the distribution of a heuristic's performance parameters therefrom. The empirical approach (Golden and Steward, 1985), on the other hand, simulates instances of the problem, applies the heuristic to each of them and uses the resulting performance measures as data in some empirical analysis. Both approaches require assumptions about the underlying distribution of instances. While in the probabilistic approach one can isolate the influence of various factors directly, its application is constrained by the potential complexity of the mathematics. The empirical approach can be applied to a more general class of problems and heuristics, but when there are different factors determining the performance of a heuristic it may be difficult to isolate them. The problems are similar to those of any other empirical, statistical analysis, with the exception that we have full control over data generation. Because of the relatively complex mathematics involved in determining the expected cost of the spatial search problem, we will apply the empirical approach in the following analysis of heuristics for the spatial search problem.

The most important performance indictor for a heuristic is the quality of the solution, i.e. how close its expected cost is to the minimum expected cost of the optimal solution. Since we want to keep the following discussion of heuristics for the spatial search problem at an exploratory level, we will generally deal with a small number of alternatives. Therefore, we will be able to compute the minimum expected cost and to use this in evaluating the heuristics. In the case of larger problems, when the optimal solution cannot be obtained, one tries to find a lower bound for the minimum expected cost to be used instead.

However, there are other performance indicators as well. Ball and Magazine (1981, 215f) provide the following list:

1. Quality of Solution,
2. Running Time and Storage,
3. Difficulty of Implementation,
4. Flexibility,
5. Robustness,
6. Simplicity and Analyzability,
7. Interactive Computing.

Some of these criteria are more important from an operational point of view. Running time and storage is of general concern. Since the reason for analyzing heuristics lies in the computational complexity (i.e. time requirement) of the optimal strategy, a heuristic is of any value only when it reduces running time considerably. Simplicity and analyzability are important criteria when we want to use a heuristic to draw conclusions about the underlying process.

5.2.2 Heuristics for the General Spatial Search Problem

As we have noted above, the complexity of the spatial search problem mainly derives from its routing component. Because of the interdependence between the stopping and routing component, in the optimal solution the two components need to be solved simultaneously.

The stopping component yields some internal weighing of the different travel cost in a spatial search strategy. Because the searcher can stop searching at each alternative, travel cost in later parts of the search strategy are of less importance for the expected cost than earlier ones. In terms of the decision tree of the spatial search problem (see figure 4.4), this means that decisions made and cost incurred in the upper part of the tree are more important for the expected cost than those in the lower parts. We can use this general observation for the construction of various heuristics.

The Nearest Neighbor Heuristic

A very simple heuristic for the spatial search problem is the nearest neighbor heuristic (see also Maier, 1991). In this heuristic we "solve" the routing part of the spatial search problem independently of the stopping part by applying a simple strategy. Reservation prices and expected cost of search are computed only for the route resulting from the earlier step. The heuristic can be described by the following algorithm:

Algorithm 5.1 Nearest Neighbor Heuristic

1. *Construct a route starting at the home location by always adding the closes not yet selected alternative. When there are no more alternatives left, return home.*

2. *Solve the search problem for the route resulting from 1.*

The nearest neighbor route can be constructed very easily. It requires at most $\frac{n(n+1)}{2}$ loops through a simple set of computational steps. Once the nearest neighbor route is identified, the expected cost are computed only for this one route.

Table 5.2 shows performance characteristics of the nearest neighbor heuristic in comparison to the optimal solution for various problem sizes. The comparison is based on 100 randomly generated incidences of the spatial search problem with identical price distributions (zero-one uniform) at the alternatives. The home and all the alternatives have randomly generated locations within the unit square (i.e. a square extending one unit

5.2. Heuristics and Approximations

number of		optimal strategy		nearest neighbor		
alt.	routes	exp. cost	comp. time	exp. cost	comp. time	% opt.
3	6	0.4162385	1.16	0.4164714	0.24	90
4	24	0.3800163	6.25	0.3809295	0.30	79
5	120	0.3500830	41.11	0.3509872	0.34	75
6	720	0.3219073	421.07	0.3229998	0.37	68
7	5040	0.3040388	2488.00	0.3059359	0.57	59

Table 5.2: Optimal Strategy and Nearest Neighbor Heuristic Performance for Various Problem Sizes

of measurement in each direction). Each point within the unit square is equally likely. Transportation cost between each pair of points is assumed to be one tenth of the euclidian distance between them.

As we can see from table 5.2, the characteristics of this spatial search problem differ markedly with problem size as we had to expect from the theoretical discussion. The expected costs of search decline when more alternatives become available. Partly because the searcher has more choices, partly because the average distance between alternatives decreases when more of them are distributed over the unit square. The cost of computing the optimal solution increase dramatically even for fairly small numbers of alternatives due to the increase in the number of routes.

The nearest neighbor heuristic performs very well in our numerical example. Figure 5.7 shows the differences in expected cost and computing time between the nearest neighbor heuristic and the optimal solution. While the difference in expected cost grows gradually over the range of alternatives, the difference in computing time accelerates very rapidly. In relative terms, for all the problem sizes the expected cost for the nearest neighbor heuristic get within 1% of the minimum expected cost. Computing time, on the other hand, drops from 57% for three alternatives to 0.05% for seven alternatives.

The last column of table 5.2 shows that the nearest neighbor heuristic yields the optimal route in a high percentage of cases. The "success rate" drops from 91% for three alternatives to 51% for seven alternatives. This seems to indicate that the nearest neighbor heuristic performs better for small graphs. However, the decline in the percentage has to be compared to the number of possible routes through the graph. Finding the optimal route out of six (for 3 alternatives) is less of an achievement than finding it out of 5040 (for 7 alternatives) possible routes as the nearest neighbor heuristic did in more than half the instances.

Despite the attractive performance the nearest neighbor heuristic has shown in our numerical example, one has to be aware that it is based

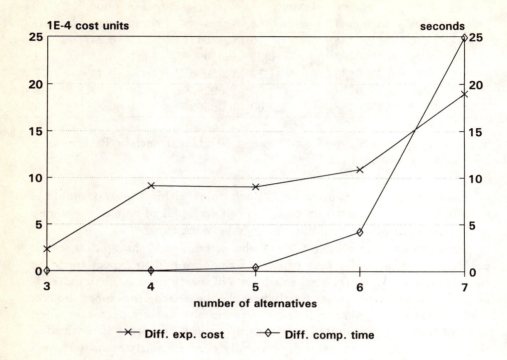

Figure 5.7: Performance of the Nearest Neighbor Heuristic

upon only part of the parameters of an instance of the spatial search problem. We only use the distance matrix to construct the nearest neighbor route; even ignoring the cost of returning home. The heuristic takes into account price distributions and cost of returning home only for the one nearest neighbor route. The potential impacts of these parameters upon the routing decision are completely left out of consideration.

In order to see whether the nearest neighbor heuristic performs well in general or only in the specific constellation used in table 5.2, we will test its sensitivity to variations in some of these parameters. Later on we will briefly discuss some possible refinements of the nearest neighbor heuristic.

We will again assume the prices to be generated by a uniform distribution. We will use the same 100 randomly generated distance matrices for all variants we want to investigate. This eliminates any impact from variations in the distance matrix. In particular, we will look into the following three parameters:

1. location of the distribution,
2. spread of the distribution,

5.2. Heuristics and Approximations

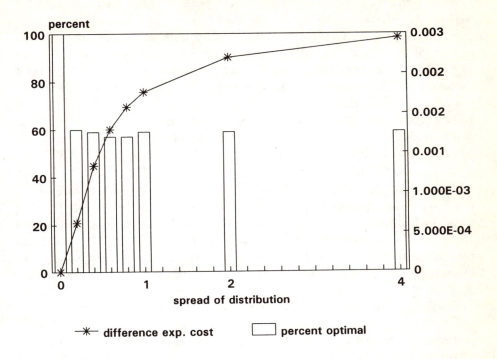

Figure 5.8: Performance of the Nearest Neighbor Heuristic: Variation in Spread of the Price Distribution

3. variation in the location of the distribution between alternatives.

In the first two cases we use the same distribution for all alternatives.

When we shift the price distribution for all alternatives by the same amount, the spatial search problem basically remains unchanged. When all the price distributions are shifted upward by, say, a units, we can view this as a constant surcharge of a to every price. Therefore, all the limits of integration in our basic recursive equation are increased by the same amount as well. As a consequence, the minimum expected cost increase by a as well (see section 4.5). Since the nearest neighbor heuristic does not take into account the price distribution, it yields the same nearest neighbor route, and consequently expected cost that are a units larger than in the original situation. As a consequence, the nearest neighbor heuristic performs equally well in terms of difference in expected cost and success rate, for whatever the location of the price distribution.

When we alter the spread of the distribution, the minimum expected cost as well as the performance characteristics of the nearest neighbor heuristic change. Figure 5.8 shows the performance characteristics for various distributions. All the distributions have identical means (2.0) and are the same for all the alternatives. The numbers under the bars of the graph represent the difference between the upper and lower boundary of the uniform distribution. So, the point to the far left represents a degenerate distribution, i.e. the situation where the price is known with certainty. In this case, there is no possible gain from searching alternatives and the searcher will therefore go to the nearest alternative, buy the product there at the given price, and return home. The nearest neighbor heuristic yields the same result. Therefore, its success rate is 100% and there is no difference in expected cost.

When we allow the distribution to spread around the mean, searching the alternatives begins to pay off for the searcher. However, at the same time the limitations of the nearest neighbor heuristic start to show. When we allow the uniform distribution to spread over 0.2 units, the success rate drops to 60% and the nearest neighbor heuristic yields slightly higher expected cost than the optimal strategy. When we increase the spread further, the success rate remains approximately at this level while the difference in expected cost increases further. However, the increase in the difference of expected cost soon starts to level off. It seems that a specific increase in the spread of the distribution affects the relative performance of the nearest neighbor heuristic more when the original spread is small than when it is large.

Finally, let us look into the effects of the alternatives having different distributions. We start with a uniform distribution between 0.5 and 1.5 and shift it by a random component. This random component has mean zero and differs over the alternatives. Figure 5.9 shows the performance parameters of the nearest neighbor heuristic. The numbers under the bars indicate the maximum amount by which the distribution may shift. The 0.2, for example, means that the distributions may shift by a maximum of 0.1 in each direction. Since the spread is the same for all alternatives, the price offers will be generated from a $0.5 + a$ to $1.5 + a$ uniform random distribution, where a is a the realization of a uniformly distributed random variable ranging between -0.1 and 0.1.

As we can see from figure 5.9 the performance of the nearest neighbor heuristic is affected most strongly in this case. This is not surprising. Since the stochastic properties now differ, some alternatives are stochastically more attractive than others. The suppliers at some alternatives tend to quote lower prices than others. The nearest neighbor heuristic does not take this into account by concentrating solely on the cost matrix. It therefore will perform poorer the more the price distributions are allowed to vary between the alternatives. Our numerical example supports this

5.2. Heuristics and Approximations

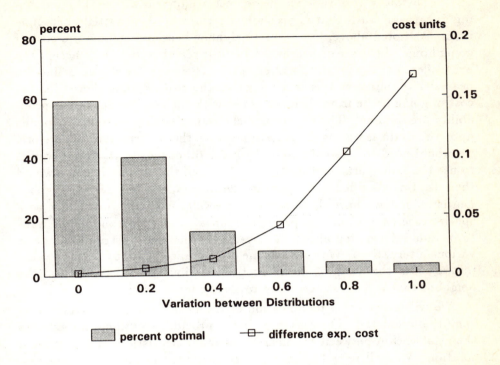

Figure 5.9: Performance of the Nearest Neighbor Heuristic: Variation in Location of the Price Distribution between Alternatives

hypothesis. As shown in figure 5.9 the success rate declines and the difference in expected cost increases as we allow greater variations. It should be noted, however, that even when we allow the largest variation the nearest neighbor heuristic performs reasonably well. In our numerical example it yields expected cost of 0.64 as compared to minimum expected cost of 0.48. This can be attributed to the fact that the searcher is assumed to perform an optimal search along the nearest neighbor route. When an unfavorable alternative appears early in the nearest neighbor route, its choice probability will be accordingly low.

Modified Nearest Neighbor Heuristics

It is interesting to see that the nearest neighbor heuristic performs quite well in most situations, despite the fact that it ignores a considerable amount of information about the spatial search problem. The simple structure of the nearest neighbor heuristic leaves room for refinements that take into account some of the additional characteristics.

An obvious way of refining the nearest neighbor heuristic is by redefining "nearness" such that it accounts for some of the omitted characteristics. As noted above, the nearest neighbor heuristic ignores the cost of going home. They are of relevance when the searcher decides to accept the price offered at the respective alternative. Therefore, we should define the nearest alternative as this one, for which the cost of going there plus the cost of going home from there weighted with the conditional choice probability are minimal. The conditional choice probability, however, depends upon the route as well as the behavior at the other alternatives. Therefore, we would need to approximate it by some other figure. A simple way is to use the same parameter λ, $0 \leq \lambda \leq 1$, for all the alternatives. We would then use this modified cost figure in algorithm 5.1. The nearest neighbor heuristic that we have discussed above results from this procedure as a special case ($\lambda = 0$) of this procedure. In a similar way one might want to include information about the location of the price distribution at the various alternatives. We could define a generalized cost figure that takes into account the mean of the respective distribution and try to find the neighbor that is nearest according to this generalized cost.

We will discuss one modification of the nearest neighbor heuristic in slightly more detail. The reason is that it provides additional insight into the relationship between the nearest neighbor heuristic and the optimal solution. We will refer to this modified heuristic as the *k-step l-nearest neighbor heuristic*. The meaning of this name will become clear soon.

When constructing the nearest neighbor route in algorithm 5.1 we n-times look for the one not yet selected alternatives that is nearest to the current one. This yields just one route through the graph. We have noted above, however, that the decisions made early in the search sequence are generally of greater importance than those made later. We may take this into account by constructing not just one but two routes in such a way that we identify the *two* alternatives nearest to the home location, use each of them as the first alternative in one of the two routes and add the other alternatives according to the nearest neighbor criterion. In a second step we may compute the expected cost for both routes and select the one providing lower expected cost.

Of course, we are not restricted to only two routes. We may use the 3, 4, or $l \leq n$ alternatives nearest to the home location and construct the corresponding number of routes. Also, we may want to apply this rational not only to the first alternative in a route, but also to the second, third, ... one. In general we may find all routes through the l-nearest neighbors for the first k steps of the search tree. In general, this is still a heuristic because it does not guarantee to yield the optimum solution of the spatial search problem. We therefore call it the k-step l-nearest

5.2. Heuristics and Approximations

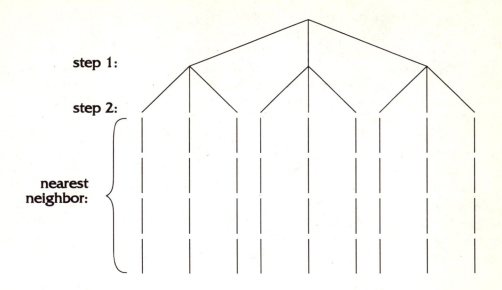

Figure 5.10: Routes Resulting from the k-Step l-Nearest Neighbor Heuristic ($k = 2$, $l = 3$)

neighbor heuristic.

Formally, this heuristic can be defined in the following way:

Algorithm 5.2 k-Step l-Nearest Neighbor Heuristic

1. Construct a set of routes, $\mathcal{R}$, starting at the home location according to the following roles:

    (a) For the first k steps, for each subroute leading to this step find the l not yet selected alternatives (when less than l alternatives are remaining use this smaller number) nearest to the current one. For each subroute leading to the current step construct the subroutes leading to the next step by adding one of the l nearest alternatives at a time.

    (b) After the first k steps, complete each subroute through the first k steps by adding the not yet selected alternatives according to the nearest neighbor criterion. When all alternatives are selected, return home.

2. Solve the search problem for every route in set $\mathcal{R}$ and select the one as the heuristic solution that provides the lowest expected cost.

Figure 5.10 illustrates the route construction for the k-step l-nearest neighbor heuristic for two steps and the three nearest neighbors. Note that the nearest neighbors are always defined relative to the current position in the route. So, the three nearest neighbors in the second step of the left branch may differ from those of the other two branches.

The nearest neighbor heuristic defined in algorithm 5.1 is a special case of the k-step l-nearest neighbor heuristic. We get to it by setting $k = l = 1$. Since we basically use the same criterion as in the nearest neighbor heuristic for constructing the route, the nearest neighbor route will always be an element of the set $\mathcal{R}$. Because we select the route with the lowest expected cost from $\mathcal{R}$ in step 2, the result of the k-step l-nearest neighbor heuristic will be at least as good as that of the nearest neighbor heuristic. In more general terms, whenever we increase k and/or l we add routes to $\mathcal{R}$ without removing any; i.e. the old set is a subset of the new one. Therefore, the heuristic solution can only improve or remain unchanged when we increase k and/or l.

When we set $k = l = n$, we perform a full enumeration of all possible routes. In the second step of the algorithm we therefore investigate all possible routes and find the best one. For $k = l = n$ the algorithm for the k-step l-nearest neighbor heuristic therefore coincides with the algorithm for finding the optimal solution (algorithm 4.1). In this sense, the k-step l-nearest neighbor heuristic bridges the gap between the optimal solution and the nearest neighbor heuristic.

In order to test the performance of the k-step l-nearest neighbor heuristic, we apply it to a case, where the nearest neighbor heuristic performed poorly. We use randomly generated graphs with 6 alternatives and allow the mean of the price distribution to vary between 0.5 and 1.5 over the alternatives. In figure 5.10 this version of the spatial search problem yielded the largest difference in expected cost and the lowest success rate. While the minimum expected cost is 0.477 in our numerical example, the nearest neighbor heuristic yields a figure of 0.645. Only in three out of one hundred repetitions the nearest neighbor route coincided with the optimal one.

Figure 5.11 shows the performance characteristics of the k-step l-nearest neighbor heuristic in this case. The different lines represent increasing values of k, while on the x-axis we find increasing numbers of l, with $l = 1$ representing the nearest neighbor heuristic. The horizontal line at the bottom of the graph represents the minimum expected cost. As the graph shows quite clearly, the performance of the k-step l-nearest neighbor heuristic increases strongly when we increase k and/or l. When we investigate the routes generated by the 4 best alternatives for the first 4 steps of the search procedure, the expected cost figure almost reaches the minimal value. In our numerical example, this version of the k-step l-nearest neighbor heuristic finds the optimal route in 74% of the repe-

5.2. Heuristics and Approximations

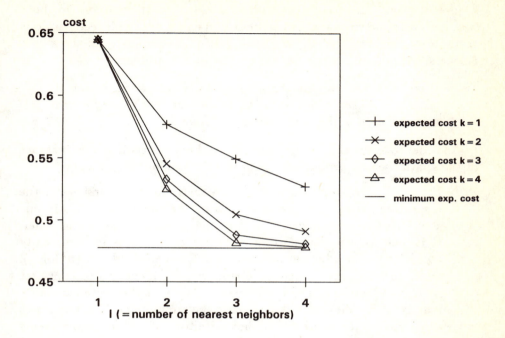

Figure 5.11: Expected Cost for Different Versions of the k-Step l-Nearest Neighbor Heuristic

titions. The graph also shows, that the marginal benefit from allowing an additional nearest neighbor (increasing l) declines rapidly. So, there is little to gain from increasing k or l.

Of course, there is a price to pay for the chance of finding a better solution. It is paid in terms of computer time. When we assume $n \geq l+k-1$, the route generation part of the k-step l-nearest neighbor heuristic yields l^k routes through the graph[6]. After these routes have been identified in the first step, in the second step we try to find the best one of them. When we increase k and/or l, computing time increases accordingly. Note, however, that the number of routes does not depend upon the size of the problem. Therefore, once k and l are determined, an increase in the number of alternatives has little impact upon the cost of computing the k-step l-nearest neighbor heuristic. We only have to find the l smallest

---

[6] When this condition does not hold, there will be steps among the first k where less than l alternatives are remaining. Therefore, in this case the number of routes will be less than l^k.

from a larger array of numbers and need to compute the – predetermined – number of expected cost over a larger number of alternatives. For both problems it is known that they can be solved efficiently. This leads directly to the following result about the computational complexity of the k-step l-nearest neighbor heuristic for the spatial search problem:

> **Theorem 5.4** *For any fixed values of k and l the k-step l-nearest neighbor heuristic yields a heuristic solution for the spatial search problem in polynomial time.*

In order to apply the k-step l-nearest neighbor heuristic to any instance of the spatial search problem we need to take the following steps:

1. For the first k steps we have to find the l smallest numbers in the respective rows of the distance matrix. We can achieve this in one step by sorting all rows of the distance matrix in ascending order. It is well known that sorting an array of size n is of complexity $O(n \log n)$. The whole matrix can therefore be sorted in $O(n^2 \log n)$.
2. Once the distance matrix is sorted we can identify the l^k routes in $\mathcal{R}$ by identifying the respective elements in the sorted distance matrix. After the first k steps we add the remaining $n-k$ alternatives according to the nearest neighbor criterion. The time requirements of this whole step are therefore linear in problem size.
3. For the l^k routes in $\mathcal{R}$ we compute the expected cost of search. This requires us to evaluate n integrals for each route. Since the number of routes is fixed, the whole step can be performed in linear time.
4. Finally, we have to identify which route yields the lowest expected cost. Since the number of routes is given the computing time required for this step is not related to problem size.

These four steps can be performed in sequence and for each one of them we have an efficient algorithm available. Therefore, the whole algorithm is efficient. This proves theorem 5.4.

At first sight theorem 5.4 seems to contradict the above mentioned observation that we can make the k-step l-nearest neighbor heuristic coincide with the optimal algorithm by setting $k = l = n$. Note, however, that in the context of theorem 5.4 we have always argued in terms of *fixed* values of k and l. When we set them equal to n they will have to increase with problem size and one condition for theorem 5.4 is not valid any more.

Figure 5.12 compares the computing time requirements of the k-step l-nearest neighbor heuristic with $k = l = 3$ with those of the optimal solution. As we can see, the time requirements for the optimal solution quickly increases beyond bounds while those for the heuristic increase only gradually.

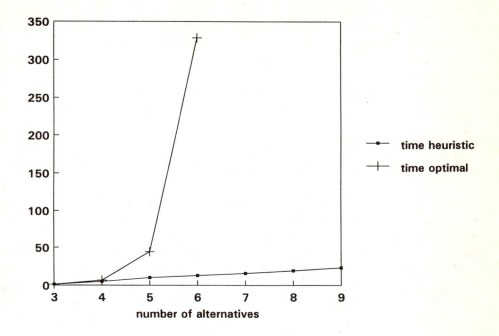

Figure 5.12: Computing Time required for k-Step l-Nearest Neighbor Heuristic ($k = l = 3$)

In principle the k-step l-nearest neighbor heuristic suffers from the same deficits as the nearest neighbor heuristic. It reduces their impact to some extent by suggesting not just one but a number of routes for closer inspection. Nevertheless, the route generation step again relies solely upon the distance matrix. It does not take into account any of the other parameters of the spatial search problem. We may try to overcome this deficit by redefining "nearness" in one of the ways that we have suggested above. When doing this, one should be aware, however, that by choosing bad parameter values one may reduce rather than improve the performance of the heuristic. This is in contrast to increases in k and/or l which are guaranteed to lead to at least the same performance of the heuristic.

A Fixed Sample Size Based Heuristic

Rogerson (1990) discusses spatial search on the basis of Stigler's fixed sample size concept. As we know from section 2, as long as there are no scale effects, entry barriers or other fixed cost associated with the search process, FSS-search is inferior to a sequential search strategy. Since our basic assumptions in section 4 (more specifically, assumption G.5) preclude such elements, applying a FSS-strategy to the problem will only yield an approximate solution. However, by using FSS-search we can derive interesting approximate results that may be helpful in the case of a spatial search problem with a large number of alternatives.

Rogerson notes that when the sample size is n^*, the searcher's total expected cost of acquiring the product are:

$$E(\min\{X_1, \ldots, X_{n^*}\}) + T(n^*) , \qquad (5.9)$$

where $T(n^*)$ is the minimal travel cost associated with the inspection of n^* alternatives.

$E(\min\{X_1, \ldots, X_{n^*}\})$ is a non-increasing function in n^*, while $T(n^*)$ is an non-decreasing function. The searcher has to balance expected savings in purchase price from increasing n^* against increases in travel cost. While the first is solely determined by the underlying price distribution, the travel cost function reflects the structure of the cost matrix. Therefore, depending on the spatial structure of the problem, the function of the searcher's total expected cost may have more than one local minimum. This is in stark contrast to the aspatial search problem. In this case the lowest minimum has to be found.

Since the parameters of the price distribution are assumed to be identical over all alternatives and in FSS-search the searcher always visits all the alternatives in the sample, $E(\min\{X_1, \ldots, X_{n^*}\})$, is independent of which alternatives are chosen for investigation and the searcher's route. Given the underlying price distribution we can compute $E(\min\{X_1, \ldots, X_{n^*}\})$ for every sample size n^*. Only $T(n^*)$ depends upon the route the searcher chooses through the n^* alternatives. Therefore, in order to "solve" the spatial search problem, we "only" need to concentrate on the second component of (5.9).

In practical terms this turns out to be complicated enough. When there is a total number of N alternatives, for each sample size n^* we would have to examine $(n^*)!\binom{N}{n^*}/2$ possible routes, "since there are $\binom{N}{n^*}$ ways of choosing a subset of n^* points from a set of N, and $(n^*)!/2$ different ways of putting a route through a given set of $n^* + 1$ points" (Rogerson, 1990, p. 340). Since we are also trying to find the optimal sample size, we would have to run through this calculation for each n^* from 1 to N. Note that just for $n^* = N$ this equals the enumeration part of the Traveling Salesman Problem. Obviously, full enumeration is not a practical approach for the FSS spatial search problem.

Instead, Rogerson uses a result by Beardwood, Halton, and Hammersley (1959), who show that for points that are randomly distributed in a plane of area A, as the number of points increases, the expected length of the traveling salesman tour through these points approaches:

$$\lim_{n \to \infty} E[T(n)] = \phi\sqrt{An} \ .$$

The scaling constant ϕ needs to be found empirically and "is believed to be 0.75" (DaGanzo, 1984).

"With N points distributed at random in the plane with density $\rho = N/A$, the expected cost of a traveling-salesman tour through both a fixed home location and the subset of n^* stores that are closest to home will be approximately" (Rogerson, 1990, p. 340)

$$E[t] \approx \phi\sqrt{\frac{(n^* - 1)n^*}{\rho}} \ . \tag{5.10}$$

The marginal cost of an additional observation is therefore

$$\frac{\phi}{\sqrt{\rho}}\left[\sqrt{n(n+1)} - \sqrt{n(n-1)}\right] \approx \frac{\phi}{\sqrt{\rho}} \ . \tag{5.11}$$

Note that this approximation is independent of the sample size.

The marginal benefit of an increase in sample size depends upon the price distribution at the stores and is independent of the searcher's route, as we have seen above. We can therefore equate marginal cost and marginal returns and solve for the optimal number of stores to visit. For uniform prices on the interval $(0, b)$, Rogerson (1990, p. 341) finds the optimal sample size n^* to be

$$n^* = \frac{1}{2}\left[\sqrt{1 + \frac{16b\sqrt{\rho}}{3}} - 1\right] \ . \tag{5.12}$$

this tells us how many but not *which* stores to visit. For the optimal sample size n^* we will have to find those n^* stores that can be visited from the given home location at minimal cost.

In the second half of his paper, Rogerson discusses alternative heuristic algorithms for this routing problem. They are based on the "nearest-neighbor" idea that we have described above, combined with improvement techniques that delete and insert alternatives in such a way that the total number remains constant, but the tour length decreases.

It is important to note, however, that Rogerson has to apply a number of approximations in order to get to this point where he can focus on the routing problem:

- By assumption the searcher is constrained to a fixed-sample-size strategy;

- since the searcher's home location is given, not all the alternatives through which a route has to be found are located randomly;
- the Beardwood, Halton, and Hammersley formula is asymptotic and contains the scaling constant ϕ;
- in order to derive an expression for marginal cost, he has to apply additional approximations to this formula.

The attractivity of Rogerson's result lies in the fact that it is based upon a *large* number of alternatives. In the first step this number is reduced to the optimal sample size n^*. The routing heuristic is then applied to this – usually much smaller – number of alternatives. In contrast to the previously discussed heuristics, this one provides for a mechanism to reduce a large number of alternatives to a smaller, more manageable set.

5.3 Summary

Building on our result about the complexity of the spatial search problem in chapter 4, in this chapter we have tried to identify computationally tractable versions of the spatial search model. Our discussion has focussed on two general strategies: first, to identify spatial structures that reduce the numbers of possible routes through the problem, and, second, to define alternative objectives that yield near-optimal solutions but lead to structures that are considerably easier to solve.

The first strategy is discussed in section 5.1. We analyze a number of obvious candidates. They have been presented in general terms in chapter 3. The most obvious version of a simplified spatial structure is linear space, where the alternatives form a path graph. As long as we do not impose any additional constraints on the spatial structure, assuming a path graph is not sufficient to allow for efficient solution of the spatial search problem. Only when we place the searcher's home location at one of the endpoints of the path graph, the spatial search problem becomes solvable in polynomial time.

The reason for the computational complexity of the spatial search model in a general path graph lies in the fact that the searcher always can choose from two sides. When the alternatives form a circle graph the searcher usually has to consider two sides. Therefore, the spatial search model is difficult to solve in this case as well.

Another special graph that we have discussed in chapter 3 is a star graph. This can be considered as a spatial search problem where the searcher has to return home after each alternative. As we can show, as long as the price distributions are identical at all alternatives, the routing problem can be solved independently from the stopping problem. The optimal routing strategy is simply to search the alternatives in increasing order of search costs. When the alternatives have different price distributions, however, this strategy does not necessarily yield the optimal route. Nor were we able to find another simple strategy for this situation. The searcher will probably have to apply the standard strategy that we have discussed in chapter 4.

The final simplified spatial structure we discussed is a separable graph. The separability of the graph suggests that we could solve the search problem in a two-step process. First, collapse each subgraph into one vertex and find the optimal route through the resulting spanning tree. Second, find the optimal route through each subgraph in a sequential way. This strategy can be optimal only, when the searcher always exhausts all the alternatives in a subgraph before he/she moves to the next one. A simple example shows, however, that this is not always the case. Therefore, the suggested strategy yields only a heuristic solution to the spatial search problem.

In section 5.2 we concentrate on the discussion of heuristic solutions for the spatial search model. First, we discuss some general aspects of heuristic solutions like performance guarantees and methods for judging the quality of a heuristic. Then we turn to strategies for the spatial search problem that yield heuristic solutions. Most of our discussion focusses upon the nearest neighbor heuristic. It uses the cost matrix for "solving" the routing problem and applies the stopping part of the problem only to the one route resulting from the first step. We suggest a generalization of the nearest neighbor heuristic, the k-step l-nearest neighbor heuristic, that is guaranteed to yield expected costs at least as low as the nearest neighbor heuristic and is computable in polynomial time. Finally, we discuss a heuristic suggested by Rogerson (1990) that is based upon a fixed sample size search strategy.

Chapter 6

The Implication of Spatial Search for Market Areas and Firm Location

Up to now we have concentrated on conceptualizing spatial search and dealing with its computational complexity. The rest of our presentation will be devoted to the implications spatial search may have for various spatial phenomena. We will implement the idea of spatial search as it was developed in the previous sections into a number of well known regional economic theories. It is our intention to find out, what the impacts of spatial search are for the basic theoretical results of those well known and well established theories.

In this chapter we will concentrate on market areas and firm location. The next chapter will be devoted to the question of agglomeration and spatial clustering of suppliers. In chapter 8 we will discuss the relationship between the spatial search model and spatial interaction models.

Until now we have looked at spatial search from the searcher's perspective. There was one individual who faces a set of options, represented by different suppliers, and who has to make decisions about where to look for the desired product and under what circumstances to buy it. In the discussion in this chapter we will look at the problem from a slightly different perspective; that of the supplier. We will usually consider one or few suppliers who face a large number of spatially distributed customers. Nevertheless, it is still the customers who search for the product and who make the same types of decisions that we have discussed so far.

From our discussion of the complexity of the spatial search problem in the previous chapters it is apparent that we cannot use the spatial search concept in its most general form for this task. We will have to rely on some of the simplified and more restrictive versions of the spatial search problem that we have developed and discussed in chapter 5. Most of the time we will use some form of linear space.

6.1 Standard Location and Spatial Price Theory

Questions of market areas and firm location are at the heart of some of the most traditional theories in Regional Science. Weber's (1909) Theory of Industrial Location and Christaller's (1933) Central Place Theory are examples. Both works have stimulated the development of a rich body of literature.

In this section we want to give an overview of the theory of location and spatial pricing as it is available now. We do not intend to provide an in-depth presentation of the theory[1]. Instead we want to discuss basic assumptions and features and demonstrate that Regional Science has developed many different versions of the theory over the years.

The basic idea of the theory of spatial pricing and location is very simple: suppliers and customers of a product usually can be found at different locations in space. For the customer to utilize the product – for consumption or as input to some production process – resources have to be used to transfer the product from one location to the other. As a consequence, what the customer pays for the product differs from what the supplier receives:

$$p^c = p^s + t(\delta) \; , \tag{6.1}$$

where p^c is the price paid by the customer, p^s the net-return received by the supplier, δ distance between the two, and t the function relating transport costs to distance. The latter is often assumed to be linear, i.e., $t(\delta) = t\delta$.

Depending on from what perspective we look at the situation – and who has to bear transportation costs – we see a price funnel or a price cone (see figure 6.1). In the first case, transportation costs are – at least partially – paid by the customer. Therefore, the further away from the producer he/she is located, the more expensive the product becomes. When demand is not completely inelastic, customers who are located further away will demand less of the product. Beyond a certain distance there will be no demand at all. In the second case, the producer bears – at least some of

---

[1] For recent comprehensive reviews see Beckmann and Thisse (1986), Greenhut et al. (1987). Earlier contributions are Greenhut (1956), Isard (1956), Smith (1971)

6.1. Standard Location and Spatial Price Theory

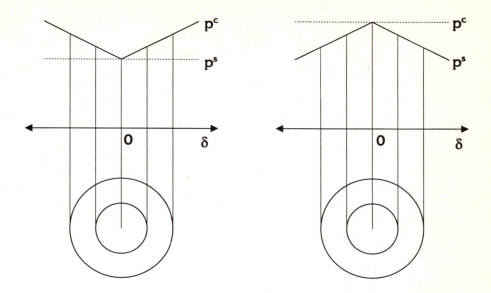

Figure 6.1: Price Funnel and Price Cone (source: Maier and Tödtling 1992, p. 49)

– the transportation costs. The further away a customer is located the lower the supplier's net return will be because larger and larger amounts have to be invested into transportation. Beyond a certain distance the supplier will refuse to deliver the product.

Equation (6.1) is fundamental to a large number of theories in Regional Economics. When we consider few suppliers and markets at specific discrete locations, and ask where a new production facility that buys from the suppliers and delivers to the markets should be located, we are in the domain of Alfred Weber's location theory. When we consider one market and suppliers scattered around it who deliver to this market, we get to von Thünen's theory of land rent. Taking into account many market areas and various products we end up in the world of Christaller and Lösch. We cannot discuss all these theories in detail here. Instead we want to briefly list some of the fundamental aspects of spatial price and location theory as they can be derived from equation (6.1). Since we will have to use a highly simplified version of spatial price and location theory in the context of spatial search[2], with the following discussion we intend to lay

---

[2] As noted by Greenhut et al., 1987, p. 271, "one of the major problems in an analysis of imperfect competition is that a slight increase in model complexity can generate an intractable increase in mathematical complexity." This is particularly the case when we introduce a concept of such high complexity as spatial search.

out the broader perspective. We will need this more general view in order to appreciate the search-based results we will derive.

Spatial price and location theory concentrates on the impact of transportation costs upon the behavior of producers and consumers. It is assumed that both sides of the market act in a neoclassical way, i.e. that they attempt to maximize profits and utility. In comparison, the treatment of the production side is usually quite simplistic. It is common in spatial price and location theory to assume constant marginal costs[3].

As far as spatial structure is concerned, linear space is a common assumption in this branch of Regional Economics. Supply and demand are located either on a (bounded or unbounded) line or on the circumference of a circle. In chapter 5 we have discussed both these simplified spatial structures in the context of spatial search.

When there is just one supplier, he/she can act as a monopolist (spatial monopoly[4]). The supplier has some control over prices and can set them according to his/her economic interests. The supplier can apply different pricing strategies. Implicitly we have already mentioned two pricing strategies in the above discussion: *mill pricing* and *uniform pricing*. Another pricing strategy that has received considerable attention in the literature is *discriminatory pricing*.

At mill pricing the supplier sells the product at the plant location for a specific price (mill price), and leaves it to the customer to get the product to his/her location. The supplier's net-return is fixed at the mill price, the price for the customer increases with distance according to (6.1). Consequently, demand declines with distance. The size of the market area is determined by the maximum distance consumer's are willing to travel for the product.

At uniform pricing the supplier delivers the product to each customer's location at a given price (uniform price). Therefore, the supplier's net-return declines with distance, while the price for the customer and his/her demand remains constant. The market area is determined by the maximum distance the supplier is willing – based on profit maximizing behavior – to transport the product.

When the supplier applies a discriminatory pricing strategy he/she sets a different price – the price which maximizes his/her profits – for every distance. Price increases with distance, but less than under a mill price strategy. As under mill pricing, the market area is determined by the maximum distance consumer's are willing to travel for the product.

---

[3] Most of the time marginal costs are set to zero.

[4] A spatial monopoly can exist even when there is a large number of suppliers in the economy as a whole. Suppliers can act as spatial monopolists when their potential market areas do not touch.

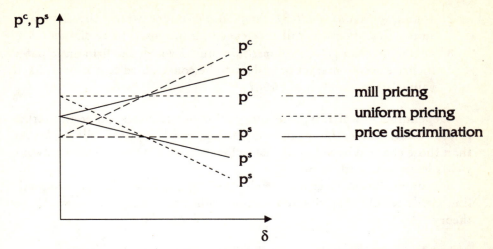

Figure 6.2: Consumer Price and Net-Return under Different Pricing Strategies

Figure 6.2 shows the prices for customers and producers (net-return) as a function of distance under the three pricing strategies.

Beckmann and Thisse (1986, p. 30ff) compare these pricing strategies and list a number of theoretical results:

- Market areas, output, and profits are the same under mill pricing and uniform pricing.
- Under linear demand and constant marginal costs, the optimal market radius, output and profit under discriminatory pricing are larger than under mill and uniform pricing.
- Assuming a uniform density of consumers "discriminatory pricing turns out to yield a lower consumer surplus but a higher social surplus than mill pricing" (Beckmann and Thisse, 1986, p. 34, see also Holahan, 1975).

The major point for our discussion lies in the observation that major parameters of the market depend upon the pricing strategy the spatial monopolist applies.

When there is more than one supplier, the strategies of a firm as well as the aggregate result of some action depend upon how competitors will or are expected to react. Although one can imagine a whole range of assumptions, three *types of competition* are of particular importance in the literature:

1. "*Löschian competition*, under which the firm presumes that its rivals will react identically to any proposed price change.

2. *Hotelling-Smithies (H-S) competition*, under which the firm presumes that its rivals will not react to a proposed price change.
3. *Greenhut-Ohta (G-O) competition*, under which the firm anticipates its price on the market boundary to be constrained to a known, fixed value." (Greenhut et al., 1987, p. 20)

Depending on which type of competition one assumes, different market prices result. Under Löschian competition, market prices will be *higher* than those charged by a monopolist, whereas only G-O competition always yields lower competitive prices.

It can be shown (Greenhut et al., 1987, p. 21) that Löschian competition yields results that violate those of traditional nonspatial competitive theory

1. "As transport costs and/or fixed costs approach zero, price will approach the nonspatial monopoly price.
2. As fixed costs and transport costs rise, prices *fall*, whereas an increase in marginal cost leads to ambiguous results.
3. As firms enter and thus competition increases, prices increase.
4. Price increases as population density increases." (Greenhut et al., 1987, p. 21)

G-O competition, on the other hand, yields the results that we expect from traditional nonspatial competitive theory.

It is important to realize that spatial competition does not rule out price strategies. The reason is that a supplier may have monopoly power over one part of the market even when he/she faces competition in another part. Let us illustrate this with the following example (following Beckmann and Thisse, 1986, p. 43ff) that will be useful in the latter discussion as well.

Suppose a set of firms selling a homogenous product is equally spaced along an unbounded linear market. Denote the distance between any two firms by l. Marginal production cost, c, is constant and uniform across firms. Transportation cost per distance unit is equal to t. Firms follow a mill price strategy. Consumers are evenly distributed over the market at a unit density. All consumers are identical and will buy one unit of the product only if the price at their location is lower or equal to some reservation price ω. The demand function of the consumer at location d of the market is therefore

$$q(\delta) = \begin{cases} 1 & \text{if } p^c(\delta) \leq \omega, \\ 0 & \text{otherwise.} \end{cases} \quad (6.2)$$

6.1. Standard Location and Spatial Price Theory

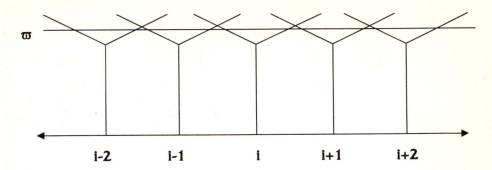

Figure 6.3: Spatial Competition between Adjacent Firms

Let us concentrate on firm i and assume that the prices for all other firms are fixed (H-S competition). Furthermore we assume $p_{i-1}^s = p_{i+1}^s > \omega - tl$ so that consumers around firm i cannot buy from firms $i-1$ and $i+1$. Figure 6.3 illustrates this situation.

We can distinguish four different cases (the non-trivial cases 2 - 4 are illustrated in figure 6.4): First, if $p_i^s > \omega$, then no consumer wants to buy from firm i. Its total demand is therefore,

$$D_i(p_{i-1}^s, p_i^s, p_{i+1}^s) = 0 \ . \tag{6.3}$$

Second, if $2\omega - p_{i-1}^s - tl < p_i \leq \omega$, then[5] firm i will serve only those customers who are not supplied from firms $i-1$ and $i+1$. The market radius of firm i is the solution R_i to $p_i + tR_i = \omega$. The total demand of firm i is therefore,

$$D_i(p_{i-1}^s, p_i^s, p_{i+1}^s) = 2\frac{\omega - p_i}{t} \ . \tag{6.4}$$

When $p_{i-1}^s - tl \leq p_i^s \leq 2\omega - p_{i-1}^s - tl$, firm i competes with its neighbors for customers (case 3; see figure 6.4b). The market is split between, say, firms $i-1$ and i such that $p_i^s + tR_i = p_{i-1}^s + t(l - R_i)$. The total demand of firm i is therefore

$$D_i(p_{i-1}^s, p_i^s, p_{i+1}^s) = \frac{p_{i-1}^s - 2p_i + p_{i+1}^s + 2tl}{2t} \ . \tag{6.5}$$

The boundary of the markets of two adjacent firms is determined by the intersection of their price (p^c) functions. When firm i lowers the price, the boundary of its market moves closer to both $i-1$ and $i+1$. By assumption the two competitors do not react to firm i's price changes.

---

[5]The first inequality can be rewritten as $p_{i-1}^s + tl - \omega > \omega - p_i^s$ (see figure 6.4a).

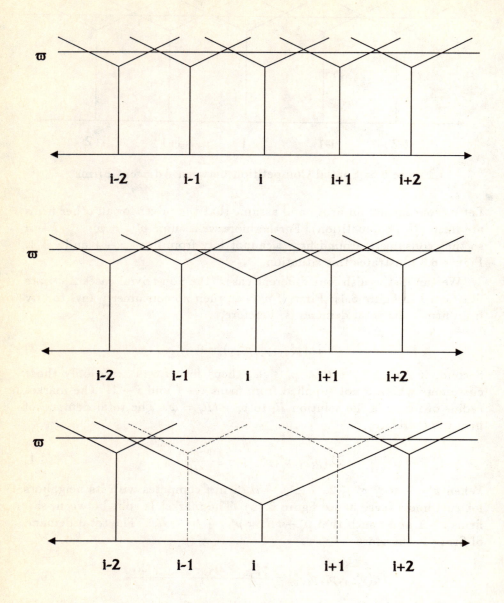

Figure 6.4: Spatial Competition between Adjacent Firms: Three Cases

6.1. Standard Location and Spatial Price Theory

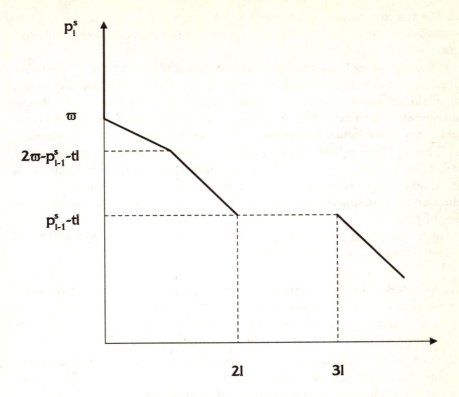

Figure 6.5: Firm i's Demand Curve

When p_i^s drops below $p_{i-1}^s - tl$ and $p_{i+1}^s - tl$, firm i undercuts the consumer prices of $i-1$ and $i+1$ at all locations (case 4). Therefore, firms $i-1$ and $i+1$ lose all their customers to firm i (see figure 6.4c). Firm i has now two new neighbors, namely $i-2$ and $i+2$. The market boundary between, say, firms $i-2$ and i is defined by $p_i^s + tR_i = p_{i-2}^s + t(2l - R_i)$. The total demand of firm i is therefore

$$D_i(p_{i-2}^s, p_i^s, p_{i+2}^s) = \frac{p_{i-2}^s - 2p_i + p_{i+2}^s + 4tl}{2t} \ . \tag{6.6}$$

The demand curve of firm i (displayed in figure 6.5; see also Beckmann and Thisse, 1986, p. 44) has three different segments. They correspond to cases 2-4 discussed above. At the transition from spatial monopoly (case 2) to the competitive situation of case 3 the demand curve is kinked because from this point on firm i feels the impact of its closest competitors (firms $i-1$ and $i+1$). The discontinuity between the competitive and the supercompetitive (case 4) segment of the demand curve occurs because at this point firm i can adds all customers located between firm $i-1$ ($i+1$)

and the market boundary between $i-1$ and $i-2$ ($i+1$ and $i+2$) to its market at once. In the supercompetitive region firm i competes with firms $i-2$ and $i+2$.

It can be shown (Beckmann 1972, Salop 1979) that for all possible values of parameters ω, c, t and l an equilibrium price[6] exists. Although, "when the impact of distance becomes negligible, the above model of spatial competition behaves like the perfect competition model (...,) perverse effects may occur when the impact of distance is significant" (Beckmann and Thisse, 1986, p. 45). The equilibrium price increases with marginal production cost, c, at some parameter constellations but is insensitive to c in others. Also, at some parameter constellations a decline in tl, i.e. a reduction in transportation cost, leads to an increase in the equilibrium price of firm i.

Let us point out some additional features of this model that will be of interest in the following discussion:

1. Whatever the parameter constellation, each customer will consider only one firm as supplier of the product or not buy at all (if $p_j^c > \omega$ for all firms j). Market areas are clearly delimited. Every consumer can be assigned to exactly one supplier.
2. The price changes of one firm directly affect only its nearest competitors with a non-empty market[7]. As long as firm i sets a price in the monopoly or competitive segment of the market, firms $i-2$, $i-3$, ... and $i+2$ $i+3$, ... remain completely unaffected.

6.2 Search Based Location and Spatial Price Structures

The spatial search model as we have discussed it up to now cannot directly be compared to the location and spatial price concept presented above. While in the previous chapters we have looked at the spatial search problem from the perspective of one consumer, standard location and spatial price theory deal with a continuum of consumers. Depending on their location these consumers are faced with different transportation costs, which lead to demand differences and market areas, and allow different price strategies of suppliers. Although we have discussed the effect of parameter changes in the spatial search model in section 4.5, we do not know

---

[6] Defined as a price p_i^{s*} such that, given p_{i-1}^{s*} and p_{i+1}^{s*}, firm i maximizes its profit.

[7] In the first three cases firms $i-1$ and $i+1$, in case 4 firms $i-2$ and $i+2$.

6.2. Search Based Location and Spatial Price Structures

yet how a marginal shift in the consumer's home location affects his/her situation in a search context.

Therefore, before we can analyze the impact of spatial search upon the concepts of standard location and spatial price theory we need to take another look at the standard search model.

While in standard location and spatial price theory the consumer is dealing with some given price, in a search context the price actually paid by the consumer depends upon the random price offers he/she receives. Before starting the search process, the consumer can compute the expected costs of search and he/she bases all relevant decisions upon this figure. As discussed in chapter 4 the expected costs determine the route the consumer follows through the search problem which, in turn, strongly influences the chances that the product is bought from one supplier as compared to the others. The expected costs of search correspond to the consumer price of section 6.1. Therefore, we will have to analyze the relationship between the consumer's location and his/her expected costs of search.

In the previous section we did not discuss what the elements of transportation costs are. We only related them to distance. Under mill pricing, implicitly we thought of them as the costs the consumer has to bear for going to the market and transporting the product back home. Under other pricing strategies the cost components may be different. In any case, there are always two trips involved: the trip to the market (or to the consumer) and the return trip. Since in the previous section both of them were over the same distance, we could ignore the distinction and integrate it into the function t.

In a search context the consumer may visit a number of suppliers and return home from any one of them. While for a given route the costs of going from one alternative to another during search are not affected by the consumer's location, the travel costs to the first alternative and the costs of returning home are. While the first cost component is clearly defined, the searcher may return home from any one of the alternatives, depending upon the price offer he/she receives. When computing the expected costs we therefore have to take into account all these options, weighted by the choice probability for the respective alternative.

This complicates the analysis. Therefore, we will proceed in two steps: first we assume that the searcher does not have to return home, i.e. we ignore the costs of the return trip. In the second step we reintroduce this cost component and analyze how this affects the overall picture.

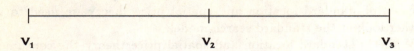

Figure 6.6: Spatial Structure

6.2.1 Consumer not Returning Home

Assume a linear market as in the previous section. To keep the analysis simple we will just consider three suppliers located as in figure 6.6. The three suppliers charge mill prices and generate price offers according to the same random distribution with identical parameters. For illustrative purposes we use an example with the following parameters: travel costs between two adjacent suppliers is 0.1, each supplier generates price offers according to a uniform 0-1 distribution.

Optimal Route and Expected Costs

When we ignore the costs of returning home[8], things are fairly simple. For a given route, say $R = (v_1, v_2, v_3)$, the searcher has to travel to the first alternative. The costs of this trip are affected by his/her home location. From then on, however, the search problem is not affected by the consumer's location any longer. Reservation prices $\bar{x}(R_1), \bar{x}(R_2), \ldots, \bar{x}(R_n)$ are independent of the consumer's location. Because of (4.6) the same is true for choice probabilities. For a consumer located a distance δ from alternative $R[1]$ – we write the corresponding travel costs as $t\delta$ – the expected costs of search can therefore be computed as:

$$\begin{aligned} y_d(R) &= C(H, R[1]) + \int_0^{\bar{x}(R_1)} x f(x)\, dx + \bar{x}(R_1)[1 - F(\bar{x}(R_1))] \\ &= t\delta + y_0(R) \ . \end{aligned}$$

Consequently, we get a "price" funnel just as in section 6.1. Figure 6.7 shows it for alternative v_1 in our example.

We have derived these expected costs based on route R. However, we know from chapter 4 that the searcher will follow this route only when it

---

[8]Note that under this simplifying assumption reservation prices and expected costs of search coincide (see (4.3)).

6.2. Search Based Location and Spatial Price Structures

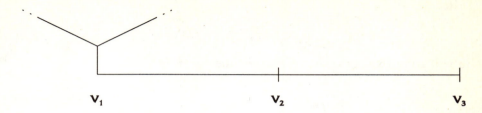

Figure 6.7: Price Funnel for One Alternative

yields the lowest expected costs. When another route yields lower expected costs from his/her location the consumer will follow this route. Over the whole range, the relevant expected costs will always be the minimal ones, i.e. those for the optimal route.

In our example route (v_3, v_2, v_1) is just the reverse of R and we get the same result. From chapter 4 we know that routes (v_1, v_3, v_2) and (v_3, v_1, v_2) can never be optimal. Also, it is easy to see that the searcher will be indifferent between routes (v_2, v_1, v_3) and (v_2, v_3, v_1). Therefore, the only route we need to analyze in our example is one of the latter two, say $S = (v_2, v_1, v_3)$.

When we compute the expected return for this route and set $\delta = 0$ we find that $y_0(S)$ is higher than $y_0(R)$. The reason for this lies in the spatial structure of the search problem. With route R distances between $R[1]$ and $R[2]$, and between $R[2]$ and $R[3]$ are both 0.1. When the search follows route S, however, alternative $S[2]$ is again 0.1 units from $S[1]$, but $S[3]$ is 0.2 units from $S[2]$. Only when the choice probability for the third alternative is zero for both routes, the two numbers are the same.

Because we have set the costs of returning home to zero, we can write the expected costs at the various steps of the search problem as

for route R:
$$\begin{aligned}
y_0(R) &= \int_0^{y_0(R_1)} x f(x)\,dx + y_0(R_1)(1 - F(y_0(R_1))) \\
y_0(R_1) &= c + \int_0^{y_0(R_2)} x f(x)\,dx + y_0(R_2)(1 - F(y_0(R_2))) \\
y_0(R_2) &= c + E(x)
\end{aligned}$$
for route S:
$$\begin{aligned}
y_0(S) &= \int_0^{y_0(S_1)} x f(x)\,dx + y_0(S_1)(1 - F(y_0(S_1))) \\
y_0(S_1) &= c + \int_0^{y_0(S_2)} x f(x)\,dx + y_0(S_2)(1 - F(y_0(S_2))) \\
y_0(S_2) &= 2c + E(x)
\end{aligned}$$
(6.7)

where c is the cost of going from one alternative to the next; e.g., from v_1 to v_2.

We see directly from (6.7) that $y_0(S_2) - y_0(R_2) = c$. Therefore, we can write

$$y_0(S_2) = y_0(R_2) + c \ . \tag{6.8}$$

Substituting (6.8) into the respective lines of (6.7) yields

$$y_0(S_1) - y_0(R_1) = \int_{y_0(R_2)}^{y_0(R_2)+c} x f(x)\,dx + c - y_0(R_2)\left[F(y_0(R_2)+c) - F(y_0(R_2))\right] - cF(y_0(R_2)+c) \ . \tag{6.9}$$

The integral in (6.9) is directly related to the expected value for the price variable between $y_0(R_2)$ and $y_0(S_2)$:

$$E(x | y_0(R_2) \leq x \leq y_0(S_2)) = \frac{\int_{y_0(R_2)}^{y_0(S_2)} x f(x)\,dx}{F(y_0(S_2)) - F(y_0(R_2))} = y_0(R_2) + \lambda c$$
$$\text{with} \quad 0 \leq \lambda \leq 1 \ . \tag{6.10}$$

The second relationship results from the fact that the conditional expectation must lie between the two conditions.

Therefore, we can rewrite (6.9) as

$$y_0(S_1) - y_0(R_1) =$$
$$[y_0(R_2) + \lambda c]\left[F(y_0(R_2)+x) - F(y_0(R_2))\right] + c$$
$$- y_0(R_2)\left[F(y_0(R_2)+c) - F(y_0(R_2))\right] - cF(y_0(R_2)+c)$$
$$= \lambda c\left[1 - F(y_0(R_2))\right] + (1-\lambda)c\left[1 - F(y_0(R_2)+c)\right] \ . \tag{6.11}$$

This yields the following relationship for the difference in expected costs:

$$c\left[1 - F(y_0(R_2))\right] \leq y_0(S_2) - y_0(R_2) \leq c\left[1 - F(y_0(R_2)+c)\right] \ . \tag{6.12}$$

We see that only when $y_0(R_2)$ is so large that the probability for proceeding to $R[3]$ is zero (i.e., $F(y_0(R_2)) = 1$) the difference between the two choice probabilities disappears. This is plausible because in this case the searcher does not travel the longer stretch in route S.

Note that (6.11) is very similar to (2.4), which is actually the marginal version of (6.11).

To derive the difference in expected costs between route R and route S we can use (6.11) and apply the same procedure again. However, much simpler is an approximate solution that we can derive from (2.4)

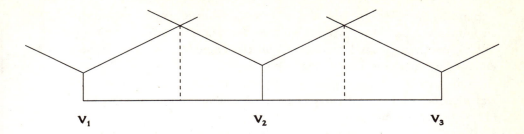

Figure 6.8: Price Funnels for all Three Alternatives

$$y_0(S) - y_0(R) \approx c\left[1 - F(y_0(R_2))\right]\left[1 - F(y_0(R_1))\right] \ . \tag{6.13}$$

As a consequence, the price funnel for alternative v_2 usually starts at a higher level than those for v_1 and v_3 ($y_0(S) \geq y_0(R)$). The slope of the funnel is again t:

$$\frac{\partial y_d(S)}{\partial \delta} = \frac{\partial (t\delta + y_0(S))}{\partial \delta} = t \ . \tag{6.14}$$

This has implications for the relative positions of the three suppliers and for their market areas. As we see from figure 6.8 consumers near the supplier at v_2 tend to have higher expected costs than corresponding consumers near suppliers v_1 and v_3. This despite the fact that all three suppliers generate their price offers from the same distribution.

Also, the supplier at v_2 will in the average receive higher payments from his/her customers than the other two suppliers. Their payments are the conditional expectations $E(x|x \leq y_0(R_1))$ and $E(x|x \leq y_0(S_1))$, respectively. Because under normal circumstances $y_0(S_1) > y_0(R_1)$, we get

$$E(x|x \leq y_0(R_1)) < E(x|x \leq y_0(S_1)) \ . \tag{6.15}$$

Determining the size of the market is more complex in a search context than in section 6.1. In a search context the consumer may buy from any available supplier. The chance that he/she buys from a particular one is given by the choice probability. The latter depends heavily upon the route the consumer chooses through the search problem.

Because the choice probabilities are constant for a given route when we ignore the costs of returning home, usually every consumer belongs to every supplier's market, irrespective of his/her location[9]. However, depending upon the route that is optimal from a searcher's location the suppliers will be able to attract his/her demand with different probability. Which route is optimal depends upon the expected cost functions at the consumer's location, i.e., which one is lowest.

This yields a picture (figure 6.8) that is very similar to that of spatial price and location theory (figure 6.3). The intersections of the price- (expected cost-) curves determine areas around the locations of suppliers. While in spatial price and location theory the consumers within a particular area always buy from the respective supplier, in the search model the consumers only visit this supplier *first* ("principal supplier"). When the suppliers are identical the choice probability is highest for the principal supplier. Nevertheless, there is usually[10] a positive probability for other suppliers to attract this demand. We call the area where a specific supplier is the principal supplier his/her "area of market domination".

As long as we assume perfectly inelastic demand (i.e., that each customer buys one unit of the product) the areas of market domination for v_1 and v_3 are unbounded. The area of market domination for the supplier at v_2 is limited by the areas of his/her competitors just as the market areas in location and spatial price theory. However, his/her area of market domination is smaller than the corresponding market area under section 6.1 because of the higher expected costs of search (see figure 6.8).

Choice Probabilities

As we know from chapter 4 (equation (4.6)) the choice probability for the first alternative in a route is directly related to the respective reservation price. Because of $y_0(S_1) > y_0(R_1)$ we get

$$P(S[1]) > P(R[1]) . \qquad (6.16)$$

Figure 6.9 illustrates this for our numerical example. Because of the change in the optimal route we observe discontinuities in choice probabilities at each border between areas of market domination. We have made similar observations in section 4.5 (routing effects). In the area of market domination of v_2 the choice probability of the principal supplier is higher than the corresponding figure for the other two suppliers. The choice probabilities for the other two suppliers coincide in this area of the

---

[9] We may make the consumer's demand a function of the expected costs. In this case demand may be zero for consumers outside a certain point.

[10] Unless the suppliers are located so far apart that all suppliers but the principle supplier represent irrelevant alternatives. In this case, the search model version reduces to the standard model discussed in section 6.1.

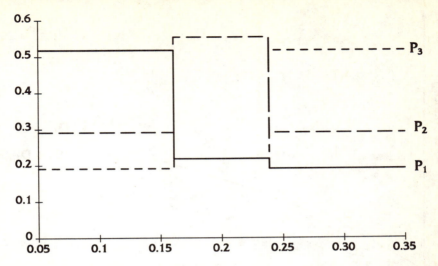

Figure 6.9: Choice Probabilities as a Function of the Consumer's Location

market because after searching v_2 every customer is indifferent between going to v_1 of to v_3 next. Interestingly, the consumers around v_2, although located near the center of the market, are more captive to their principal supplier than the other consumers.

The supplier in the center is spatially constrained by his/her competitors but within this area enjoys less competition than the other suppliers. Is the net effect positive or negative? Is the central location economically advantageous or disadvantageous? We will use the overall demand as an indicator.

Demand

Because we have assumed perfectly inelastic demand, as long as we do not constrain the spatial size of our problem demand for all three suppliers grows beyond bounds. Therefore, we will exogenously constrain the size of the overall market and look at the demand the three suppliers can attract at various sizes. We do so by expanding the market symmetrically around the location of v_2, the center of the market.

Because by assumption each customer is buying the same amount – one unit – of the product and customers are equally distributed over the linear market, we derive the demand figures simply by integrating the choice probability functions displayed in figure 6.9 over the distance from v_2. Figure 6.10 shows the result for our numerical example. As we see, up to the boundary of his/her area of market domination the centrally located supplier has been able to accumulate a considerable excess demand

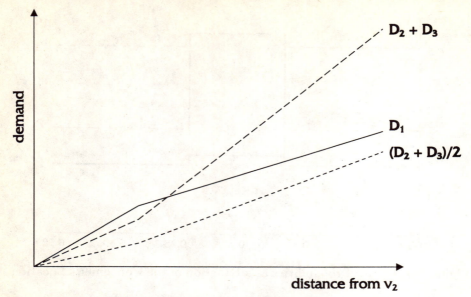

Figure 6.10: Aggregate Demand as a Function of Market Size

over the competitors. Beyond the boundary of the area of market domination, the other two suppliers gain ground but only very gradually. This is because by expanding the overall market symmetrically we not only add customers to the area of market domination of the supplier at, say, v_1 where this supplier has the highest choice probability, but also to the area of market domination of the supplier at v_3 where the choice probability for supplier 1 is lowest. In both areas the centrally located supplier experiences the second highest choice probabilities. Therefore, our numerical example indicates that up to a considerable size of the market the central location is more advantageous than peripheral locations[11].

6.2.2 Consumer Returning Home

Now let us return to our standard constellation where we also take into account the costs of the trip back home. As we will see, introducing this cost component yields a quite different picture. In a first step we will analyze the expected costs of search of the consumers located at the supply locations. In a second step we will look at the effects of deviations

---

[11]When we drop the assumption of perfectly inelastic demand and make demand a function of the expected costs (see chapter 4, assumption G.3) the size of the overall market is determined endogenously. Because outside customers will demand less and less the further away from the market center they are located the advantage of the central supplier will be even more pronounced in this case.

6.2. Search Based Location and Spatial Price Structures

from these base locations. More graphically argued, in the first step we will look at the bases of the "price" funnels, in the second step at their shapes.

The Base of the "Price" Funnel

When we calculate the respective figures for our numerical example we see that the expected costs are identical for all base locations (i.e., locations of suppliers). More extensive numerical tests indicate that this seems to be the case for any number of alternatives. We summarize this feature in the following theorem:

> **Theorem 6.1** *In a spatial search problem with any number of identical suppliers located at equal intervals in linear space and with search costs proportional to distance, all the customers whose locations coincide with that of suppliers ("base locations") have identical expected costs of search.*

We will prove this theorem in two steps: first we will show that the optimal route in this specific search problem follows a simple pattern, second we will show that all search strategies that follow this pattern yield identical search costs.

As we know from theorem 5.1, chapter 5, the searcher will never skip an alternative in linear space. Therefore, at each step of the search process the searching customer has to select at most from two alternatives: the next one to his/her left and the next one to his/her right. We have already discussed this structure in a more general form in section 5.1. There we have found that this spatial structure is still too general to allow for an efficient solution for the spatial search problem.

The problem described in theorem 6.1 differs from that in section 5.1 by three additional assumptions: first, that all suppliers are identical (i.e., they generate price offers according to the same distribution function), second, that they are located at equal distances from one another, and, third, that the customers under consideration are located at the same locations as the suppliers. We can show that under these additional assumptions the searcher's optimal route can be described as follows:

1. The customer searches the supplier at his/her home location.
2. The customer selects one side of the market at will and searches all its suppliers in sequence.
3. Only when he/she has exhausted all the suppliers at the one side of the market the searcher turns to the other side and searches all suppliers there in sequence.

That the customer searches his/her home supplier first and that he/she searches suppliers at each side of the market in sequence follows directly from theorem 5.1. The only new point in the argument is therefore that the searcher has to exhaust one side of the market before turning to the other.

Because of our additional assumptions we can simplify equation (4.5) that relates the reservation prices of the search sequence. Because all the suppliers use the same distribution function we can write

$$\int_0^{\bar{x}(R_i)} x f(x)\, dx + \bar{x}(R_i)[1 - F(\bar{x}(R_i))] = \mathcal{H}(\bar{x}(R_i)) \ . \tag{6.17}$$

Equation (4.5) then becomes

$$\bar{x}(R_{i-1}) = C(R[i-1], R[i]) + (C(R[i], H) - C(R[i-1], H)) + \mathcal{H}(\bar{x}(R_i)) \ . \tag{6.18}$$

Let R be the route described above. Suppose that the searcher is not located at one of the endpoints of the linear space[12]. After searching the supplier at his/her home location the customer can choose between two suppliers next, both search costs c away, one to his/her left and one to his/her right. Which one ever the consumer chooses, when we substitute the corresponding cost figures into 6.18 we see that

$$\bar{x}(R) = 2c + \mathcal{H}(\bar{x}(R_1)) \ . \tag{6.19}$$

Assume for a moment that the consumer has selected the alternative to his/her right[13] and that there is more than one alternative at this side of the market. Then, the next alternative in route R is again search costs c away. Substituting again into 6.18 we get

$$\bar{x}(R_1) = c + 2c - c + \mathcal{H}(\bar{x}(R_2)) = 2c + \mathcal{H}(\bar{x}(R_2)) \ . \tag{6.20}$$

As long as the searcher moves through this side of the market the next alternative is always c away and the costs of going home also increase by c. Therefore, until the searcher has exhausted this side of the market, the following relationship holds for the reservation prices:

$$\bar{x}(R_{i-1}) = 2c + \mathcal{H}(\bar{x}(R_i)) \ . \tag{6.21}$$

---

[12]In this case the optimality of route R results directly from theorem 5.1.

[13]Actually, the consumer is indifferent between searching the alternative to his/her right or left next. He/she will pick each one of them with probability 1/2. As we will show, the choice at this point implies a specific route through the remaining alternatives.

6.2. Search Based Location and Spatial Price Structures

When the right hand side of the market is exhausted, the next alternative is the first one on the other side of the market, search costs c to the left of the customer's home location. When the last alternative on the right hand side of the market is rc from home, the reservation price is:

$$\bar{x}(R_{i-1}) = (r+1)c + c - rc + \mathcal{H}(\bar{x}(R_i)) = 2c + \mathcal{H}(\bar{x}(R_i)) \ . \quad (6.22)$$

We see that (6.21) holds for all the alternatives in route R with $\mathcal{H}(\bar{x}(R_n)) = E(x)$.

Now consider a route S that differs from R in such a way that the customer searches only $r-1$ alternatives in the right hand side of the market in sequence, then exhausts the left hand side of the market and at the end returns to the last alternative at the right.

When we apply the same argument as above we see that (6.21) holds for all the $r-1$ alternatives the customer searches in the right hand side of the market, for the transition to the left hand side, and all the alternatives there. However, when the searcher has exhausted the left hand side and returns to the right hand side to search the remaining alternative there, substituting into (6.18) yields

$$\bar{x}(S_{n-1}) = 2rc + E(x) \ . \quad (6.23)$$

Whenever $r > 1$, $\bar{x}(S_{n-1}) > \bar{x}(R_{n-1})$. Because (6.21) holds for all the other reservation prices, the expected costs of search along route S must be larger than those of route R[14].

The same line of argument can be applied to any other route and we see that whenever a route does not conform to the above definition it yields higher expected costs. Therefore, route R and any other route that follows the above definition must be optimal.

The final proof of theorem 6.1 follows directly from this argument. Irrespective of the customer's home location, $\bar{x}(R)$ results from the same number of recursive applications of (6.21). Because $y(R_i) = \bar{x}(R_i) + C(R[i], H)$ (see (4.3)), and because $\bar{x}(R)$ is measured at the home location (i.e., $C(R[0], H) = 0$), $y(R)$ is the same for all base locations. This proves theorem 6.1.

Before we turn to the second part of our analysis of search based location and spatial price structures let us point out a few additional features following from the proof of theorem 6.1.

The customers at the base locations all face exactly the same search problem. Because each one has the same number of alternatives available

---

[14] When $r = 1$ there is no alternative to be left on the right hand side of the market.

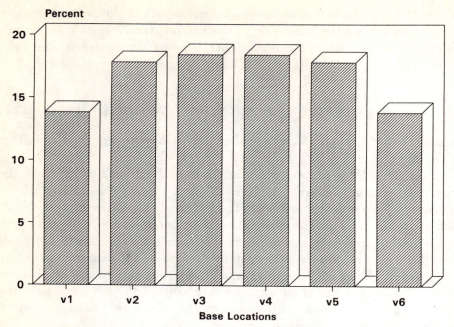

Figure 6.11: Distribution of Demand over 6 Suppliers

with the reservation prices derived from the respective number of recursive applications of (6.21) each customer at a base location bases search on the same sequence of reservation prices. Because of (4.6) he/she selects the alternatives in the respective optimal route with the same choice probability.

Because of theorem 6.1 the customers are indifferent between the base locations. Each base location yields exactly the same search costs. The suppliers, however, are not indifferent between these locations. Depending on their location they can occupy different relative positions within the optimal routes of the customers at the various base locations. Because in the optimal route the alternatives within each side of the market are searched in sequence, only the alternatives at the endpoints of the market can be last in a search sequence. Alternatives near the center of the market can never occupy this unfavorable relative position in a search sequence and experience the correspondingly low choice probability.

For a numerical example with 6 alternatives[15] and the same number of consumers at each base location we find that the suppliers at v_3 and v_4, the two central locations, will each attract 18.43% of demand, the suppliers at v_2 and v_5 17.84%, and the suppliers at the endpoints v_1 and

---

[15] We use again a uniform 0-1 distribution and $c = 0.1$.

v_6 only 13.82% each. Figure 6.11 shows this result graphically. In this situation suppliers will prefer locations closer to the center of the market over peripheral ones.

Another interesting result is based on (6.21). This equation relates the reservation price at one point in the search sequence recursively to the remaining alternatives. Under the current set of assumptions each reservation price is related to the next one in exactly the same way (as described by (6.21)). This does not mean that the reservation prices are identical because there are fewer and fewer alternatives left, the numbers are therefore based on fewer and fewer recursive applications of (6.21). However, when we assume an infinite number of identical alternatives lined up equidistantly in linear space, at every step the searcher has an infinite number of alternatives remaining and we can write

$$\begin{aligned}\bar{x}(R) &= 2c + \mathcal{H}(\bar{x}(R)) \\ &= 2c + \int_0^{\bar{x}(R)} x f(x)\,dx + \bar{x}(R)\left[1 - F(\bar{x}(R))\right] \quad . \end{aligned} \quad (6.24)$$

From this relationship we get

$$2c = \int_0^{\bar{x}(R)} (\bar{x}(R) - x) f(x)\,dx \quad , \qquad (6.25)$$

the basic equation of the standard search model of economics (see equation (2.6)). Because of the need of a return trip search costs are twice the costs of going from one alternative to the next. Since the reservation prices are constant throughout the search sequence, so are the conditional choice probabilities. Therefore, the choice probability declines geometrically over the search process.

The Shape of the "Price" Funnel

In the second step of our analysis we concentrate on the shape of the "price" funnel. Together with the expected costs at the base locations it determines the areas of market domination and the expected costs of search for consumers outside the base locations.

Introducing the costs of returning home adds too much complexity to the problem to derive general equations for the shape of the "price" funnels. However, some basic features of the search problem will allow us to reach some interesting insights into the shape of the funnels, areas of market domination, and optimal routes of the searcher. The question we try to answer now is the following: When the consumer is located anywhere on the linear market what are his/her expected costs of search, how does it relate to those of the consumers at the base location, and what are the implications for the spatial structure of the market.

The first thing we note is that because the expected costs at the base locations are all identical (theorem 6.1) and the consumer acts rational by assumption we only have to deal with the central part of each price funnel; the part from the respective base location to the locations of the nearest two suppliers. We will use this observation in the following arguments in order to focus the attentions and demonstrate later that it is indeed correct. Because the price funnel gives the additional expected costs a consumer has to bear as compared to a consumer at the respective base location, each price funnel also represents a specific route through the search problem.

The second thing we note is that there is an upper bound for the shape of the "price" funnel. Suppose the searcher applies the following – suboptimal – search strategy. He/she selects one of the nearby base locations, applies the same search strategy as a consumer at this base location and then returns home. Denote the distance between home and this base location as δ. In this case the extra costs of this searcher over the customer at the respective base location are $2t\delta$, the slope of the "price" funnel is $2t$. This yields "price" funnels with identical base costs and slopes, just like those discussed in section 6.1. However, this strategy is suboptimal because it may lead to the situation that when returning to the base location after accepting a price offer the customer passes his/her home. In this case the customer could save resources by stopping at home. Therefore, the slope of the "price" funnel based on the optimal strategy can be at most $2t$.

When the customer is located somewhere between two suppliers he/she can start search with the supplier on either side. Denote the distances between the searcher's home location and the two adjacent suppliers by δ_1 and δ_2. Note that[16]

$$t(\delta_1 + \delta_2) = c \ . \tag{6.26}$$

We will use (6.18) that describes the relationship between reservation prices for a specific route through the search problem. Because all the suppliers are assumed to be identical we can concentrate on the various cost components.

When the searcher proceeds through the search problem, we can distinguish various cases[17] that are illustrated in figure 6.12:

---

[16] As a convention we denote the distance to the supplier on the left of the searcher's home as δ_1.

[17] Because of theorem 5.1 the searcher will never skip an alternative.

6.2. Search Based Location and Spatial Price Structures

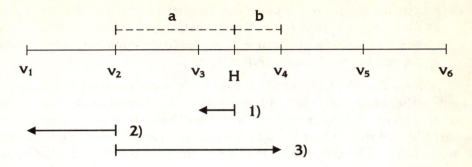

Figure 6.12: Search in Linear Space: Various Cases

1. The searcher has to go to the first alternative in his/her optimal route. Because of theorem 5.1 this can only be one of two alternatives; the first supplier to the left or to the right of the searcher's home location. When substituting the corresponding cost components we find that

$$\bar{x}(R) = 2t\delta_1 + \mathcal{H}(\bar{x}(R_1)) \quad \text{or} \quad \bar{x}(R) = 2t\delta_2 + \mathcal{H}(\bar{x}(R_1)) \qquad (6.27)$$

depending on whether the supplier to the left or to the right of the consumer's home is the first one searched.

2. The searcher proceeds from one alternative to the next one available on the same side of the market. Because of theorem 5.1 and the specific assumptions of this section the cost of going to this alternative is always c. Suppose the costs of returning home from the current alternative is a, as indicated in figure 6.12. Therefore, whenever $R[i]$ and $R[i-1]$ are both on the same side of the searcher's home location the reservation prices are related by

$$\bar{x}(R_{i-1}) = c + (a+c) - a + \mathcal{H}(\bar{x}(R_i)) = 2c + \mathcal{H}(\bar{x}(R_i)) \ . \qquad (6.28)$$

This is just equation (6.21) above.

3. The searcher changes from one side of the market to the other. Suppose the searcher's current alternative and the one he/she is going to visit next are search costs a and b from home, respectively (see figure 6.12). Then,

$$\bar{x}(R_{i-1}) = 2b + \mathcal{H}(\bar{x}(R_i)) \quad \text{or} \quad \bar{x}(R_{i-1}) = 2a + \mathcal{H}(\bar{x}(R_i)) \ , \qquad (6.29)$$

depending on the direction the searcher has to go. Whatever the direction, it is important to note that only the costs of going from home to the new alternative ($R[i]$) enter the equation. These costs depend upon δ_1 and δ_2, respectively.

We see that the location of the searcher's home, expressed by δ_1 or δ_2, enters the search costs only on those links that either originate from home or pass home. In other words, the location of home is relevant only for the first link and those where the searcher changes from one side of the market to the other. The expected costs of a specific route therefore depend upon how often and when in the search process the searcher changes from one side of the market to the other. In any case, as noted in equation (6.27) above, the costs associated with the first link are $t\delta$, where δ is either δ_1 or δ_2 depending on which alternative the searcher investigates first.

One simple routing strategy would be that the searcher begins with one side of the market, searches all its alternatives, and then changes to the other side of the market where he/she searches all alternatives in sequence. In this case there is only one link after the first one when search costs are not equal to $2c$, i.e. when the searcher changes sides. When substituting for a or b in (6.29) we find that the costs for this link are $2(c - t\delta)$[18]. Two points are important to note here: First, because $0 \leq t\delta \leq c$ the costs for changing market sides are usually[19] lower than those for proceeding to the next alternative in the same side of the market. Second, a similar relationship as (2.4) in chapter 2 for expected costs can be found for reservation prices:

$$\frac{\partial \bar{x}(R_{i-1})}{\partial \bar{x}(R_i)} = \frac{\partial \mathcal{H}(\bar{x}(R_i))}{\partial \bar{x}(R_i)} = 1 - F(\bar{x}(R_i)) \leq 1 \;, \qquad (6.30)$$

with the equality holding only when the reservation price is so low that any price is acceptable.

Therefore, the searcher reduces his/her expected costs by changing to the other side of the market. However, for a given δ the cost reduction will be lower the later this link occurs in the search sequence. As a consequence, when the searcher is located midways between two suppliers (i.e., $\delta_1 = \delta_2$) following the above sketched route he/she will find it advantageous to investigate the *shorter* side of the market first.

However, there might be another search strategy superior to the simple one sketched above. Because of the spatial structure of the problem

---

[18]More generally, the costs are $2((r+1)c - t\delta)$ with r being the number of alternatives already investigated on the other side of the market. When the searcher changes sides the first time, $r = 0$.

[19]When $t\delta = 0$ or $t\delta = c$ the searcher's location coincides with one of the base locations. This case has been discussed above and is not of interest here.

this would need to be a strategy where the searcher had to change sides more than once. It is easy to see from our discussion above and from the definition of a and b that the costs for changing back to the original side of the market is $2(rc + t\delta)$, where $r \geq 1$ is the number of alternatives the searcher has investigated before he/she had changed market sides the first time.

The searcher should try to change market sides the first time as early as possible in his/her search sequence. For two reasons: first, because the cost saving effect of the change itself is larger, and, second, because the costs of changing back to the original side of the market are smaller. It is easy to see that among all the routes that change market sides twice the following one is optimal: the searcher investigates the first alternative on one side of the market (cost: $2t\delta$), changes to the other side (cost: $2(c - t\delta)$) and searches all alternatives there (costs: $2c$ each). When all alternatives there are exhausted he/she changes back to the original side of the market (cost: $2(c + t\delta)$) and searches the remaining alternatives (cost: $2c$ each). With which side the searcher should begin depends upon the searcher's home location and the number of alternatives on each side of the market. Note that when the searcher's home is midways between two suppliers ($\delta_1 = \delta_2$) he/she is usually *not indifferent* between the two sides of the market. Rather, he/she will begin searching the shorter side of the market. In this case the number of alternatives to search between changing market sides is maximal. This implies that the "price" funnels usually do not intersect at $\delta_1 = \delta_2$, only when it is the center of the market (i.e., when the same number of alternatives is available on either side).

What about routes where the searcher changes market sides more than twice? It is easy to see that these routes are always suboptimal. When the searcher changes the market side for the third time he/she is heading to a side where he/she has already searched at least on alternative. The cost for this link are therefore $2(2c - t\delta)$ or larger. The costs are therefore larger[20] than the costs on a regular link ($2c$). Also, the searcher cannot compensate the higher costs for some cost saving later on, because the costs when he/she changes back again are even $2(2c + t\delta)$ or larger.

This leaves us with two candidate strategies for optimal route (each one actually consisting of two routes): the one where the searcher changes market sides only once (he/she exhausts one side of the market before changing to the other side), and the one where the searcher changes market sides twice. The second strategy has the advantage that the cost-saving change of market sides occurs earlier. Its disadvantage is that later on the searcher will have to change market sides again at higher costs. Although

---

[20]Remember that $t\delta \leq c$ with the equality holding only when the searcher's home is at a base location.

we cannot demonstrate the general superiority of one strategy over the other, in numerical tests the second strategy always yields lower costs. Therefore, we will base our further argument on the second strategy.

We can now analyze the shape of the "price" funnel by calculating the partial derivative of the expected costs – which is identical to the reservation price $\bar{x}(R)$ – with respect to δ:

$$\frac{\partial \bar{x}(R)}{\partial \delta} = 2t + \frac{\partial \mathcal{H}(\bar{x}(R_1))}{\partial \bar{x}(R_1)} \frac{\partial \bar{x}(R_1)}{\partial \delta} \ . \tag{6.31}$$

The first term of the summation results directly from (6.27). Depending on the home location of the searcher, the second term can assume different values[21]. When the searcher is located outside the first or the last alternative in the linear market (i.e., he/she faces only one market side), (6.28) applies to all the remaining alternatives. Therefore, $\partial \bar{x}(R_1)/\partial \delta = 0$ in this case and (6.31) reduces to

$$\frac{\partial \bar{x}(R)}{\partial \delta} = 2t \ . \tag{6.32}$$

When the searcher's home location is just inside the first or last alternative of the linear market, $R[1]$ will be this first or last alternative and for the rest of the search sequence the searcher will just exhaust the only remaining market side. In this case:

$$\frac{\partial \bar{x}(R_1)}{\partial \delta} = -2t + \frac{\partial \mathcal{H}(\bar{x}(R_2))}{\partial \bar{x}(R_2)} \frac{\partial \bar{x}(R_2)}{\partial \delta} = -2t$$

because $\partial \bar{x}(R_2)/\partial \delta = 0$, and (6.31) reduces to

$$\frac{\partial \bar{x}(R)}{\partial \delta} = 2t + (1 - F(\bar{x}(R_1)))(-2t) = 2t F(\bar{x}(R_1)) \ . \tag{6.33}$$

Note that this usually yields a smaller positive number than (6.32).

From the discussion above we know that the two steps that lead to (6.33) – the searcher investigates one alternative and then changes to the other side of the market – are common to all supposedly optimal routes. They differ from the route behind (6.33) only insofar as later in the search sequence the searcher has to change back to the original side of the market (at cost $2(c + t\delta)$). Therefore, in the general optimal route

$$\frac{\partial \mathcal{H}(\bar{x}(R_2))}{\partial \delta} > 0 \ . \tag{6.34}$$

The size of (6.34) depends upon when the searcher will change back to the original market side. However, from the discussion above we know

---

[21] From (6.30) we know that $\frac{\partial \mathcal{H}(\bar{x}(R_1))}{\partial \bar{x}(R_1)} = 1 - F(\bar{x}(R_1))$.

6.2. Search Based Location and Spatial Price Structures

that he/she can save costs by doing this step as late as possible in the search sequence. Therefore, and because of (6.30) the impact of (6.34) on expected costs will be small as compared to that of the first two steps. However, we can derive an upper bound for the slope of the "price" funnel based on the general supposedly optimal route. We do this by assuming that the searcher has to change back to the original side of the market immediately after the first two steps. From this assumption we get

$$\frac{\partial \bar{x}(R_2)}{\partial \delta} = 2t , \qquad (6.35)$$

which in turn leads to

$$\begin{aligned}\frac{\partial \bar{x}(R)}{\partial \delta} &= 2t + (1 - F(\bar{x}(R_1)))[-2t + (1 - F(\bar{x}(R_2)))2t] \\ &= 2t[1 - F(\bar{x}(R_2)) + F(\bar{x}(R_1))F(\bar{x}(R_2))] . \end{aligned} \qquad (6.36)$$

Consequently, as long as the searcher's home location is between the first and the last supplier in the linear market the following relationship must hold:

$$2tF(\bar{x}(R_1)) \leq \frac{\partial \bar{x}(R)}{\partial \delta} \leq 2t[1 - F(\bar{x}(R_2)) + F(\bar{x}(R_1))F(\bar{x}(R_2))] .$$

Because δ also may have an impact upon the reservation prices, (6.33) and (6.36) are nonlinear functions in δ. Taking the second derivative we get

$$\frac{\partial^2 \bar{x}(R)}{\partial \delta^2} = -4t^2 f(\bar{x}(R_1)) < 0 \qquad (6.37)$$

for (6.33), and for (6.36):

$$\frac{\partial^2 \bar{x}(R)}{\partial \delta^2} = -4t^2 \left\{ f(\bar{x}(R_1))[F(\bar{x}(R_2))]^2 + f(\bar{x}(R_2))[1 - F(\bar{x}(R_1))] \right\} < 0 . \qquad (6.38)$$

We see that the "price" funnel is formed by concave functions of distance.

It is evident from our discussion of the optimal route that the searcher will usually follow different routes depending on at which side of the base location he/she is located. Consider two customers, each located distance δ from base location v_i. Suppose further that there are fewer alternatives to the left of v_i than to the right. When δ is small enough, both customers will begin by searching v_i. Then, each customer will pass his/her respective home location and search the remaining alternatives at this side in sequence. When the alternatives on this side are exhausted, each customer will turn to the other side of the market to search the alternatives there. As we know from (6.29) the costs for this transition are $2(c + \delta)$.

The situation of the two customers differs only by when in their search sequence they have to change to the other side of the market. The customer to the left of v_i will have to take this step earlier. Therefore, he/she will have to bear the extra costs earlier in the search sequence, and – as long as the choice probability is non-zero for at least one alternative on the other side of the market – his/her expected costs must be higher than those of the customer to the right of v_i. We can conclude from this argument that the "price" funnel must be steeper toward the shorter side of the market than toward the longer one. Moreover, this effect will be more pronounced the larger the difference in the number of alternatives at the two sides.

This has implications for the areas of market domination. When we move from one base location to the other away from the center of the market the number of alternatives on the outer side of the respective base location declines while that on the inner side increases. Therefore, the side of the "price" funnel toward the end of the market will become steeper while that toward the market center will grow flatter. Because the shapes of the curves depend upon the price distribution and also change with the customer's location (see (6.31)) it is difficult to derive exact results. However, we can apply the same argument we used above to the midpoints between two base locations ($\delta = c/2t$) to get some idea about the size and direction of this effect.

When the customer's location is to the left of the market center there are more alternatives to his/her right than to the left. As we have noted above, in this situation the searcher will turn to the shorter side of the market first and apply the standard procedure: he/she will investigate one alternative, move past home to the other side of the market which is searched until the end. Only when the alternatives on this side are exhausted the searcher will go back to the shorter side of the market and search all alternatives there. The reason for choosing the shorter side first is the same one as above: the customer will have more alternatives to search under this strategy before he/she must change back to the shorter side of the market at extra cost.

As a consequence, two adjacent "price" funnels usually will not intersect at the midpoint between their respective base locations. The expected costs will be higher at this point for that base location that is nearer to the market center. Moreover, this difference tends to be higher further away from the market center. As compared to the market areas of standard location and spatial price theory (section 6.1) the areas of market domination in a search model that takes into account the costs of returning home are shifted toward the center of the market. Figure 6.13 illustrates this point. We will extend these results to the plane in section 6.3.

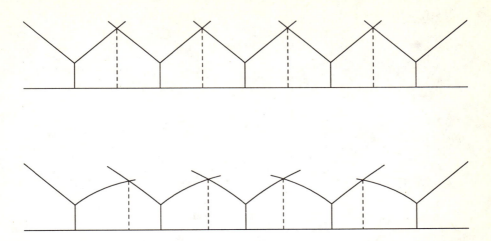

Figure 6.13: Market Areas in Standard Theory and in a Search Based Model

Choice Probabilities

Because of the close relationship between reservation prices and choice probabilities, the complex relationships that we have found above carry over to choice probabilities as well. Therefore, we cannot derive strong analytical results for choice probabilities. However, we can draw some conclusions from the above discussion.

Figure 6.14 shows the choice probabilities for our numerical example. As compared to figure 6.9 the picture becomes more complex. Again, we see numerous points where routing effects occur. They are the borders between areas of market domination, and base locations. Between these points choice probabilities are not constant any more as in section 6.2.1, but display different types of segments. When the customer is located outside the first or last alternative, his/her search problem remains unaffected by location and the choice probabilities (and reservation prices) are therefore constant. In all other cases the complex interplay of costs and reservation prices yields increasing and decreasing segments of choice probabilities.

Because of theorem 6.1 the choice probabilities at the base locations are all identical. Also, we see the impact of the shift of the areas of market domination toward the center of the market on choice probabilities. Because the boundaries between areas of market domination are points where routing effects occur, the graphs around v_2 (location = 0.20) and v_4 (location = 0.40) are clearly asymmetric with the longer branch extending toward the center of the market.

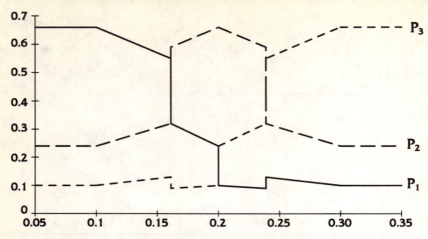

Figure 6.14: Choice Probabilities as a Function of the Consumer's Location

Demand

While the choice probabilities at the base locations are now identical – contrary to section 6.2.1 – the supplier at the center of the market is now squeezed in between his/her competitors, whose areas of market domination are skewed toward the market center. On the other hand, the supplier at the market center is able to reach relatively high choice probabilities outside his/her area of market domination as well.

When we integrate the choice probabilities for the various suppliers over the whole market range we get the total demand each of them can expect. Because we have assumed perfectly inelastic demand, the size of our market is unlimited and demand may grow beyond bounds. As in section 6.2.1 we will again analyze demand as a function of exogenously given market size.

Figure 6.15 shows the resulting graphs. It corresponds to figure 6.10 in section 6.2.1. Again, we expand symmetrically around the center of the market (v_3). Figure 6.15 shows basically the same result as figure 6.10. Up to a considerable size of the market the centrally located supplier can attract more demand than his/her more peripheral competitors.

6.3 Fetter's Law of Markets and Search

In the previous discussion we have derived results about the location and shape of the price funnel under search conditions in a linear market. From this we could extract some results about the size of market areas (areas

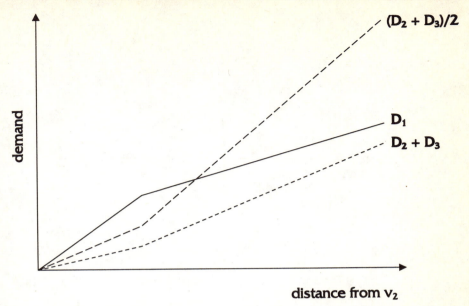

Figure 6.15: Aggregate Demand as a Function of Market Size

of market domination). Do these results extend to market areas on the plane?

In 1924, F.A. Fetter published a fundamental result about the shape of market areas: "The boundary line between the territories tributary to two geographically competing markets for like goods is a hyperbolic curve. At each point on this line the difference between freights from the two markets is just equal to the difference between the market prices. ... The relation of prices in the two markets determines the location of the boundary line: the lower the relative price the larger the tributary area" (Fetter, 1924, p. 252). This result is known as *Fetter's law* (Gillen, Guccione, 1993).

Assume two suppliers at locations v_1 and v_2, charging fixed mill prices p_1^s and p_2^s, respectively. According to (6.1) a customer at location H therefore pays

$$p_1^c = p_1^s + t(2\delta_{1H})$$

when shopping at v_1, and

$$p_2^c = p_2^s + t(2\delta_{2H})$$

when shopping at v_2, where δ_{1H} and δ_{2H} are the distance between home and v_1 and v_2 respectively.

The customer will be indifferent between the two suppliers at those locations where $p_1^c = p_2^c$. This condition yields

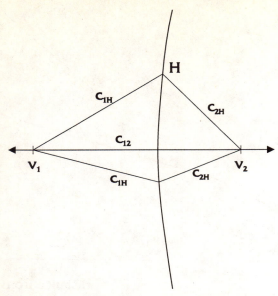

Figure 6.16: Boundary between Market Areas according to Fetter's Law

$$\delta_{2H} - \delta_{1H} = \frac{p_1^s - p_2^s}{2t} \ . \tag{6.39}$$

When the prices are given the right hand side of (6.39) is a constant and the boundary of the market area is a branch of a hyperbola (see figure 6.16).

Gillen and Guccione (1993) argue that Fetter's law also holds in a search environment. Their argument is the following: Suppose we have two suppliers at v_1 and v_2 and customers located anywhere on the plane. The customers charge prices randomly generated from probability density functions $f_1(x)$ and $f_2(x)$, respectively. Each customer can choose from two routes through the search problem:

$$R = (v_1, v_2) \ , \qquad S = (v_2, v_1) \ .$$

The boundary between the market areas of v_1 and v_2 is formed by those points, where the customer is indifferent between route R and route S.

Let the costs of going from v_1 to v_2 be c_{12}, and the costs of going from home to v_1 and v_2 be c_{1H} and c_{2H}, respectively. Assume that the costs are symmetric (i.e., $c_{12} = c_{21}$, $c_{1H} = c_{H1}$, etc.) and proportional to distance. We can write the reservation prices after the first alternative in the route as:

$$\bar{x}(R_1) = c_{12} + [c_{2H} - c_{1H}] + \int_{-\infty}^{\infty} x f_2(x)\, dx \; ,$$
$$\bar{x}(S_1) = c_{12} + [c_{1H} - c_{2H}] + \int_{-\infty}^{\infty} x f_1(x)\, dx \; .$$

Note that when the home-location of the customer changes such that the difference $c_{1H} - c_{2H}$ remains unchanged, $\bar{x}(R_1)$ and $\bar{x}(S_1)$ do not change either.

The reservation prices for the whole routes can be derived as ($F_1(x)$ and $F_2(x)$ are the cumulative density functions of the price distributions at v_1 and v_2, respectively):

$$\bar{x}(R) = 2c_{1H} + \int_{-\infty}^{\bar{x}(R_1)} x f_1(x)\, dx + \bar{x}(R_1)\left[1 - F_1(\bar{x}(R_1))\right] \; ,$$
$$\bar{x}(S) = 2c_{2H} + \int_{-\infty}^{\bar{x}(S_1)} x f_2(x)\, dx + \bar{x}(S_1)\left[1 - F_2(\bar{x}(S_1))\right] \; .$$

This yields the following condition for the boundary of the market areas (i.e., $\bar{x}(R) = \bar{x}(S)$):

$$2[c_{2H} - c_{1H}] = \int_{-\infty}^{\bar{x}(R_1)} x f_1(x)\, dx + \bar{x}(R_1)\left[1 - F_1(\bar{x}(R_1))\right] -$$
$$\int_{-\infty}^{\bar{x}(S_1)} x f_2(x)\, dx - \bar{x}(S_1)\left[1 - F_2(\bar{x}(S_1))\right] \; . \quad (6.40)$$

Both sides of this equation remain constant when the searcher's home-location changes such that $c_{1H} - c_{2H}$ does not change. Therefore, the boundary of the market area is a branch of a hyperbola in this situation as well.

However, this result of Gillen and Guccione (1993) holds in this general form only when there are no more than two suppliers. To demonstrate this, let us add a third supplier at v_3 that can be reached from v_2 at costs c_{23} (see figure 6.17). Let us consider the boundary between the market areas of v_1 and v_2. From the discussion above we know that this boundary is formed by the condition

$$\bar{x}(R) = \bar{x}(S)$$

with

$$R = (v_1, v_2, v_3) \; ,$$
$$S = (v_2, v_1, v_3) \; . \quad (6.41)$$

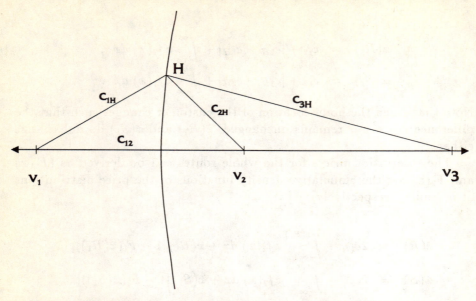

Figure 6.17: Boundary between Market Areas with Three Suppliers

The reservation prices for these routes are ($c_{13} = c_{12} + c_{23}$):

$$\bar{x}(R_2) = c_{23} + [c_{3H} - c_{2H}] + \int_{-\infty}^{\infty} x f_3(x)\, dx \,, \tag{6.42}$$

$$\bar{x}(S_2) = c_{13} + [c_{3H} - c_{1H}] + \int_{-\infty}^{\infty} x f_3(x)\, dx \,, \tag{6.43}$$

$$\bar{x}(R_1) = c_{12} + c_{2H} - c_{1H} + \int_{-\infty}^{\bar{x}(R_2)} x f_2(x)\, dx + \bar{x}(R_2)\left[1 - F_2(\bar{x}(R_2))\right] \,,$$

$$\bar{x}(S_1) = c_{12} + c_{1H} - c_{2H} + \int_{-\infty}^{\bar{x}(S_2)} x f_1(x)\, dx + \bar{x}(S_2)\left[1 - F_1(\bar{x}(S_2))\right] \,,$$

$$\bar{x}(R) = 2c_{1H} + \int_{-\infty}^{\bar{x}(R_1)} x f_1(x)\, dx + \bar{x}(R_1)\left[1 - F_1(\bar{x}(R_1))\right] \,,$$

$$\bar{x}(S) = 2c_{2H} + \int_{-\infty}^{\bar{x}(S_1)} x f_2(x)\, dx + \bar{x}(S_1)\left[1 - F_2(\bar{x}(S_1))\right] \,. \tag{6.44}$$

The boundary of the market areas is again given by (6.40). However, when the searcher's home-location changes such that $c_{1H} - c_{2H}$ does not change the right hand side of (6.40) does not remain constant any longer. The reason is that $\bar{x}(R_2)$ and $\bar{x}(S_2)$ now depend upon c_{3H} as well, which has to change when we move the searcher's home location along the branch of the hyperbola. Because of the recursive relationship in (6.44), the difference between $\bar{x}(R)$ and $\bar{x}(S)$ now also depends upon the price distribution at v_1 and v_2. Consequently, the border between the market areas cannot be a branch of a hyperbola any longer.

6.3. Fetter's Law of Markets and Search

When we change the search problem slightly, Fetter's law can be recovered. Assume that the searcher cannot travel home from v_3 directly, but has to follow the linear market to v_2. In this case, we get

$$c_{3H} = c_{23} + c_{2H} \tag{6.45}$$

Substituted into (6.42) and (6.43) we get:

$$\begin{aligned}
\bar{x}(R_2) &= c_{23} + [c_{23} + c_{2H} - c_{2H}] + \int_{-\infty}^{\infty} x f_3(x)\, dx \;, \\
&= 2c_{23} + \int_{-\infty}^{\infty} x f_3(x)\, dx \;, \\
\bar{x}(S_2) &= c_{13} + [c_{23} + c_{2H} - c_{1H}] + \int_{-\infty}^{\infty} x f_3(x)\, dx \;, \\
&= c_{13} + c_{23} + [c_{2H} - c_{1H}] + \int_{-\infty}^{\infty} x f_3(x)\, dx \;.
\end{aligned}$$

The two reservation prices do not change when the searcher's home location moves such chat $c_{1H} - c_{2H}$ remains unchanged. Consequently, the right hand side of (6.40) remains constant and Fetter's law is re-established.

We can use the results of section 6.2 to extend this discussion. Let us go back to the linear market with equidistant suppliers of section 6.2. We have found there that when we move away from market center the outer side of the "price" funnel will become steeper while the inner side will become flatter. As a consequence, the boundary points between the areas of market domination on the linear market will be skewed more and more toward the market center.

In general, these boundary points are given by the intersection of (6.40) with the linear market. The routes R and S are the optimal routes that begin with the first alternative to the left and to the right of the customer's location, respectively. The right hand side of (6.40) can also be viewed as the difference in expected total costs of search of the two routes calculated immediately *before* the first alternative. As we know from the discussion of section 6.2 the absolute value of this difference tends to be larger the further we are from the market center. Therefore, the cost difference on the left hand side that represents the market boundary must be larger in absolute terms as well.

When we generalize the assumption in (6.45) in such a way that we allow the searcher to depart from the linear market on his/her trip home only at the alternatives immediately adjacent to his/her home location, Fetter's law holds in this general case as well. Equations (6.28) and (6.29) give the only costs we have to take into account in this situation. While (6.28) is independent of the searcher's home location, the cost term in (6.29) is a function of the difference of the costs of going from the market

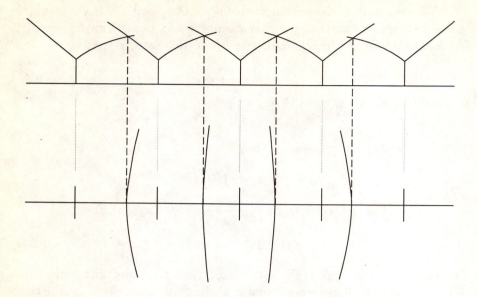

Figure 6.18: Boundaries between Market Areas

boundary at the linear market to the two adjacent suppliers (i.e., $\delta_1 - \delta_2$[22]). As a result, the boundaries of the areas of market dominance between two adjacent suppliers are branches of hyperbolas. Moreover, because the right hand side of (6.40) is larger in absolute terms the further we go away from the market center, the hyperbolas will become more and more curved (see figure 6.18).

6.4 Summary

In this chapter we have analyzed the implications of spatial search based consumer behavior on the size and shape of market areas and firm location. In the first part of the chapter we have reviewed standard location and spatial price theory and its implications for market areas and firm location. In the second part of the chapter we have assumed each consumer to perform spatial search, and have again derived implications for market areas and firm location. Because of the complexity of the general spatial search problem (see chapter 4) we have to employ a highly simplified spatial structure in our analysis, namely linear space with equally spaced suppliers. Fortunately, this structure is frequently used in the standard theory as well.

---

[22]Note that because of $t(\delta_1 + \delta_2) = c$ we get $2t\delta_1 = c + t(\delta_1 - \delta_2)$.

6.4. Summary

In section 6.1 we review standard location and spatial price theory. It is the main purpose of this section to present the baseline against which the theoretical results of the latter sections can be compared. However, we also discuss aspects that are important in the standard form of location and spatial price theory but cannot be taken into account here in the search based framework. The most important examples are pricing strategies and different types of spatial competition.

As it turns out, in standard location and spatial price theory market areas are clearly separated. Each customer considers only one supplier, that who offers the lowest delivered price. As a consequence, strategic actions of one supplier directly affect only his/her nearest competitors. Other suppliers may be affected indirectly via the reactions of the nearest competitors (Mulligan, Fik, 1989).

These results are in clear contrast to the situation where spatial search is allowed. We discuss this model extension in section 6.2. When customers are uncertain about the exact price each supplier charges and therefore search for a good deal, the market areas of suppliers overlap. We can distinguish different segments of the linear market that are dominated by one of the suppliers (areas of market domination). However, there is usually a positive probability that customers in these areas buy from another supplier. Therefore, activities of one of the suppliers tend to influence all other suppliers and not just the nearest ones on either side.

We discuss two different versions of the search based model of spatial market areas. In the first one we assume that the searcher will not have to return home after making the final purchase; we ignore the costs of returning home. In the second version we make allowance for this cost component, i.e., we return to the standard version of our search model. In both cases we assume that suppliers are located at equal distance from one another and that they generate price offers according to the same probability function. Therefore, suppliers differ only by their location in relation to their competitors.

In both versions of the model we find significant variation over the market area. When we ignore the customer's costs of returning home their expected costs form a "price" funnel of the usual form. Expected costs increase linearly with distance from the supplier's location. However, expected costs at the locations of the various suppliers differ and are higher for more centrally located suppliers. Therefore, the area of market domination is smaller for the supplier in the center of the market than for a more peripheral one. Also, areas of market domination tend to be skewed toward the market center. When we compute the expected demand, however, we find that centrally located suppliers can attract more demand than peripheral ones. The reason for this result is that in the average centrally located suppliers are higher up in the customer's search sequence than peripheral ones.

Qualitatively the results we derive for the second model version are quite similar. Again, areas of market domination are skewed toward the center of the market, but centrally located suppliers can attract more demand than peripheral ones. However, the results differ markedly in some important details. When we account for the costs of returning home, expected costs are identical at all base locations (locations of suppliers). What differs now is the shape of the "price" funnels. They are formed by concave functions of distance. These functions are flatter on the side of the supplier's location toward the market center and become flatter when we move away from the market center. The branch of the price funnel on the outer side, however, becomes steeper at the same time. This yields the aggregate results that were mentioned above.

In section 6.3 we transfer the results that we have derived in section 6.2 for linear space into two-dimensional space. Our point of reference in this section is Fetter's law that states that the market boundaries between two competitors are branches of hyperbolas. We show that in the search based model this result holds only in a very special case and that even in this case the shape of the hyperbola depends upon the location with respect to the market center.

Chapter 7

Spatial Search and Agglomeration

"Agglomeration" and "agglomeration factors" are important and well established concepts in Regional Science[1] (see Mulligan, 1984; Norton, 1992). The latter describes "the economic advantages which accrue to a firm by locating in an area which contains a number of related industries, and/or in a large city or metropolitan area" (Stafford, 1979, p. 91). The term "agglomeration" refers either to the process that results from agglomeration factors or to the resulting spatial pattern of economic activities[2].

In economic terms, agglomeration factors are externalities, i.e., non-market relationships between economic actors. Positive agglomeration factors attract one economic agent to another and, thus, lead to a clustered location pattern. Negative agglomeration factors repel activities from one another resulting in a dispersed location pattern. The existence of agglomeration factors is usually identified by analysis of the resulting location patterns (see, e.g. Latham, 1976; Carlino, 1978). The agglomeration factors themselves are "notoriously difficult to measure" (Richardson, 1978, p. 304) and quite vaguely defined also in theoretical terms. Because agglomeration is "a 'catch-all' concept" (Richardson, 1978, p. 304) or "an umbrella term" (Stafford, 1979, p. 91), the list of mechanisms that are thought to be responsible for agglomerated – or dispersed – locational patterns is long and usually confined only by the imagination of the researcher (see, e.g. Smith, 1971, p. 83; Carlino, 1978, p. 12f).

Agglomeration factors are classified in various ways in the literature. A common distinction (e.g. Carlino, 1978; Maier and Tödtling, 1992) is

---

[1] Usually Alfred Weber (1909) is credited for introducing the concept into the literature (Carlino, 1978, p. 7).

[2] Sometimes, "agglomeration" is used synonymous to "agglomeration factors" (see, e.g., Stafford, 1979).

between

- localization factors (or, localization economies), and
- urbanization factors (or, urbanization economies),

where the former refer to forces acting between different firms of the same industry, the latter to forces acting between different industries or different types of economic agents (e.g., consumers and producers). The border line between these two types of agglomeration factors is fuzzy[3] because it depends upon the definition of industry.

Another possible classification is by the recipient of the agglomeration effects. Carlino (1978, p. 6), for example, distinguishes

- "consumer agglomeration economies",
- "business agglomeration economies", and
- "social agglomeration economies".

The effects in the third category "affect all groups in society, although somewhat differently. Probably the most preeminent example under this heading is efficiency in public services" (Carlino, 1978, p. 6).

In recent years, the idea of agglomeration factors resulting from non-market relationships between economic actors has reappeared in a number of other concepts. So in the discussion of networks and their role in helping firms "to mobilize resources and information, to increase flexibility, and to reduce uncertainty" (Bergman, et al., 1991, p. 4; see also Håkanson, 1987; Johansson, 1991; Kamann, 1991), and in the literature on innovative industrial districts (see, e.g. Garofoli, 1992; Pyke and Sengenberger, 1992) which stresses, among other factors, the importance of "an efficient system of transmitting information at the local level (...) [and] 'face-to-face' relationships between economic actors" (Garofoli, 1991, p. 126). Outside Regional Science agglomeration factors play a prominent role in the works of Porter (1990) and Krugman (1991).

In this chapter we will analyze to what extent search processes may bring about forces toward agglomeration. As we know from chapter 4 the number of alternatives is an important determinant for the expected costs of a search problem. When we add an alternative to a specific search problem, the expected costs will usually decline (see corollary 4.1). Consequently, at least for the customers, an agglomeration of alternatives seems to be beneficial. We will discuss this question in more detail in section 7.2.

---

[3] Just as that between localization economies and urbanization economies on the one hand and scale economies on the other. While they differ markedly in terms of their economic consequences, they lead to similar spatial structures.

For the analysis of agglomeration in a retail context, Hotelling's "principle of minimum differentiation" serves as an important reference point. His 1929 paper on "Stability in Competition" stimulated a long and still ongoing discussion. We will review this discussion in section 7.1 in order to lay the theoretical basis for the discussion of the search-related mechanisms in section 7.2.

7.1 Hotelling's Principle of Minimum Differentiation

Howard Hotelling (1929) used a spatial framework to discuss the relationship between two companies competing for the same market. The theoretical result he derived which was very influential also outside Spatial Economics (see, e.g., Graitson, 1982; Phlips, 1988; Beath and Katsoulacos, 1991) became known as the "principle of minimum differentiation".

Hotelling's main argument goes as follows: Suppose there are two suppliers serving a linear, bounded market with evenly distributed customers with inelastic demand. When the suppliers act rational – under some additional assumptions which we will discuss below – they will locate back to back in the middle of the market. Each one will serve half the market. If one of them were located somewhere else, say at one quarter of the length of the market, the other supplier could capture more and more of the demand between them by moving closer to the first supplier's location. This would go on until they were both located at one quarter, with the first supplier serving 1/4 of the market, the other one 3/4. In this situation the first supplier could improve his/her situation by jumping to the other side of the second supplier's location. There he/she would serve the long side of the market and leave the other supplier with just 1/4 of the total number of customers. The second supplier could apply the same strategy, and they would leapfrog until they have reached the middle of the market with each supplier serving one half of the market.

Hotelling's argument is intuitively appealing, but the result he derives depends upon a number of critical assumptions:

- the market is bounded,
- demand is completely inelastic,
- the good supplied is homogeneous,
- transport costs are constant per unit of distance.

Before we discuss these assumptions, let us present the Hotelling-model in more formal terms. Let l be the length of the market and α the distance of the first supplier's location from one end of the market, β the other supplier's distance from the other end of the market. Therefore

$$\alpha + \beta \leq l \qquad \alpha, \beta \geq 0 \ .$$

Since the product is homogeneous, each customer will buy from that supplier whose delivered price (mill price set by supplier plus transportation costs) is lowest at his/her location. The suppliers have to decide about two parameters: location and mill price. When mill prices are identical, each supplier serves all the customers from his/her location to the nearest end of the market, plus half of the customers between the two suppliers. Suppose for simplicity that mill prices are identical, that customers are distributed with unit density, and that each customer buys one unit of the product. Then the suppliers will sell the following quantities:

$$q_1 = \alpha + l - \frac{\alpha + \beta}{2} = l + \frac{\alpha}{2} - \frac{\beta}{2}$$
$$q_2 = \beta + l - \frac{\alpha + \beta}{2} = l + \frac{\beta}{2} - \frac{\alpha}{2} \ .$$

It is trivial to see that each supplier will gain from increasing the distance to his/her end of the market. The reaction of q_1 (q_2) to a marginal increase of α (β) is 1/2 because the suppliers can increase the protected side of their market by one marginal unit, but lose only half that number of customers at the competitive side of the market.

The price mechanism has received considerable attention in the literature. As has been shown by d'Aspremont et al. (1979), Hotelling's solution for the location part of the problem implies zero prices and profits (see also Beath and Katsoulacos, 1991, p. 16). The suppliers can realize positive profits only when they locate apart from one another.

However, the suppliers have to locate sufficiently far from one another for equilibrium prices to exist. As demonstrated by d'Aspremont et al. (1979, p. 1146) their locations must satisfy the conditions

$$\left[l + \frac{\alpha - \beta}{3}\right] \geq \left[\frac{4}{3}\right] l(\alpha + 2\beta) \ ,$$
$$\left[l + \frac{\beta - \alpha}{3}\right] \geq \left[\frac{4}{3}\right] l(\beta + 2\alpha) \ . \qquad (7.1)$$

Outside this range, Nash equilibrium prices do not exist. When the two suppliers locate symmetrically, i.e., $\alpha = \beta$, these conditions reduce to

$$\alpha = \beta \leq \frac{l}{4} \ ,$$

7.1. Hotelling's Principle of Minimum Differentiation

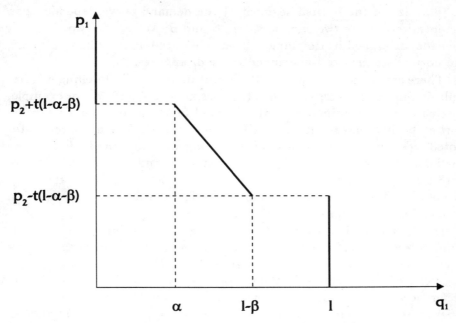

Figure 7.1: Demand of First Supplier

i.e., both suppliers have to locate in the outer quartiles of the market. In this range, however, the partial derivatives of profits at equilibrium prices with respect to the size of the supplier's protected market side (α and β, respectively) are strictly positive for both suppliers. Therefore, both suppliers will tend to move out of the area of price stability.

The reason for this "existence problem" of the Hotelling model lies in the fact that the suppliers are faced with discontinuous demand curves that result from the spatial structure of the model: Each supplier in the Hotelling model has two sides of his market; an inner side between his/her location and his/her competitor's, and an outer side between his/her location and the market boundary. Competition between the two suppliers occurs usually only at their respective inner sides of the market. However, with locations and the competitor's price given, a supplier may reduce his/her price so much to capture all the demand of his/her inner side of the market. When the price is reduced slightly more, he/she can capture all the customers at the competitor's outer side – and consequently all the customers in the market – at once. So, at this price level the demand curve the supplier faces is discontinuous. Another discontinuity occurs when the price is raised so much that the competitor can capture the whole demand on the outer side. Figure 7.1 displays the demand curve of the first supplier.

The size of the normal segment of the demand curve depends upon the locations of the two suppliers, i.e., α and β. When the two locations coincide, as argued in Hotelling's "principle of minimum differentiation", the normal segment of the demand curve disappears.

There are various attempts in the literature to "save" Hotelling's "principle of minimum differentiation". D'Aspremont et al. (1979), for example, eliminate the discontinuities in the demand functions by assuming transport costs that increase quadratically with distance[4]. When one replicates Hotelling's analysis under this new set of assumptions, one finds that the partial derivatives of profits with respect to α and β, respectively, are both strictly negative, now. The suppliers will try to locate as far apart as possible; the "principle of minimum differentiation" is replaced by a "principle of maximum differentiation".

De Palma et al. (1985) were able to restore the "principle of minimum differentiation" under the assumption of large enough heterogeneity in consumer's tastes. They "recognize that (1) inherent characteristics of firms cause differentiation in their products, (2) consumers have specific preferences for these products, and (3) firms cannot determine a priori differences in consumers' tastes" (De Palma et al., 1985, p. 767) and reformulate the Hotelling-model accordingly. They use a random utility function as it is common in Discrete Choice Theory (see, e.g. Ben-Akiva and Lerman, 1985; Maier and Weiss, 1990; chapter 8 below) to introduce a stochastic component into the decision of the consumer. This is interpreted as heterogeneity between consumer's tastes, unobservable for the suppliers. De Palma et al. (1985) demonstrate that whenever heterogeneity is sufficiently large in relation to transportation costs suppliers tend to cluster at a central location. The discontinuities in the demand curves are smoothed out by the stochastic component so that under sufficient heterogeneity the existence problem disappears.

With the concentration on the instability of the price mechanism the recent discussion has somewhat overlooked the important role other assumptions play for Hotelling's "principle of minimum differentiation". This despite the fact that earlier discussions of Hotelling's model (Lerner and Singer, 1937; Smithies, 1941) have concentrated on these assumptions.

In the following discussion we will concentrate on the first two of Hotelling's assumptions as we have listed them above, namely (1) that the market is bounded, and (2) that demand is completely inelastic. For

---

[4]While this assumption may be valid in the case of product differentiation, where "distance" is usually interpreted as the gap between a customer's preferences and the characteristics of the supplied products, it is not very meaningful in a real spatial application where there are different modes of transportation (see, e.g., Maier and Tödtling, 1992, p. 53).

7.1. Hotelling's Principle of Minimum Differentiation

simplicity we will assume mill prices to be exogenously given. When we think about what happens when one supplier moves toward the other in Hotelling's model, it becomes intuitively evident that these two assumptions are crucial for the "principle of minimum differentiation": when he/she moves closer to the competitor, the supplier's outer side of the market increases at the expense of the inner side which is reduced by the decreasing distance to the competitor. But since consumers' demand is assumed to be completely inelastic, the increased distance to consumers at the outer side of the market does not reduce their demand. Because the market is bounded, the size of the outer side of the market increases in proportion to the distance moved by the supplier. The inner side of the market is reduced by the same amount. But because market shares at this side are determined by the respective delivered prices of the two suppliers, the loss of demand to the first supplier is lower than what he/she has gained at the outer side of the market.

More formally, let us relax one assumption at a time. Instead of a bounded linear market let us assume that consumers and suppliers are located on a circle. This removes the assumption of a bounded market. Let l be the length of the circle and α the clockwise distance along the circle from firm 1 to firm 2. Then the clockwise distance along the circle from firm 2 to firm 1 is $l - \alpha$.

When we use the same basic assumptions as above (identical mill prices, customers distributed with unit density, each customer buys one unit of the product), demand for both suppliers is given by

$$Q_1 = Q_2 = \frac{\alpha}{2} + \frac{l-\alpha}{2} = \frac{l}{2} \ . \tag{7.2}$$

Demand is independent of the location of the suppliers. Wherever on the circle they locate, they will always serve half the customers.

For the customers the location of the suppliers makes a difference. Since we have assumed a unit density of consumers, their aggregate transportation costs are

$$T = 2 \left(\int_0^{\frac{\alpha}{2}} \delta \, d\delta + \int_0^{\frac{l-\alpha}{2}} \delta \, d\delta \right) = \frac{2\alpha^2 - 2l\alpha + l^2}{4} \ . \tag{7.3}$$

It is easy to see that transportation costs are at a minimum for $\alpha = l/2$. When the suppliers occupy opposite locations on the circle, their customers will have to bear the lowest transportation costs. Since the suppliers are not affected by their location, this is also socially the optimal constellation.

The supplier's indifference results from the missing feedback from customer's costs to supplier's sales because of the assumption of perfectly inelastic demand. When customers reduce demand in reaction to higher prices suppliers will prefer opposite locations as well. Assume a simple linear demand function

$$q(\delta) = a + b(p^c(\delta)) , \qquad (7.4)$$

where $p^c(\delta)$ is the delivered price to the nearest supplier. Let a be positive and b non-positive. In order to avoid the need to distinguish different cases, let l, a, b, p^s, and t be such that demand is positive on the whole circle irrespective of the suppliers' location.

Substituting (6.1) for p^c, the demanded quantity can be written as

$$q(\delta) = a + bp^s + bt\delta . \qquad (7.5)$$

Supplier one[5] therefore will be able to sell the following quantity to the customers in his/her market area:

$$\begin{aligned} Q_1 &= \int_0^{\frac{\alpha}{2}} (a + bp^s + bt\delta)\, d\delta + \int_0^{\frac{l-\alpha}{2}} (a + bp^s + bt\delta)\, d\delta \\ &= \frac{(a - bp^s)l}{2} + \frac{btl^2}{8} - \frac{btl\alpha}{4} + \frac{bt\alpha^2}{4} . \end{aligned} \qquad (7.6)$$

Note that with $a = 1$ and $b = 0$ we just get (7.2).

Taking the derivative with respect to α we find that the optimal value of α is

$$\alpha^* = \frac{l}{2} . \qquad (7.7)$$

When b is negative the suppliers will maximize their sales when they locate as far apart from one another as possible.

To what extent does this result depend upon the assumption of an unbounded (circular) market? Let us transfer this concept into Hotelling's bounded linear market. To avoid the need to consider different cases we again assume that parameters are such that the linear demand function yields non-negative values for all possible locations. More specifically, we assume[6] $a \geq -b[p^s + t(l - \beta)]$.

The demand of an individual customer is again described by (7.5), where δ is the distance to the supplier that charges the lowest delivered price. Assume again that mill prices are identical for the two suppliers and given. Supplier 2 is located a distance $\beta \leq l/2$ from one end of the

---

[5]The constellation is perfectly symmetric for the two suppliers. So, the following argument holds for supplier two as well.

[6]Note that $b \leq 0$.

7.1. Hotelling's Principle of Minimum Differentiation

market. As we know from the earlier discussion, in the original Hotelling model supplier one has an incentive to move closer and closer to his/her competitor. Where will his/her optimal location be when we allow for elastic demand?

Under the above set of assumptions, the size of the outer side of the market of supplier one is α, his/her distance from the market boundary. The size of the inner side is $(l - \alpha - \beta)/2$, half the distance to the competitor's location. Therefore, the total demand for supplier one is

$$\begin{aligned} Q_1 &= \int_0^\alpha [a + b(p^s + t\delta)]\, d\delta + \int_0^{\frac{l-\alpha-\beta}{2}} [a + b(p^s + t\delta)]\, d\delta \\ &= \frac{5bt\alpha^2}{8} + \left(\frac{a}{2} + \frac{bp^s}{2} - \frac{bt(l-\beta)}{4}\right)\alpha + \\ &\quad \frac{al}{2} - \frac{a\beta}{2} + \frac{bp^s(l-\beta)}{2} + \frac{btl^2}{8} - \frac{btl\beta}{4} + \frac{bt\beta^2}{8}. \end{aligned}$$

Taking the derivative with respect to α we find the first supplier's optimal distance to the market boundary, α^*, to be

$$\alpha^* = \frac{(l-\beta)}{5} - \frac{2a}{5bt} - \frac{2p^s}{5t} . \qquad (7.8)$$

Usually it will *not* coincide with the location of the other supplier. Substituting the lowest value we have allowed for a ($= -b[p^s + t(l-\beta)]$), yields an α^* of

$$\alpha^* = \frac{3}{5}(l-\beta) . \qquad (7.9)$$

It is worthwhile to take a closer look at equation (7.8). Since b is non-positive, the first two terms of the summation are positive while the last one is negative. Under our assumptions about a the sum of the second and third term is always positive[7]. Since the first term of the summation is non-negative by definition we see that the first supplier will never locate at the market boundary.

When the distance between the market boundary and the other supplier's location (i.e. $l - \beta$) increases, either because of an increase in l or a decrease in β, the first supplier relocates away from his/her market

---

[7]When a is below this threshold, market areas may not extend all the way to the market boundaries. In this case, the size of the market is determined endogenously. This complicates the mathematical argument because we have to distinguish different cases but does not alter the basic result, namely that the suppliers do not agglomerate.

boundary. However, he/she does so only by 1/5 of the extra distance. The distance to the other supplier increases by four fifth of the extra distance.

An increase in autonomous demand, which is expressed in a rise in a, leads to an increase in α^*, i.e. a more clustered location pattern:

$$\frac{\partial \alpha^*}{\partial a} = -\frac{2}{5bt} > 0 \ . \tag{7.10}$$

The reason for this is that with the extra demand the loss of demand at the inner side of the market is more easily compensated by demand at the outer side of the market.

A similar result is derived for a price change:

$$\frac{\partial \alpha^*}{\partial p^s} = -\frac{2}{5t} < 0 \ . \tag{7.11}$$

For the same reason, an increase in mill prices[8] forces the second supplier to move away from his/her competitor.

A change in transportation technology yields ambiguous results. The partial derivative is

$$\frac{\partial \alpha^*}{\partial t} = \frac{1}{5t^2}\left(\frac{1}{b}+1\right) \ . \tag{7.12}$$

Depending on the slope of the demand curve, the first supplier reacts with a more or less clustered location:

$$\frac{\partial \alpha^*}{\partial t} \begin{cases} > 0 & : \ b < -1 \\ = 0 & : \ b = -1 \\ < 0 & : \ b > -1 \end{cases} \ . \tag{7.13}$$

We see, as soon as we allow for elastic demand in the Hotelling model the optimal location of a supplier depends upon all the parameters and the "principle of minimum differentiation" will not hold.

We can conclude from this brief discussion, that minimum differentiation actually results from the very specific set of assumptions Hotelling used, and by no means represents a general "principle". As noted by Brown (1993, p. 201) in summarizing numerous theoretical studies dealing with the Hotelling model, "the bulk of studies support Eaton and Lipsey's (1979: 422) contention that 'the Hotelling model is not able to explain the local clustering of firms. ... Indeed, once the assumptions are relaxed very slightly in the direction of realism, Hotelling's model predicts that no two firms should be clustered together.' "

This negative theoretical result is in stark contrast to the outcome of many empirical investigations. They "all appear to agree that sellers of the

---

[8]Remember, that they are identical and exogenously given.

same or similar categories of merchandise tend to cluster closely together. There is a general consensus, moreover, that the degree of clustering is inversely related to the order of the good (Kivell and Shaw, 1980). In other words, high order retail trades, like ladies outfitters or department stores exhibit the most clustered distributions, whereas low order retail businesses such as convenience stores and personal services are least agglomerated of all" (Brown, 1993, p. 200). "Similarly, it has been shown that the degree of agglomeration is a function of transportation costs. When freight rates are high or are met by the seller, a dispersed pattern of outlets results. Agglomeration, on the other hand, is encouraged by low freight rates or when costs are paid by the consumer (Gannon 1973; D'Aspremont et al. 1979; Heal 1980)" (Brown, 1993, p. 200).

As we will see in the next section, agglomeration with all these regularities can be "explained" by a Hotelling-type model that is based on spatial search.

7.2 Spatial Search and Agglomeration

As we have seen in the previous discussion, the tendency toward agglomeration disappears in the Hotelling model when we assume a circular market (see, e.g, Eaton, 1976). With this assumption we remove the influence of the market boundaries. Under the remaining assumptions of the Hotelling model, suppliers were indifferent between various locations whereas aggregate costs for customers were minimal when the suppliers located at maximum distance. When we allowed for a declining demand curve, suppliers as well preferred to locate on opposite sides of the circle.

We will use the same constellation in the context of spatial search. Suppose we have a circular market of length l with customers evenly distributed along the circle. There are 2 suppliers serving this market with a homogeneous product. They are charging prices generated from the same probability distribution. Because there are no border effects, we can fix the location of one of the suppliers at 12 o'clock on the circle without loss of generality. As a consequence, we only have to analyze the optimal location for the other supplier.

We denote the location of the second supplier by a, the clockwise distance from supplier 1 to supplier 2 along the circle. Because the situation is symmetric we can restrict the second supplier's location to one side of the market

$$0 \leq a \leq l/2 \ . \tag{7.14}$$

Because there are only two suppliers, it is easy to identify the searcher's

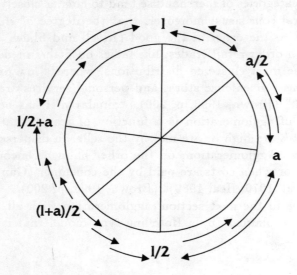

Figure 7.2: Segments in a Circular Market

optimal route through the spatial search problem. As in chapter 6 we can identify different segments of the market (see figure 7.2).

I   All customers between location 0 and $a/2$ will first visit supplier 1, then pass their home location, visit supplier 2, and return home.
II Customers between location $a/2$ and a will do the same but visit supplier 2 first and then supplier 1.
III Customers between a and $\frac{l}{2}$ will visit supplier 2, continue in the same direction to supplier 1, and then turn around and go the same way back home.
IV Between $\frac{l}{2}$ and $\frac{l+a}{2}$ the customers will visit supplier 2, supplier 1, and then continue in the same direction to their home location.
V   Also the customers between $\frac{l+a}{2}$ and $\frac{l}{2} + a$ will eventually travel the whole circle. They will start off with supplier 1, continue to supplier 2, and then proceed in the same direction to home.
VI The last group of customers is located between $\frac{l}{2} + a$ and l. They visit supplier 1, supplier 2, then turn around and go back home.

In figure 7.2 these routing patterns are market by arrows that have to be read from inside out. As can be seen from the figure, this pattern is symmetrical around $a/2$. Therefore, it is sufficient in the following analysis to analyze segments II to IV; i.e. to restrict i, the location of the customers, to

7.2. Spatial Search and Agglomeration

$$\frac{a}{2} \leq i \leq \frac{l+a}{2} .\qquad(7.15)$$

In principle the situation is similar to that in section 6.2 and we can draw on some of the results we have developed there. For the general argument we use again $\mathcal{H}$ as defined in (6.17):

$$\mathcal{H}(\bar{x}(R_i)) = \int_0^{\bar{x}(R_i)} x f(x)\, dx + \bar{x}(R_i)[1 - F(\bar{x}(R_i))] .\qquad(7.16)$$

Since there are only two suppliers, we always get:

$$\mathcal{H}(\bar{x}(R_2)) = E(X) ,\qquad(7.17)$$

with $E(X)$ being the expected value of the price distribution.

Let t be the travel costs per distance unit along the circle. Following the argument in section 6.2 – in particular equation (6.18) – we get the following results for reservation prices $\bar{x}(R_1)$ and $\bar{x}(R)$ for customers located in the three relevant segments of the circle:

II Customers in segment II first visit supplier 2, then pass home to go to supplier 1. The reservation prices are therefore

$$\bar{x}(R_1) = 2ti + E(X) ,\qquad(7.18)$$

and

$$\bar{x}(R) = 2t(a - i) + \mathcal{H}(\bar{x}(R_1)) .\qquad(7.19)$$

III Customers in segment III first visit supplier 2, then goon in the same direction (counterclockwise) to supplier 1. To return home they travel the circle clockwise. The reservation prices are:

$$\bar{x}(R_1) = 2ta + E(X) ,\qquad(7.20)$$

and

$$\bar{x}(R) = 2t(i - a) + \mathcal{H}(\bar{x}(R_1)) .\qquad(7.21)$$

IV When they are located in segment IV customers first visit supplier 2, then goon in the same direction (counterclockwise) to supplier 1, just as the customers from segment III. To return home, however, they proceed along the circle counterclockwise. This yields reservation prices of:

$$\bar{x}(R_1) = tl - 2t(i - a) + E(X) , \qquad (7.22)$$

and

$$\bar{x}(R) = 2t(i - a) + \mathcal{H}(\bar{x}(R_1)) . \qquad (7.23)$$

The choice probability for alternative $R[1]$, i.e., the probability that a customer shops at supplier 2, is in all three segments:

$$P(R[1]) = F(\bar{x}(R_1)) \qquad (7.24)$$

We can derive a few interesting results from this set of equations: First, note that $\bar{x}(R_1)$ in segment III does not depend upon the location of the customer. Therefore, this reservation price as well as the respective choice probability are constant over the whole segment:

$$\frac{\partial P(R[1])}{\partial i} = \frac{\partial \bar{x}(R_1)}{\partial i} = 0 \quad \text{in segment III} . \qquad (7.25)$$

The marginal change of expected costs with a change of i in this segment is therefore

$$\frac{\partial \bar{x}(R)}{\partial i} = 2t \quad \text{in segment III} . \qquad (7.26)$$

For the other two segments we get:

II

$$\frac{\partial \bar{x}(R_1)}{\partial i} = 2t , \qquad (7.27)$$

$$\frac{\partial \bar{x}(R)}{\partial i} = -2tF(\bar{x}(R_1)) . \qquad (7.28)$$

IV

$$\frac{\partial \bar{x}(R_1)}{\partial i} = -2t , \qquad (7.29)$$

$$\frac{\partial \bar{x}(R)}{\partial i} = 2tF(\bar{x}(R_1)) . \qquad (7.30)$$

The derivatives for segments II and IV look quite similar. When we plot expected costs and choice probabilities for all the customers on the circle[9]

---

[9] We used the following parameter values: $l = 72$, $a = 19$, $t = 1/7$. For the price distribution we assumed a 0-1 uniform distribution.

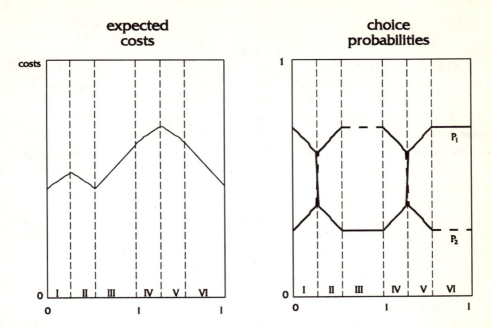

Figure 7.3: Expected Costs and Choice Probabilities along a Circular Market

(figure 7.3) the choice probabilities in segments II and IV seem to be just mirror images.

That this is indeed the case can be seen when we reformulate (7.18) and (7.22) slightly. We express the reservation prices as functions of the distance, k, from the outside border of their segment ($a/2$ and $(l+a)/2$, respectively). For the two segments we can write

$$\begin{aligned} i &= a/2 + k & \text{for segment II} \\ i &= (l+a)/2 - k & \text{for segment IV} \end{aligned} \qquad (7.31)$$

with k running from 0 to $a/2$.

Substituting for i in (7.18) and (7.22) yields in both cases

$$\bar{x}(R_1) = ta + k + E(X) . \qquad (7.32)$$

With this result it becomes clear that the slopes in (7.27) and (7.29) differ only by the sign. It also has implications for the slope of the expected costs function (equations (7.28) and (7.30)). Since $\bar{x}(R_1)$ are identical for the same value of k, so is $F(\bar{x}(R_1))$. As a consequence, also the slopes for the expected costs function differ only by the sign. As can be seen on the left hand side of figure 7.3, the absolute expected costs differ between the two segments. But because of this result and because of the symmetry of the routing pattern, the graph of the expected costs function in segments I and II is duplicated – at a higher level – in segments IV and V.

This sets the stage for our analysis of agglomerative forces in the search model. Of course, agglomeration will only occur when it is economically advantageous. Usually, we would derive the profit functions of the suppliers, analyze the relationship between location and profits, and see whether there are forces toward a stable concentration of suppliers. It is quite common in location sciences to assume constant – usually zero – marginal costs. Under this assumption profit maximization is equivalent to maximizing of sales.

The quantity $D_j(i)$ supplier j expects to sell to the customer at location i is influenced by two factors: the quantity $D(i)$ the customer at location i plans to buy and the probability that this customer will shop at supplier j:

$$D_j(i) = D(i)P_j \qquad \text{with } j=1,2 \ .$$

According to our basic assumption G.3 in chapter 4, the consumer's demand, $D(i)$, is a function of his/her expected costs. For simplicity we assume a linear demand function[10]:

$$D(i) = D_0 + b\bar{x}(R,i) \qquad \text{with } b \leq 0$$

To simplify the argument we assume that the autonomous demand, D_0, is large enough so that $D(i)$ is always positive.

Each supplier is attempting to maximize his/her total sales that can be derived as:

$$D_j = \int_0^l D_j(i)\,di \ .$$

However, under our current set of assumptions the two suppliers are identical, and identical customers are evenly distributed along a circular market; i.e., a market with no border effects. Under these circumstances the two supplier always face the same situation. Consequently, wherever the second supplier locates, they always face the same demand[11]:

$$D_1 = D_2 \ .$$

Because of this, when supplier 2 locates such as to maximize his/her sales he/she also maximizes the first supplier's sales as well as total sales. Therefore, we can consider the supplier's objective function to be:

---

[10] Where the reservation price depends upon the location of the customer (segment II and IV) we make this dependence explicit by including reference to i.

[11] Note that this holds only for total demand, not at all for a single customer.

7.2. Spatial Search and Agglomeration

$$D = D_1 + D_2 = \int_0^l P_1 D(i)\, di + \int_0^l (1 - P_1) D(i)\, di = \int_0^l D(i)$$
$$= \int_0^l D_0 + b\bar{x}(R,i)\, di = D_0 l + b \int_0^l \bar{x}(R,i)\, di \quad . \tag{7.33}$$

The only element that varies with a, the second supplier's location, is $\int_0^l \bar{x}(R,i)\, di$. It is the sum of the expected costs of all the customers. We denote it as $C(a)$.

When demand is perfectly inelastic, i.e. $b = 0$, every customer buys D_0 irrespective of the price or expected costs. This is the assumption of the traditional Hotelling model. Each supplier sells $D_0 l/2$, whatever a or the value of other parameters (see also section 7.1). Therefore, when demand is perfectly inelastic supplier 2 is always indifferent between all possible locations.

As we have seen in section 7.1, although the total sales of suppliers are unaffected by their location in a circular market with perfectly inelastic demand, the total expected costs of the customers, $C(a)$, are not. They can be used as an alternative, social, objective function in the special case of perfectly inelastic demand.

When $b < 0$, i.e. demand reacts to changes in expected costs, we see from (7.33) that total demand, D, and total expected costs, $C(a)$, are inversely related. The location that maximizes total demand – as well as the expected demand of each supplier – must be the same location that minimizes the total expected costs of all customers. Therefore, we can concentrate our analytical efforts on the latter figure.

What we want to find in the following analysis is the value of a that minimizes the sum of the expected costs for all customers. Equations (7.19), (7.21), and (7.23) give the expected costs of a customer at i as a function of a, the location of supplier 2 (in relationship to that of supplier 1). In order to derive the expected total costs we need to integrate these functions over the respective range and add them:

$$\begin{aligned}
C(a) &= \int_0^l \bar{x}(R,i)\, di \\
&= 2\int_{\frac{a}{2}}^{a} 2t(a-i) + \mathcal{H}(\bar{x}(R_1,i))\, di + 2\int_a^{\frac{l}{2}} 2t(i-a) + \mathcal{H}(\bar{x}(R_1))\, di \\
&\quad + 2\int_{\frac{l}{2}}^{\frac{l+a}{2}} 2t(i-a) + \mathcal{H}(\bar{x}(R_1,i))\, di \\
&= t\left(a^2 - la + \frac{l^2}{2}\right) + 4\int_{\frac{a}{2}}^{a} \mathcal{H}(\bar{x}(R_1,i))\, di + \mathcal{H}(\bar{x}(R_1))(l - 2a) \quad .
\end{aligned}$$
$$\tag{7.34}$$

Since the reservation prices in segments II and IV are mirror images, the following relationship must hold:

$$\int_{\frac{a}{2}}^{a} \mathcal{H}(\bar{x}(R_1, i)) \, di = \int_{\frac{l}{2}}^{\frac{l+a}{2}} \mathcal{H}(\bar{x}(R_1, i)) \, di \ . \tag{7.35}$$

This yields the second term of the summation on the right hand side of (7.34).

The cost function (7.34) is difficult to analyze in this general form. Therefore, we assume again that prices are generated by a 0-1 uniform distribution[12]. When we substitute the corresponding functions, the cost function becomes:

$$C(a) = 2\left\{ \frac{5}{6} t^2 a^3 + \left(\frac{t}{4} - t^2 l \right) a^2 + \frac{tl^2}{4} + \frac{3}{16} l \right\} \ . \tag{7.36}$$

Cost function (7.36) is valid only when

$$l \leq \frac{1}{2t} \ , \tag{7.37}$$

because only in this case $\bar{x}(R_1)$ does not exceed the upper bound of the price distribution for all valid values of a. When condition (7.37) does not hold, we have to distinguish two other segments on the circle.

When

$$\frac{1}{4t} < a < \frac{1}{2t} \tag{7.38}$$

for some $a \leq l/2$, the reservation price $\bar{x}(R_1)$ may exceed the upper bound of the price distribution for some customers. These customers will patronize only one supplier[13] and will never visit the other one.

From (7.18) and (7.22) we see that these customers are located between

$$o_1 = \frac{1}{4t} \quad \text{and} \quad o_2 = \frac{l}{2} + a - \frac{1}{4t} \ . \tag{7.39}$$

Figure 7.4 illustrates this situation. As can be seen and is clear from (7.38) and (7.39), the range of customer locations with positive choice probabilities for both suppliers is narrowed in this situation. Therefore, we have to calculate the total expected costs as:

---

[12] The only substantial part in this assumption is that of a specific functional form. With the upper and lower limit of the distribution we only fix the scale for transportation costs. When we change the difference between the upper and lower bound and transportation costs by the same factor the basic results remain the same.

[13] Supplier 2 in the part of the market we analyze.

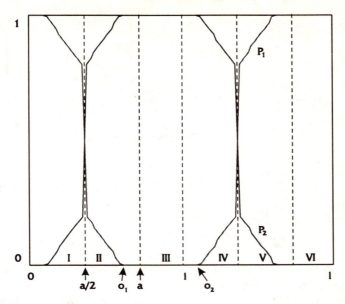

Figure 7.4: Choice Probabilities Along a Circular Market, Case 2

$$\begin{aligned} C(a) &= \int_0^l \bar{x}(R,i)\, di \\ &= 2\left\{ \int_{a/2}^{o_1} 2t(a-i) + \mathcal{H}(\bar{x}(R_1,i))\, di \right. \\ &\quad + \int_{o_1}^{a} 2t(a-i) + \frac{1}{2}\, di + \int_{a}^{o_2} 2t(i-a) + \frac{1}{2}\, di \\ &\quad \left. + \int_{o_2}^{\frac{l+a}{2}} 2t(i-a) + \mathcal{H}(\bar{x}(R_1,i))\, di \right\} \\ &= 2\left\{ \frac{t^2 a^3}{6} + \frac{ta^2}{4} + \frac{a}{8} - \frac{tal}{2} - \frac{1}{48t} + \frac{l}{4} + \frac{tl^2}{4} \right\} \,. \quad (7.40) \end{aligned}$$

When $a \geq 1/(2t)$, all customers will visit only one supplier. In this constellation, the search process vanishes from the model. The total expected costs therefore simplify to:

$$C(a) = \int_0^l \bar{x}(R,i)\, di$$

condition	cost equation	range
$t \leq 1/(2l)$	7.36	$0 \leq a \leq l/2$
$1/(2l) \leq t \leq 1/l$	7.36	$0 \leq a \leq 1/(4t)$
	7.40	$1/(4t) \leq a \leq l/2$
$t \geq 1/l$	7.36	$0 \leq a \leq 1/(4t)$
	7.40	$1/(4t) \leq a \leq 1/(2t)$
	7.41	$1/(2t) \leq a$

Table 7.1: Summary of Cost Functions and Parameter Ranges

$$= 2\left\{\int_{a/2}^{a} 2t(a-i) + \frac{1}{2}\,di + \int_{a}^{\frac{l+a}{2}} 2t(i-a) + \frac{1}{2}\,di\right\}$$

$$= 2\left\{\frac{ta^2}{2} - \frac{tal}{2} + \frac{tl^2}{4} + \frac{l}{4}\right\} . \tag{7.41}$$

Depending on the relationship between the length of the market, l, transportation costs, t, and the spread of the price distribution that we have exogenously fixed[14] one, two, or all three of the above segments can be found on the circular market. Table 7.1 and figure 7.5 summarize the conditions for the various segments.

Cost function (7.41) is a polynomial of second degree in a, functions (7.36) and (7.40) are polynomials of third degree. Therefore, the first function has one extreme value while the other two functions have two. We get the following results for the extreme values:

1 For (7.36) we derive the extreme values from

$$\frac{\partial C(a)}{\partial a} = 5t^2 a^2 + (t - 4t^2 l)a , \tag{7.42}$$

which yields the following two solutions

$$a_1^* = 0$$
$$a_2^* = \frac{1}{5}\left(4l - \frac{1}{t}\right) .$$

Substituting these solutions into the second derivative of the cost function shows that

---

[14]It just sets the scale for the other parameters.

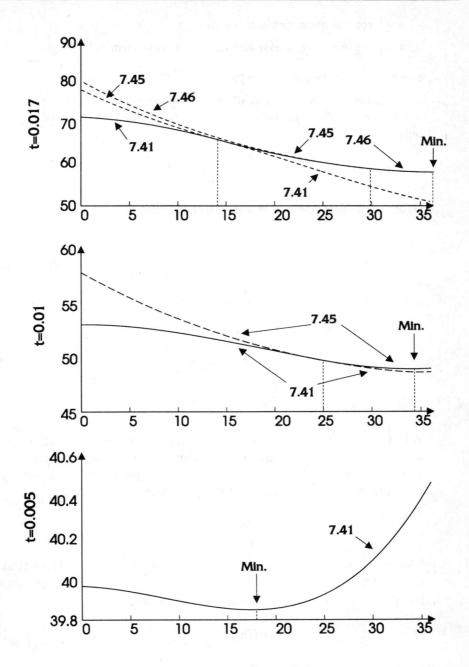

Figure 7.5: Market Segments for Different Parameter Values

- a_1^* represents a minimum and a_2^* a maximum for $t < \frac{1}{4l}$;
- a_1^* represents a maximum and a_2^* a minimum for $t > \frac{1}{4l}$.

For $t = 1/(4l)$ we get $a_1^* = a_2^* = 0$.

From table 7.1 we see that $a_1^* = 0$ is always in the range of valid values for a. The second solution, a_2^*, falls into the range of (7.36) only when

$$t \leq \frac{9}{16l} . \qquad (7.43)$$

Otherwise, a_2^* is not a relevant extreme value.

2 For (7.40) we derive the extreme values from

$$\frac{\partial C(a)}{\partial a} = t^2 a^2 + ta + \frac{1}{4} - tl , \qquad (7.44)$$

which yields the following two solutions

$$a_3^* = -\frac{1}{2t} + \sqrt{\frac{l}{t}}$$

$$a_4^* = -\frac{1}{2t} - \sqrt{\frac{l}{t}} .$$

When substituting into the second derivative we see that a_3^* represents a minimum, a_4^* a maximum. However, a_4^* is always negative and therefore outside the range of valid values for a. Solution a_3^* falls into the range of valid values only when

$$\frac{9}{16l} \leq t \leq \frac{1}{l} . \qquad (7.45)$$

This condition holds only in the second row of table 7.1. Note that $a_3^* = l/2$ for $t = 1/l$, the maximum valid value of t in this segment.

3 For (7.41) we derive the extreme values from

$$\frac{\partial C(a)}{\partial a} = 2ta - tl , \qquad (7.46)$$

which yields

$$a_5^* = \frac{l}{2} \qquad (7.47)$$

as minimum of the function. This always coincides with the maximum valid value for a.

This set of results leads to an interesting economic interpretation. When transportation costs[15] are large – at least $1/l$ – for a given size of the market and a given price distribution, cost function (7.41) is relevant for the location behavior of the second supplier. His/her optimal location is determined by $a_5^* = l/2$. The supplier will locate at the maximum distance from the competitor at the other pole of the circular market. In this case both suppliers have clearly defined market areas of equal size. Market areas do not overlap. Search does not occur in this situation because every customer patronizes only one supplier, namely the nearer one. The reason for this is that the transportation costs between the locations of the two suppliers are too large for the customers to benefit from visiting both of them. The search option is not utilized by the customers for economic reasons. The outcome of the model in this case is exactly the situation of the standard location and spatial price theory that we have discussed in section 6.1. It also coincides with the result we derived in section 7.1 for a circular market.

When transportation costs decline below the threshold $1/l$, (7.40) becomes the relevant cost function. It becomes beneficial for some customers located around the former market boundary (see (7.39)) to consider both suppliers as potential source for the respective product. These customers begin to search in the sense that they may reject the price requested by one of the supplier and go to the other one. In this segment a_3^* is the condition for the optimal location of the second supplier. It is smaller than $l/2$ for $t < 1/l$ and declines with declining transportation costs. In other words, it becomes economically attractive[16] for the second supplier to locate at less than maximum distance from his/her competitor. This force toward agglomeration becomes stronger when transportation costs continue to decline. At the same time the range of locations where customers patronize only one supplier decreases.

When transportation costs reach $t = 9/(16l)$, the optimal location of customer 2 has declined to $a_3^* = a_2^* = 4l/9$. From this point on the market areas of the two suppliers overlap completely. Every customer considers both suppliers and acts according to the search concept. For transportation costs below this threshold, (7.36) is the relevant cost function. The optimal location of supplier 2 is determined by a_2^*. As long as $t > 1/(4l)$

---

[15]Transportation costs always need to be considered in relation to the exogenously fixed spread of the price distribution.

[16]Remember that with elastic demand the location that minimizes total expected costs for all customers also maximizes the sales of each supplier.

the two suppliers choose separate locations. Only when transportation costs are $1/(4t)$ or smaller, the two locations coincide as determined by a_1^*. Only then the two suppliers agglomerate in the strict sense.

The model is able to display both dispersed and agglomerated location patterns. When transportation costs are high as compared to the spread of the prices distribution locational patterns are dispersed. In this case the possible gain from searching the other supplier cannot compensate the high costs of overcoming the distance between them. When transportation costs decline or prices become more dispersed, the possible gains from search become more important relatively to transportation costs. These potential gains are higher when the suppliers locate nearer to one another. When transportation costs are low in relation to the spread of the price distribution, for the average customer it is better to have two suppliers at greater distance than only one close by.

The transition from a dispersed to an agglomerated location pattern is not abrupt. Dispersed and agglomerated patterns are just the extreme ends and there is a smooth transition between them. How close together the two suppliers should locate depends upon the transportation rate in relation to the spread of the price distribution. For a given rate they may locate too far apart as well as to close. In both cases the total expected costs are higher than necessary. So, our model allows for "more or less" clustered location patterns. They will be more clustered when prices are more variable[17] and/or transport costs are lower. Both these factors have been found important in empirical investigations (for a summary see Brown 1993 as quoted at the end of section 7.1).

7.3 Summary

In this chapter we have analyzed in which way agglomeration forces may result from spatial search behavior. As we note in the introductory paragraphs of this chapter, agglomeration and agglomeration forces are well established concepts in Regional Science, but are difficult to derive from a microeconomic framework. It was the purpose of this chapter to investigate whether and to what extent agglomeration factors may be the result of spatial search processes.

Hotelling's "principle of minimum differentiation" represents a famous theoretical argument for the spatial concentration of two suppliers. The underlying model has been analyzed in section 7.1. As it turns out, "minimum differentiation" results only from a specific set of assumptions. When

---

[17]Although we have based our argument solely on prices, price variability can also be seen as a substitute for quality variation, product differentiation, etc.

7.3. Summary

any one of these assumptions is dropped, suppliers do not cluster in space any longer. They are indifferent about their location or even tend to locate as far apart as possible. Even when we accept Hotelling's original set of assumptions, recent literature has shown that spatial concentration of suppliers leads to price instability that lets the respective market collapse. A stable market can only be achieved in the framework of the Hotelling model when the two suppliers are located sufficiently far apart.

In section 7.2 we have introduced spatial search into a Hotelling type model. In order to avoid the irregularities that occur at the endpoints of a bounded linear market, as discussed in section 7.1, we use a circular market with two suppliers and a large number of customers evenly distributed along the circle. Depending on where the two suppliers locate on the circle customers will follow different optimal routes through the circular market. This allows us to identify six segments on the circle. Because of the symmetry of the spatial structure three of the segments are just mirror images of the other three.

We derive expected cost equations for the customers in each segment and integrate them over all customers to yield total expected costs as a function of the location of one of the suppliers (the location of the other supplier is fixed). The optimal location of this supplier is where the total expected cost function is minimal in the range of valid locations. As we can show, when demand is not completely inelastic this location also maximizes the total expected sales of the two suppliers.

As it turns out, the structure of the total expected costs equation depends upon the relationship between the transport rate and the spread of the price distribution. When the transport rate is high relative to the spread of the price distribution it is optimal for the suppliers to locate as far apart from each other as possible. Each supplier has a clearly defined market of equal size. Each customer patronizes only one supplier, search does not occur in this situation. Therefore, market areas do not overlap. When transportation becomes cheaper relative to the spread of the price distribution, customers around the former market boundary begin to consider searching both suppliers. In this segment of the circle market areas now overlap. Customers closer to each supplier still patronize just their nearest supplier. Because of the customers who search both suppliers it becomes attractive for the suppliers to move closer to one another. This effect is stronger the lower the transportation rate becomes.

From a certain point on, the market areas of the two suppliers overlap completely. Spatial search has become the exclusive behavior of customers. The optimal locations of the suppliers have moved fairly close together, but are still separated. Only when the transport rate declines further relative to the spread of the price distribution, the optimal locations of the suppliers collapse into one location.

As compared to the Hotelling model the search based model displays this tendency toward agglomeration for a broad set of assumptions. In addition and as discussed above, the model shows the transition from clearly separated market areas with no search activity at all – the structure of traditional location theory – to completely overlapping markets with many or all customers being engaged in spatial search. Only under the latter constellation the model shows a tendency toward spatial agglomeration of suppliers.

Chapter 8

Spatial Search and Spatial Interaction Models

Until now our discussion of spatial search has focused mainly on the behavioral side. We have discussed the searcher's optimal strategy in terms of route choice and stopping behavior, investigated the relationship between the two, and drawn conclusions about complexity, market areas, and expected costs.

One basic result of this discussion is that there is usually no one-to-one relationship between the searcher and the available alternatives but that the searcher will select each alternative with some probability (choice probability). This was the main factor contrasting the standard theory of market areas from its search based version (see chapter 6).

The same basic structure also applies to spatial interaction models, a whole family of other important spatial models. In this chapter we will investigate whether this similarity is the result of some fundamental relationship between spatial search and spatial interaction models. In particular we will deal with the gravity model and the intervening opportunities model. In the course of this analysis we will also discuss discrete choice models, a family of models that has found considerable attention in spatial analysis and is closely related to the gravity model.

Until now our discussion of the spatial search model was oriented toward deriving theoretical results about the structure of the model. We did not take any steps toward operationalizing the model for empirical application. Discrete choice models, on the other hand, are fully operationalized and ready for empirical application. When discussing the relationships between spatial search models and discrete choice models, among others, in this chapter, we will also be able to derive some basic insights into the empirical side of spatial search models.

In section 8.1 we will focus on the most prominent type of spatial interaction model, the gravity model. Section 8.2 will present the intervening opportunities model. In section 8.3 we will present discrete choice models, a family of models that has become quite popular in spatial analysis and provides a behavioral basis for spatial interaction models. In section 8.4 we will focus on the relationship between these models and the spatial search model.

8.1 The Gravity Model

The gravity model[1] is probably the most widely used type of model in spatial analysis (for more detailed discussions see, e.g., Fotheringham and O'Kelly, 1989; Haynes and Fotheringham, 1984). It has been applied to a wide range of problems. Recent examples are Cho (1993), Thompson and Caves (1993), and Maier (1993b).

Basic Structure and Model Versions

The gravity model is based on the following hypothesis that is in analogy to Newtonian physics: the interaction between two points in space will tend to be stronger

1. the larger the mass of the two points, and
2. the smaller the distance between them.

This basic relationship has been formalized in many different ways. A very simple one is:

$$T_{ij} = k M_i^\alpha M_j^\beta d_{ij}^\gamma , \tag{8.1}$$

where T_{ij} is the number of interactions of some type between location i and location j, M is a measure for the size of i and j, respectively, often called a *mass term*, d_{ij} is a measure of the distance between the two points, and k, α, β, γ are parameters. We expect k, α, and β to be positive, γ to be negative. M_i, M_j, and d_{ij} are positive.

Even in the form of (8.1) the gravity model may deal with both directed and undirected interactions. When α and β are allowed to be different, T_{ij} represent the interactions *from i to j*. When we restrict α to be equal to β, $T_{ij} = T_{ji}$ as for undirected interactions.

In the more general case of directed interactions, M_i, the mass term for the origin, is a measure for the force that generates a flow, M_j, the mass term for the destination, a measure for the attractiveness of j, i.e.

---

[1]Actually, there is not just *one* gravity model. Rather the term describes a whole family of models.

8.1. The Gravity Model

its ability to attract flows. The parameters α and β determine the relative weight of the two masses in generating the interaction as well as the model's return to scale. Depending on whether the sum of α and β is smaller than, equal, or larger than one, the model displays decreasing, constant or increasing returns to scale[2]. The term d_{ij} is supposed to measure the friction of the distance (distance decay) between the two locations. The corresponding parameter γ determines how severely interaction is hampered by the distance between any two points.

The parameter k is a scaler that brings both sides of (8.1) to the same scale of measurement. When we know the total number of interactions in the system, T, the parameter k is determined by

$$T = \sum_i \sum_j T_{ij} = k \sum_i \sum_j M_i^\alpha M_j^\beta d_{ij}^\gamma \;,$$

which yields

$$k = \frac{T}{\sum_i \sum_j M_i^\alpha M_j^\beta d_{ij}^\gamma} \;. \qquad (8.2)$$

Substitution of (8.2) into (8.1) leads to the following form of the gravity model:

$$T_{ij} = T \frac{M_i^\alpha M_j^\beta d_{ij}^\gamma}{\sum_{i'} \sum_{j'} M_{i'}^\alpha M_{j'}^\beta d_{i'j'}^\gamma} \;. \qquad (8.3)$$

We will comment on this model form later in the discussion.

Various factors may contribute to the mass terms and to the distance measure in (8.1). In a commuting model, for example, the mass term for the origin may depend upon the size of the labor force, the level of unemployment, wage level, educational level, age structure of the population, etc. The mass term for the destination may be a function of the number of jobs, number of job vacancies, wage level, industrial mix, etc. Distance friction may be measured in terms of physical distance, car travel time, travel time by public transport, etc. For other types of application very different variables will be of relevance.

There is no need to restrict mass terms and distance friction of the gravity model to just one variable. In an empirical investigation we will be particularly interested in allowing for various variables in order to identify those that are determining the type of spatial interaction under investigation. We can view each one of the independent variables in (8.1) as a

---

[2]This means that when the mass terms of both locations are increased by the same factor, the number of interactions grow by less, equal or more than this factor.

function of a whole set of underlying variables. We will discuss this important generalization of the gravity model later on. For the discussion of the structure of the model we will stay with the simple notation, keeping in mind that each variable may stand for a whole vector of influences.

In many applications of the gravity model we have more information available than just (8.1). For example, we may know the number of interactions originating from each location i. This piece of information yields the following additional constraint:

$$\sum_j T_{ij} = O_i , \qquad (8.4)$$

where O_i is the number of interactions originating from location i. Because the number of interactions produced in each location are a-priorily given in this model, it is usually termed a *production constrained* gravity model.

Substituting (8.1) into constraint (8.4) yields

$$O_i = \sum_j T_{ij} = k M_i^\alpha \sum_j M_j^\beta d_{ij}^\gamma \qquad (8.5)$$

or

$$k M_i^\alpha = \frac{O_i}{\sum_j M_j^\beta d_{ij}^\gamma} .$$

Substituting this relationship into (8.1) yields the following basic function for the production constrained gravity model:

$$T_{ij} = O_i \frac{M_j^\beta d_{ij}^\gamma}{\sum_{j'} M_{j'}^\beta d_{ij'}^\gamma} . \qquad (8.6)$$

It is trivial to see that the summation over all possible destinations indeed yields O_i as required by constraint (8.4).

Basically the same line of argument can be applied to a situation where we know a-priorily how many interactions terminate at each destination[3]. The *attraction constrained* gravity model that results from this constraint can be written as:

$$T_{ij} = D_j \frac{M_i^\beta d_{ij}^\gamma}{\sum_{i'} M_{i'}^\beta d_{i'j}^\gamma} \quad \text{with} \quad D_j = \sum_i T_{ij} .$$

Of particular interest are those situations where we know both, the vector of originating (O_i) and the vector of terminating (D_j) interactions. In this case our model has to fulfill both constraints simultaneously. This cannot

---

[3]Constraint (8.5) does not hold in this context.

8.1. The Gravity Model

be achieved with just one scale parameter. We must allow k to vary over destinations.

Consequently, the *production attraction constrained* gravity model[4] is characterized by the following set of equations:

$$T_{ij} = k_j M_i^\alpha M_j^\beta d_{ij}^\gamma$$
$$O_i = \sum_j T_{ij}$$
$$D_j = \sum_i T_{ij} \ . \qquad (8.7)$$

It is equivalent to a production constrained gravity model with a set of destination specific parameters k_j:

$$T_{ij} = O_i \frac{k_j M_j^\beta d_{ij}^\gamma}{\sum_{j'} k_{j'} M_{j'}^\beta d_{ij'}^\gamma} \qquad (8.8)$$

$$\text{with} \quad k_j = \frac{D_j}{M_j^\beta \sum_i M_i^\alpha d_{ij}^\gamma} \ . \qquad (8.9)$$

The destination specific parameters k_j rescale the model for each destination such that it produces the given number of interactions arriving at each destination. Note that we have to impose an additional constraint in order to identify β and all k_j. If we don't do so, we can set β to any value we like. Because M_j^β is in the denominator of (8.9), k_j adjusts such that $k_j M_j^\beta$ remains unaltered. Only when we set β or one of the k_j, we can identify the rest of the parameters. Obvious choices are $\beta = 1$ or $k = 1$ for one of the destinations. We will come back to this problem in section 8.4 when discussing the relationship between discrete choice models and the gravity model.

While the nominator of the equation for k_j in (8.9) simply gives the known number of arrivals at j, the denominator represents the number of arrivals at j predicted by the model in the absence of a scaling factor (i.e., for $k = 1$). The latter part contains an interesting element that is the basis for another class of spatial models. The term

$$\sum_i M_i^\alpha d_{ij}^\gamma \qquad (8.10)$$

is usually called a *potential*. It is a weighted sum of the mass terms of all possible origins of an interaction with j where the weights are related to the

---

[4] Also known as *doubly constrained* gravity model.

distance between the locations. The potential represents a measure for the impact the respective interaction may have on location i. Because we have derived the potential formula (8.10) from the gravity model formulation it contains the parameters of our gravity model. In empirical applications of the potential model (see, e.g. Bergman and Maier, 1991) one usually has to set the parameter values or derive them from other sources. Frequently, α is assumed to be 1, and γ is extracted from statistics on commuting, shopping trips, trade relations, or whatever basis seems most appropriate. Also other functional forms for the distance friction are used. Quite frequently an exponential function is substituted for the power function[5].

The Gravity Model Derived from Entropy Maximization

The gravity model as we have discussed it above lacks a sound theoretical basis. It builds on some – plausible – ad-hoc assumptions that are drawn in analogy to physics. Wilson (1967) used another concept borrowed from physics, entropy maximization, to give some theoretical basis to the gravity model. It must be underlined, however, that Wilson's approach to the gravity model does not have to be interpreted as a Social Science application of the second law of thermodynamics. As argued by Webber (1977, 1980) and others the mathematical procedure can also be seen as deriving the most likely interaction pattern or that pattern that minimizes the amount of unsupported information.

The basic idea of the derivation (for details see Wilson, 1967, 1970; Wilson, Bennett, 1985, pp. 236-243) is that interactions are the result of the behavior of individuals. So, in an interaction matrix with

$$\sum_i \sum_j T_{ij} = \sum_j O_i = \sum_j D_j = T$$

there are T individuals making interactions. Instead of compiling the interaction information in an interaction matrix we could write down all the individuals and the interactions they make in a long list (with T entries). This list is called a *micro-state* of the system. It is obvious that a particular interaction matrix may result from a number of different micro-states. When we write the interaction matrix as $\boldsymbol{T}$ and the number of micro-states giving rise to this matrix as $W(\boldsymbol{T})$, one can write (see Wilson, Bennett, 1985, p. 239)

$$W(\boldsymbol{T}) = \frac{T!}{\prod_{ij} T_{ij}!} .$$

---

[5]The same is true for the gravity model formulation.

8.1. The Gravity Model

When all micro-state are equally probable, the probability that a particular interaction matrix can be observed is proportional to the number of micro-states that give rise to this particular matrix. However, micro-states cannot occur without restrictions. When we know all O_i and D_j only those micro-states are relevant that are in accordance with the second and third equation in (8.7). Moreover, Wilson adds the constraint that the total interaction costs $\sum_{ij} T_{ij} c_{ij}$, where c_{ij} is the costs for interaction from i to j, are fixed to some value C.

In order to derive the most probable interaction matrix we have to solve the following maximization problem:

$$\max_{\boldsymbol{T}} \frac{T!}{\prod_{ij} T_{ij}!}$$

subject to

$$\sum_j T_{ij} = O_i \, ,$$

$$\sum_i T_{ij} = D_j \, ,$$

$$\sum_i \sum_j T_{ij} c_{ij} = C \, .$$

Applying standard maximization techniques yields

$$T_{ij} = \exp(-\lambda_i^{(1)}) \exp(-\lambda_j^{(2)}) \exp(-\lambda^{(3)} c_{ij}) \qquad (8.11)$$

and the constraints of the optimization problem. $\lambda_i^{(1)}$, $\lambda_j^{(2)}$, and $\lambda^{(3)}$ are the Lagrangian multipliers corresponding to the three constraints. We can use the first two constraints to get

$$\exp(-\lambda_i^{(1)}) = \frac{O_i}{\sum_j \exp(-\lambda_j^{(2)}) \exp(-\lambda^{(3)} c_{ij})} \, ,$$

$$\exp(-\lambda_j^{(2)}) = \frac{D_j}{\sum_i \exp(-\lambda_i^{(1)}) \exp(-\lambda^{(3)} c_{ij})}$$

$$= k_j M_{ij}^{\beta} \, .$$

In the last equation we have substituted the scaling factor[6] from (8.8) for the scaling factor $\exp(-\lambda_j^{(2)})$. When we substitute into (8.11) and set

---
[6] Keeping in mind the need for an additional constraint that we have discussed above.

$\gamma = -\lambda^{(3)}$ we get a doubly constrained gravity model that differs from (8.8) only by the functional form of the distance decay function:

$$T_{ij} = O_i \frac{k_j M_j^\beta \exp(\gamma c_{ij})}{\sum_{j'} k_{j'} M_{j'}^\beta \exp(\gamma c_{ij'})} \ . \tag{8.12}$$

Alternatively, we may make $-\lambda_j^{(2)}$ a function of attributes of region j and a destination specific scaling factor[7] k_j. In this case we get

$$T_{ij} = O_i \frac{\exp(k_j + \boldsymbol{X}_j \boldsymbol{\beta} + \gamma c_{ij})}{\sum_{j'} \exp(k_{j'} + \boldsymbol{X}_{j'} \boldsymbol{\beta} + \gamma c_{ij'})} \ , \tag{8.13}$$

where $\boldsymbol{X}_j$ is a vector of attributes describing destination j, $\boldsymbol{\beta}$ the corresponding vector of parameters.

Formulation (8.13) can be viewed as a logit-model. We will discuss this and related model types in section 8.3. Now we just note that there is this relationship between the gravity model and the logit model. It can be used to develop a sound behavioral basis for the gravity model.

8.2 The Intervening Opportunities Model

"The intervening opportunities model was first developed by Stouffer (1940) to explain migration between origins and destinations" (Maier and Rogerson, 1986, p. 3). The more sophisticated version of the model that has become standard is due to Schneider (1959). We will concentrate on this latter version.

The intervening opportunities model assumes that when a decision maker considers some activity that will lead to spatial interaction, the alternatives are in some natural sequence. "The underlying assumption of the model is that the tripper considers each opportunity, as reached, in turn, and has a definite probability that his needs will be satisfied" (Wilson, 1970, p. 151). Let L be the probability that a particular alternative satisfies the decision maker's needs. Then, the probability that the decision maker will be traveling beyond the first D_j alternatives is

$$(1 - L)^{D_j} \ .$$

When in the next zone, say zone k, there are D_k alternatives, the probability of stopping at one of these alternatives is

$$p(k) = (1 - L)^{D_j} - (1 - L)^{D_j + D_k} \ . \tag{8.14}$$

---

[7]Here, again, we face the need for an additional constraint.

8.2. The Intervening Opportunities Model

When there is only one alternative in zone k, i.e., $D_k = 1$, (8.14) becomes

$$p(j+1) = (1-L)^{D_j} L , \qquad (8.15)$$

where $j+1$ denotes the next alternative after the first D_j.

Function (8.15) is the probability density function of the geometric distribution. For an infinite number of available alternatives the respective probabilities sum to 1. When there is only a finite number of alternatives, say D_N, we have to rescale (8.15) in order to guarantee this basic property of a probability:

$$p(j+1) = b(1-L)^{D_j} L \quad \text{with} \quad b = \frac{1}{1-(1-L)^{D_N}} \qquad (8.16)$$

where the denominator represents the sum over (8.15) over the first D_N alternatives.

More common is the following continuous version of the intervening opportunities model (see Wilson, 1967, 1970; Wilson and Bennett, 1985). We approximate the probability that the decision maker travels beyond the first D_1 alternatives, Q_1, by

$$Q_1 = 1 - LD_1 ,$$

where L is again the probability for stopping at one of the alternatives. To travel beyond the first $A_2 = D_1 + D_2$ alternatives, the decision maker must not stop at one of the first D_1 alternatives and must not stop at any one of the D_2 alternatives in the second zone:

$$Q_2 = Q_1(1 - LD_2) .$$

In general terms we get the relationship

$$Q_j = Q_{j-1}(1 - LD_j) .$$

This can be rewritten as

$$\frac{Q_j - Q_{j-1}}{Q_{j-1}} = -L(A_j - A_{j-1}) . \qquad (8.17)$$

Assuming that we can transfer to continuous variation, (8.17) can be expressed as

$$\frac{dQ}{Q} = -L\,dA .$$

This equation can be integrated to the following exponential function

$$Q = ke^{-LA},$$

where k is the constant of integration. Note that this is just one minus the cumulative density function of the exponential distribution.

The probability that the decision maker selects one of the alternatives in zone j can therefore be written as

$$p(j) = k(e^{-LA_{j-1}} - e^{-LA_j})$$

The constant k serves the same role as b in the discrete version (8.16) and can be determined in the same way as

$$k = \frac{1}{1 - \exp(-LA_N)},$$

where A_N is the total number of alternatives available.

So far we have only made statements about the probability of one decision maker choosing an alternative in a particular zone. In a spatial interaction model we need to derive the number of individuals that we predict to interact between origin i and destination j. This transition is fairly simple. Assuming that we have O_i interactions originating from i we get

$$T_{ij} = b_i O_i \left[(1-L)^{D_j} - (1-L)^{D_j + D_k} \right]$$

for the discrete version, and

$$T_{ij} = k_i O_i \left[e^{-LA_{j-1}} - e^{LA_j} \right]$$

for the continuous version of the intervening opportunities model. We have made the scaling parameters origin specific, because there may be a different number of alternatives available for decision makers from different origins.

8.3 Discrete Choice Models

The General Structure of Discrete Choice Models

Discrete choice models (for a more detailed discussion see, e.g. Maddala, 1983; Ben-Akiva and Lerman, 1985; Pudney, 1989; Maier and Weiss, 1990) have become famous in Regional Science in recent years (e.g., Anas, 1982; Maier and Fischer, 1985; van Lierop, 1986; Golledge and Timmermans,

8.3. Discrete Choice Models

1988; Hughes and McCormick, 1989; Evers, 1989; Fischer et al., 1990). Their basic structure is well suited for many spatial phenomena. Because they are built upon the assumption of utility maximization, discrete choice models are also in accordance with standard economic theory.

Discrete choice models deal with the following situation: A decision maker – characterized by subscript k – has to choose one alternative out of a set of I_k mutually exclusive alternatives. He/she evaluates each alternative based on their characteristics and his/her utility function. The decision maker can assign a utility to each alternative in his/her choice set:

$$U_{1k}, U_{2k}, \ldots, U_{I_k k} \quad ,$$

and will choose that alternative that yields the highest utility.

The fundamental problem when analyzing this situation is that we can only observe the decision maker's final choice. As long as no other alternative becomes the best one, we cannot observe any reaction to a change in the characteristics of the alternatives. The decision maker does not continuously adjust behavior but rather reacts in discrete transitions.

Discrete choice models are based upon the concept of random utility. The observer recognizes the fact that even in the best situation he/she cannot perfectly observe all the factors influencing the decision maker's evaluation. Therefore, from the researcher's point of view the utility the decision maker assigns to an alternative is a random variable. By analyzing the situation the decision maker is in and the characteristics of the alternatives he/she has available, the researcher can account for some of the utility. However, there always remains an unobserved component. The essence of this argument can be captured in the following equation (for details see Maier and Weiss, 1990, p. 98ff):

$$U_{ik} = V(\boldsymbol{C}_{ik}, \boldsymbol{S}_k, \boldsymbol{\beta}) + \epsilon_{ik} \quad . \tag{8.18}$$

The indices i and k refer to the alternative and the decision maker, respectively. $\boldsymbol{C}_{ik}$ is a vector of variables characterizing alternative i for individual k, $\boldsymbol{S}_k$ is a vector of variables that characterizes the decision maker. V is the function that combines these variables to that part of utility the researcher can account for (*deterministic* utility, V_{ik}). It is determined up to a vector of parameters, $\boldsymbol{\beta}$. The remaining random component is characterized by ϵ_{ik}.

Based on (8.18) we recognize that there is no chance to predict with certainty the decision maker's behavior. All we can make is a probability statement:

$$P_{ik} = \text{Prob}(U_{ik} \leq U_{jk}, \quad j=1,\ldots,I_k) \qquad (8.19)$$
$$= \text{Prob}(V_{ik} + \epsilon_{ik} \leq V_{jk} + \epsilon_{jk}, \quad j=1,\ldots,I_k) \qquad (8.20)$$
$$= \text{Prob}(V_{ik} + \epsilon_{ik} - V_{jk} \geq \epsilon_{jk}, \quad j=1,\ldots,I_k) \qquad (8.21)$$
$$= \text{Prob}(V_{ik} - V_{jk} \geq \epsilon_{jk} - \epsilon_{ik}, \quad j=1,\ldots,I_k) \,. \qquad (8.22)$$

The probability that individual k chooses alternative i, P_{ik}, equals the probability that the random utility for alternative i is the largest one for all alternatives.

It is reasonable to assume $(\epsilon_{1k},\ldots,\epsilon_{I_k k})$ to be a continuous random variable with joint density function

$$f_k(\epsilon_{1k}, \epsilon_{2k}, \ldots, \epsilon_{I_k k}) \,.$$

With this assumption we can write the probability that individual k will choose the first alternative[8] as:

$$P_{1k} = \int_{-\infty}^{\infty} \int_{-\infty}^{V_{1k}+\epsilon_{1k}-V_{2k}} \cdots \int_{-\infty}^{V_{1k}+\epsilon_{1k}-V_{I_k k}} f_k(\epsilon_{1k}, \epsilon_{2k}, \ldots, \epsilon_{I_k k}) \, d\epsilon_{I_k k} \cdots d\epsilon_{2k} d\epsilon_{1k}$$

Depending on what distributional assumption we make for $(\epsilon_{1k},\ldots,\epsilon_{I_k k})$ we derive different types of discrete choice models. It can be shown (see Maier and Weiss, 1990, p. 107ff) that discrete choice models are in accordance with the standard properties of utilities.

Based on random utility theory and the assumption of utility maximization we were able to derive a vector of probabilities, P_{ik}, describing the chance that individual k will choose alternative i. These probabilities characterize the individual's choice situation. For each individual there are I_k discrete and mutually exclusive possible outcomes, each characterized by a choice probability. For a given number of decisions of the individual – usually one – the individual's choice situation can be viewed as a random event following a multinomial distribution. The individual's actual – and observable – behavior is a realization of this random event.

This leads us to the estimation of the parameters (β) of a discrete choice model. Suppose the decision maker has made the respective decision Y_k-times where the decisions are independent from one another. We know, how often he/she has selected each alternative. We write these numbers as y_{ik} and combine them to the vector

---

[8]To simplify the notation we write the choice probability for the first alternative only. This does not restrict the generality of the argument because we can reorder alternatives as we like.

$$y_k = (y_{1k}, y_{2k}, \ldots, y_{I_k k}) .$$

When the decision has been made only once, y_k is one for the element corresponding to the selected alternative and zero for all other.

The probability for observing a specific y_k can be written[9] as

$$P(y_k) = B_k \prod_{i \in A_k} [P_{ik}(\boldsymbol{\beta})]^{y_{ik}} .$$

with

$$B_k = \frac{(\sum_i y_{ik})!}{y_{1k}! y_{2k}! \cdots y_{I_k k}!} .$$

For a one-time decision (i.e. $Y_k = 1$) B_k is just 1.

Assuming that the individuals decide independently from one another, we can write the likelihood of observing a particular sample of decisions as:

$$L(\boldsymbol{\beta}) = \prod_{k=1}^{K} P(y_k) ,$$

where $L(\boldsymbol{\beta})$ represents the likelihood function of the sample and K the number of individuals in the sample. Taking the derivatives with respect to the parameters and setting them equal to zero yields – provided the conditions for a maximum hold – maximum likelihood estimators for the parameters.

The Logit Model

As noted above, different distributional assumptions for the random utility component yield different types of discrete choice models. By far the most important one is the *logit model*. It is based on the assumption that the ϵ are independent identically Gumbel-distributed. The Gumbel-distribution[10] is characterized by the following cumulative distribution function:

$$P(X \leq x) = F(x) = \exp\left[-e^{-\mu(x-\eta)}\right] \qquad \mu > 0 .$$

where η is a location parameter and μ a scale parameter. It has the following properties that are important in our context as well (Ben-Akiva and Lerman, 1985, p. 104-105; Maier and Weiss, 1990, p. 135-136):

---

[9] We make explicit the dependence of P_{ik} on the vector of unknown parameters.

[10] For a more detailed discussion of the Gumbel distribution see Johnson and Kotz, 1970; Domencich and McFadden, 1975; Ben-Akiva and Lerman, 1985; Maier and Weiss, 1990.

1. The modus of the distribution is η.
2. The expected value is $\eta + \gamma/\mu$ where γ is Euler's constant.
3. The variance is $\pi^2/6\mu^2$.
4. Is ϵ Gumbel-distributed with parameters (η,μ) then $\alpha\epsilon + V$, with V and $\alpha > 0$ being any constants, is again Gumbel-distributed with parameters $(\alpha\eta + V, \mu/\alpha)$.
5. When ϵ_1 and ϵ_2 are independently Gumbel-distributed random variables with parameters (η_1,μ) and (η_2,μ), their difference, $\epsilon^* = \epsilon_1 - \epsilon_2$ is logistically distributed with cumulative distribution function

$$F_{\epsilon^*}(x) = \frac{1}{1 + e^{\mu(\eta_1 - \eta_2 - x)}} \ .$$

6. When ϵ_1 and ϵ_2 are independently Gumbel-distributed random variables with parameters (η_1,μ) and (η_2,μ), respectively, their maximum, $\max(\epsilon_1, \epsilon_2)$, is a Gumbel-distributed random variable with parameters

$$\left(\frac{1}{\mu}\ln\left(e^{\mu\eta_1} + e^{\mu\eta_2}\right), \mu\right) \ .$$

7. Applying property 6 repeatedly shows that the maximum of J independently Gumbel-distributed random variables with parameters $(\eta_1,\mu), \ldots, (\eta_J,\mu)$ is Gumbel-distributed with parameters

$$\left(\frac{1}{\mu}\ln \sum_{j=1}^{J} e^{\mu\eta_j}, \mu\right) \ .$$

These properties of the Gumbel-distribution lead to choice probabilities of the following form for the logit model (A_k characterizes the choice set of individual k; for the derivation of the logit model from the Gumbel distribution see Domencich and McFadden, 1975, p. 63ff; Ben-Akiva and Lerman, 1985, p. 106; Maier and Weiss, 1990, p. 136f):

$$P_{ik} = \frac{e^{\mu V_{ik}}}{\sum_{j \in A_k} e^{\mu V_{jk}}} \ . \tag{8.23}$$

Note the similarity of (8.23) with the fraction on the right hand side of (8.13). We will discuss this relationship in section 8.4.

We cannot estimate the parameter vector, β, and the scale parameter of the Gumbel-distribution, μ, with the available information. Therefore, μ is set to some arbitrary positive value, usually 1. This determines the

8.3. Discrete Choice Models

scale of the elements of β which can only be interpreted in relative terms, therefore.

The logit model is characterized by the independence of irrelevant alternatives (IIA) property. It means that the ratio of the choice probabilities of two alternatives is independent of availability and characteristics of other alternatives. This follows immediately from (8.23):

$$\frac{P_{ik}}{P_{jk}} = \frac{\exp(\mu V_{ik})}{\sum_{h \in A_k} \exp(\mu V_{hk})} \bigg/ \frac{\exp(\mu V_{jk})}{\sum_{h \in A_k} \exp(\mu V_{hk})} = e^{\mu(V_{ik} - V_{jk})} \ .$$

The logit model is often criticized for its restrictive nature that results from the IIA-property[11]. It is a direct result of the assumption of independent error terms.

The Nested Logit Model

A generalization of the logit model that is of particular importance in our context is the *nested logit model*. It attempts to overcome the rigidity of the IIA-property of the logit model without too high an increase in model complexity[12].

In many situations some alternatives in the choice set are more closely related than others. In these situations the IIA-property of the logit model, which results from the assumption of independently distributed error terms, is a potential problem. It cannot account for the possible correlation between the error terms of the related alternatives[13].

The nested logit model subdivides the choice problem into various interrelated subproblems. Each one of them can be treated as a standard logit model. To illustrate this assume a shopping problem[14]. Suppose there are two shopping centers, C_1 and C_2, with three and four relevant shops, respectively. We denote these alternatives[15] as

---

[11] Although, often the IIA-property is misinterpreted (for a discussion see Maier and Weiss, 1990, p. 141ff)

[12] The nested logit model can also be derived as a special case of the generalized extreme value model (see McFadden, 1978; Ben-Akiva and Francois, 1983; Maier and Weiss, 1990).

[13] We will not discuss the statistical properties of the nested logit model and its relationship to the model structure because we do not need it in the context of spatial search. The interested reader is referred to, e.g., Ben-Akiva and Lerman, 1985; Maier and Fischer, 1985; Maier and Weiss, 1990.

[14] It is important to notice that we do *not* take into account any search process here. We will discuss the differences and similarities between the search approach and the discrete choice approach in section 8.4.

[15] To simplify the notation we drop the index for the individual in the following discussion.

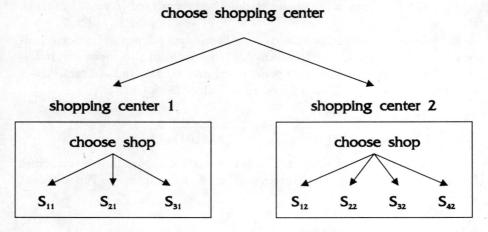

Figure 8.1: Nested Logit Structure: Example

$$(S_{11}, S_{21}, S_{31}, S_{12}, S_{22}, S_{32}, S_{42}) \ ,$$

where the first index refers to the shop within the shopping center, the second index to the shopping center.

In a standard logit model we would have all seven alternatives in the choice set. However, it is reasonable to assume that some factors that influence the decision maker's perception of the shops are common to all the shops in the same shopping center. Therefore, it is likely that the IIA-property of the standard logit model is too restrictive.

In the nested logit approach we subdivide the choice situation into two levels (see figure 8.1). At the upper level the decision maker decides between shopping centers, at the lower level he/she chooses between the shops at one of the shopping centers.

Although we break apart the overall choice problem, it is still assumed that the decision maker optimizes over all the alternatives. The lower level decisions are conditional upon the choice of the shopping center. The choice between shopping centers, on the other hand, takes into account characteristics of the alternatives at the lower level.

Suppose the decision maker has selected one of the shopping centers. Applying the logit structure to the lower level decision we can therefore write the choice probabilities as:

$$P(S_{i1}|C_1) = \frac{\exp(\mu V_{i1})}{\sum_{S_{j1} \in C_1} \exp(\mu V_{j1})} \qquad P(S_{i2}|C_2) = \frac{\exp(\mu V_{i2})}{\sum_{S_{j2} \in C_2} \exp(\mu V_{j2})} \ .$$

8.3. Discrete Choice Models

Note that the choice probabilities are conditional on the selection of shopping center and that the summation in the denominator is only over the shops in the respective shopping center.

At the upper level the rational decision maker will select the shopping center with the shop that provides the highest utility level. Therefore, he/she will choose between the two shopping centers based upon the maximum utility of their respective shops:

$$W_1 = \max(U_{11}, U_{21}, U_{31}) \, , W_2 = \max(U_{12}, U_{22}, U_{32}, U_{42}) \, .$$

From property 7 of the Gumbel-distribution we know that W_1 and W_2 are Gumbel-distributed random variables with scale parameter μ and location parameters defined by:

$$I_i = \frac{1}{\mu} \ln \sum_{S_{ji}} \exp(\mu V_{ji}) \, , \qquad (8.24)$$

where i runs over the number of alternatives in the upper level decision, i.e. 1 and 2 in our example. The I_i in (8.24) are known as *inclusive value* in the literature and they give an aggregate measure of the lower level decisions.

With the appropriate distributional assumption (see Maier and Weiss, 1990, p. 157) we can model the upper level decision as logit model as well. The choice probabilities for the choice of shopping center[16] can be written as:

$$P(C_i) = \frac{\exp(\mu' I_i)}{\sum_{C_j} \exp(\mu' I_j)} \, ,$$

where μ' is the scale parameter of the upper level decision. It can be shown that $\mu' \leq \mu$ must hold (e.g., Maier and Weiss, 1990, p. 161).

We can combine the decisions at the two levels to derive the choice probabilities for all the alternatives (all the shops in our example). It is just the product of the conditional lower level choice probability with the respective marginal upper level choice probability:

$$P(S_{ij}) = P(S_{ij}|C_j)P(C_j) = \frac{\exp(\mu V_{ij})}{\sum_{S_{hj} \in C_j} \exp(\mu V_{hj})} \frac{\exp(\mu' I_j)}{\sum_{C_{j'}} \exp(\mu' I_{j'})} \, . \qquad (8.25)$$

It is easy to show that the standard logit model is a special case of the nested logit model. It is derived from (8.25) when we set $\mu' = \mu$. When

---

[16]Implicitly we assume that there are no measurable characteristics distinguishing the two shopping centers. When such characteristics are available they have to be included in separate deterministic utility terms.

the two scale parameters are equal, all the random utility components are independent. Substituting this assumption into (8.25) yields:

$$\begin{aligned} P(S_{ij}) &= \frac{\exp(\mu V_{ij})}{\sum_{S_{hj} \in C_j} \exp(\mu V_{hj})} \frac{\exp(\mu I_j)}{\sum_{C_{j'}} \exp(\mu I_{j'})} \\ &= \frac{\exp(\mu V_{ij})}{\sum_{S_{hj} \in C_j} \exp(\mu V_{hj})} \frac{\sum_{S_{hj} \in C_j} \exp(\mu V_{hj})}{\sum_{C_{j'}} \sum_{S_{hj'} \in C_{j'}} \exp(\mu V_{hj'})} \\ &= \frac{\exp(\mu V_{ij})}{\sum_{C_{j'}} \sum_{S_{hj'} \in C_{j'}} \exp(\mu V_{hj'})} \ . \end{aligned} \quad (8.26)$$

Since the two sums in the denominator of the last term in (8.26) together run over all the available stores, (8.26) is just a standard logit model.

The nested logit model can easily be generalized to more than two levels. We only have to apply the above logic to any additional levels. In the extreme, we can even put each alternative on a separate level and link them via conditional probabilities and inclusive values. When all the scale parameters are identical, we know from (8.26) that it is equivalent to a simple standard logit model. Although no researcher would probably want to approach the standard logit model in this way in an empirical application, it will proof useful for our context in section 8.4.

8.4   Search, Spatial Interaction, Discrete Choice

In the previous sections (sections 8.1 and 8.2) we have briefly presented the gravity and the intervening opportunities models of spatial interaction. In section 8.3 we gave an overview of discrete choice modeling, particularly concentrating on the logit model and the nested logit model. In this section we will discuss the relationships between these models and relate them to the concept of spatial search. This comparison can be made on two levels. First, in terms of the logical and behavioral structure of the models, and, second, in terms of their mathematical structure. As we will see, comparisons at the two levels yield different results and allow for interesting transitions from one model to the other.

Discrete Choice Models and the Gravity Model

The formal relationship between the gravity model and discrete choice models follows almost immediately from the presentation in sections 8.1 and 8.3. In terms of their logical structure the two models are quite different, however.

The gravity model attempts to capture spatial interaction[17] between various spatial units at a macro scale. It is the regularities at the macro scale the model focuses upon. The gravity model in its standard form lacks a sound behavioral basis and has often been criticized for this.

The behavioral theory is really at the heart of discrete choice models. They are derived from a microeconomic theory of a decision maker's choice between mutually exclusive, discrete alternatives. That many of the decisions underlying spatial interaction are of this type, makes discrete choice models so important for spatial interaction analysis.

In this sense, discrete choice models and the gravity model are complementary. The decisions of individuals that discrete choice models deal with at the micro scale, produce gravity model type spatial interactions at the macro scale.

For an individual who is deciding about some spatial interaction, the various spatial units can be viewed as discrete alternatives. Using a logit model the probability that decision maker k selects to interact with spatial unit j can be written as (see 8.23)

$$P_{jk} = \frac{e^{\mu V_{jk}}}{\sum_{j' \in A_k} e^{\mu V_{j'k}}} \ . \qquad (8.27)$$

When all the O_i individuals in origin i are identical, we will expect

$$T_{ij} = O_i \frac{e^{\mu V_{ji}}}{\sum_{j'} e^{\mu V_{j'i}}} \ . \qquad (8.28)$$

where V_{ji} is the deterministic utility of spatial unit j for an individual from i.

Equation (8.28) differs from (8.6) only by the functional form in the nominator and denominator of the fraction. When we define the deterministic utility to be[18]

$$V_{ji} = \beta \ln(M_j) + \gamma \ln(d_{ij}) \ , \qquad (8.29)$$

the two equations are identical. When we derived the production constrained gravity model from entropy maximization in (8.12) we found the cost of distance friction to be in the exponent. In (8.13) we even derived the logit formulation directly.

While the power function in the traditional gravity model is based on an ad-hoc formulation without any behavioral basis, the discrete choice

---

[17] Although the gravity model has been transferred to other areas of application. Examples are .

[18] Note that we have defined M_j and d_{ij} to be positive in section 8.1.

based version (8.28) is derived from an elaborate behavioral theory. However, the deterministic utility in (8.28) is undefined. We may define the deterministic utility as

$$V_{ji} = k_j + \boldsymbol{X}_j\boldsymbol{\beta} + \gamma c_{ij}$$

to derive (8.13), as

$$V_{ji} = \ln(k_j) + \beta \ln(M_j) \gamma d_{ij}$$

to derive (8.12), or as in (8.29) to end up at (8.6). Which function, or combination of functions, is the best one is to some extent an empirical question. It can be tackled by use of discrete choice models which allow for all of them (see Maier and Weiss, 1990, p. 169ff). By use of a Box-Cox-transformation we can allow for a linear as well as a logarithmic function (see Maier and Weiss, 1990, p. 126f).

While in the traditional gravity model only the size of the destination is of relevance, the utility theory behind the discrete choice formulation provides the basis for inclusion of many more variables. Whatever characteristic of a potential destination we think may influence the utility of a decision maker can be included in the model. The size of the destination is usually just one out of many characteristics; and one that requires special treatment: In most spatial interactions the size of the destination is a proxy for the number of potential partners for interaction within the destination. So, when we look carefully, the relevant alternatives are not the spatial units directly, but the inhabitants, workplaces, companies, etc. within the spatial unit. Following the argumentation of the nested logit model, the decision maker will interact with a particular spatial unit only when he/she finds the best contact partner there.

At the macro level we usually cannot distinguish the potential partners at a specific spatial unit. Therefore, we have to assign each one of them the same deterministic utility (v_{ji}) and treat the obvious difference between them as Gumbel-distributed random influence. From section 8.3 (equation (8.24)) we know that the maximum utility level of all the partners at the spatial unit is Gumbel distributed with location parameter

$$I_j = \frac{1}{\mu} \ln \sum_{j'=1}^{N_j} e^{\mu v_{ji}} = \frac{1}{\mu} \ln N_j + v_{ji} \ ,$$

where N_j is the number of basic alternatives (potential partners) at destination j. We see that variables that reflect the size of a spatial unit should enter the deterministic utility of a discrete choice model in logarithmic form. Adding a parameter and substituting into (8.27) yields a function like (8.12).

Until now we have concentrated on the relationship between the logit model and the production constrained gravity model. As we see from (8.3), the unconstrained gravity model shows the same basic structure as (8.6). The only difference is that the alternatives have to be defined as a combination of origin and destination. Because in a discrete choice model we focus upon the decision maker and assume that he/she has to choose one of the alternatives[19], the attraction constrained gravity model appears behaviorally dubious.

Much of the discussion in 8.1 was devoted to the doubly constrained gravity model. We can construct this model type from a standard logit model by adding a full set of alternative specific constants. It turns out that they are just the k_j of 8.1 (see (8.13); the respective parameters in (8.12) and (8.8) are the exponentiation of the alternative specific constants) which had the effect of adjusting the flows in such a way that the constraint for the destination is met. That alternative specific constants of a logit model have the same effect can be seen from the first order condition for the maximum of the likelihood function (see Maier and Weiss, 1990, p. 145). The necessity to fix one of the parameters in order to identify the rest applies to the alternative specific constants as well.

Summarizing this discussion, we see that we can replicate any behaviorally meaningful gravity model by use of a logit model. The behavioral as well as the statistical theory behind the logit model therefore transfer easily to the gravity model. Moreover, because discrete choice models are based on a theory of microeconomic behavior, this equivalence allows for the disaggregation of the gravity model.

In our context this equivalence is of particular importance. As we will show below, we can derive the choice probability of the logit model from the spatial search approach. This not only allows us to utilize the well developed statistical theory of discrete choice models for empirical applications of the spatial search model. It also links the spatial search model to the gravity model and provides an alternative behavioral basis for the latter.

The Intervening Opportunities Model and Spatial Search

The basic argument that leads to the intervening opportunities model is very similar to the spatial search concept. The decision maker investigates the alternatives in sequence and decides at each one whether to accept it or not. Once he/she has found an acceptable alternative, the process terminates.

---

[19]We can always define the set of alternatives in such a way that this is the case.

In both models we derive some probability that a particular alternative produces an acceptable value. The main difference lies in how this probability is derived. In the intervening opportunities model this probability is assumed to be constant (L). This leads to a geometric or exponential decline of choice probabilities, depending on whether we use the discrete or continuous version of the intervening opportunities model. In the spatial search model this probability is determined endogenously. It is based upon the reservation price which takes into account the costs of reaching other alternatives, the number of remaining alternatives, and their price distributions.

The spatial search model produces a constant conditional choice probability only in very rare and unrealistic cases. As we know from chapter 2 the assumptions of the basic search model of economics yield a constant reservation price and consequently also constant conditional choice probabilities. The assumptions are

- an unlimited number of alternatives,
- identical price distributions, and
- constant marginal costs.

Under these assumptions the reservation price, $\bar{x}$, can be determined from the following equation (see also (2.6) in chapter 2):

$$c = \int_0^{\bar{x}} (\bar{x} - x) f(x)\, dx \ ,$$

where c is the costs of going to the next alternative (including the increase in the costs of going home), and $f(x)$ is the density function of the price distribution. The conditional choice probability, p, is determined as:

$$p = F(\bar{x}) = L \ ,$$

where $F(x)$ is the cumulative density function of the price distribution.

In more realistic circumstances reservation prices and conditional choice probabilities will not be constant throughout the search process. They will reflect differences in costs or in the price distribution, or the fact that the searcher risks running out of alternatives. This implicit adjustment of the reservation price in the spatial search model also guarantees that the choice probabilities sum to one. It avoids the ad-hoc adjustments that are necessary in an intervening opportunities model with a finite number of alternatives. Moreover, it becomes apparent that adjusting all choice probabilities by a common scaling factor is inadequate. Since this rescaling is necessary because the individual uses up the available alternatives, the choice probabilities of alternatives later in the sequence should be rescaled more than earlier ones.

Another problem of the intervening opportunities model lies in the assumption of a given sequence of the alternatives. This sequence is determined outside the model. How, remains unclear. By contrast, the spatial search model provides a mechanism for determining the optimal sequence of alternatives endogenously. As we know from chapter 4, it leads to the computational complexity of the spatial search model.

We can conclude from this discussion that the intervening opportunities model and the spatial search model are based on the same behavioral process. Because of its basic assumptions about conditional choice probabilities and the route through the alternatives, the intervening opportunities model turns out to be much more restrictive than the spatial search model. It coincides with the latter one under some quite unrealistic assumptions.

Consequently, the spatial search model can be used to provide a firmer behavioral basis to the intervening opportunities model. It allows for a much broader set of situations without having to rely on questionable ad-hoc assumptions. Of course, this flexibility comes at the expense of higher computational complexity of the spatial search model.

Discrete Choice Models and Spatial Search

The logical structure of the discrete choice framework differs considerably from that of the search concept. While in discrete choice models the decision maker is assumed to know all the available alternatives and chooses the best one of them, in a search model the alternatives are investigated one after another. Discrete choice models are based upon a simultaneous decision, the spatial search model upon a sequential decision.

As a consequence, the ordering of alternatives is irrelevant in discrete choice models. At the time of decision the decision maker has all the information he/she can have about all the alternatives. In the spatial search model, on the other hand, the decision maker learns about one alternative and forms expectations about the result of searching the remaining alternatives. He/she then decides based upon the comparison of the available alternative and the expectations.

Despite this difference in the logical structure, we can link the formal structure of the two models. More specifically, we can construct a spatial search model with logit-model choice probabilities. To do this we use the nested logit version of the standard logit model (see (8.26)).

As we have seen in section 8.3, the standard logit model is a special case of the nested logit model. Therefore, we can write every logit model

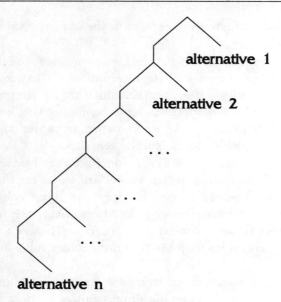

Figure 8.2: Nested Logit Model: Extreme Structure

in the form of a nested logit model. In a discrete choice modeling context it usually does not make sense to write a standard logit model in this form, since the standard logit model is easier to handle than the nested logit model. In our context, however, this form of writing the logit model turns out to be useful.

When we take the nested logit model to the extreme, we can put each alternative on a separate level. This yields the structure shown in figure 8.2, which is similar to the basic structure of the standard search model (see figure 2.1 in chapter 2). It is important to note that the model still reflects a simultaneous decision. At each level the decision maker compares the alternative at this level with the best alternative of the lower levels and feeds the result into the next higher level. Consequently, at the highest level the decision maker is able to identify the best alternative of the choice set.

Since the utility levels of the alternatives are random variables for the analyst, at each level the model compares two random variables. The result is a new random variable, the maximum value of the first two. Under the distributional assumptions of the logit model all three random variables are Gumbel-distributed. The choice probabilities represent the chance that the utility of a particular alternative is highest.

In the search model at each level the decision maker has to draw from a random distribution. In order to make the correct stopping decision, he/she computes the expected costs of the decision tree below the current

8.4. Search, Spatial Interaction, Discrete Choice

level. This threshold (reservation price) is a constant, not a random variable. Therefore, at each level we compare a random variable (the unknown price) with a constant (the reservation price). The choice probability is the chance that the price at this level is the first one that falls below the respective reservation price.

In mathematical terms we can go from one type of decision to the other. As we have seen in section 8.3 we can express the choice probability of a discrete choice model in both ways. In (8.19) - (8.21) we use different versions of the first form, whereas in (8.22) we bring the deterministic parts of utility to one side and the random parts to the other and compare the difference of deterministic utilities to the difference of the random components. Since the difference in deterministic utilities is a constant, this is just the type of comparison we have associated above with the search model.

As we know from section 8.3, the difference of two Gumbel-distributed random variables is logistically distributed. This suggests that by assuming prices to be logistically distributed in a search model we may end up with logit-type choice probabilities.

In the way we have discussed the models, discrete choice models are based on utility maximization, whereas the objective we have used for the search model is to minimize expected total costs. As we have noted in chapter 2, we can turn a minimization problem into a maximization problem by multiplying the objective function by minus one. Therefore, in the following discussion we try to maximize the negative expected total costs in the search model.

Suppose that the decision maker uses route R to search the alternatives. The reservation price for this maximization problem is (see (4.5))

$$\bar{x}(R_{i-1}) = -C(R[i-1], R[i]) - [C(R[i], H) - C(R[i-1], H)] + \int_{\bar{x}(R_i)}^{\infty} x f_i(x)\, dx + \bar{x}(R_i) F_i(\bar{x}(R_i)) \;. \quad (8.30)$$

Assume that the prices are generated by a logistic distribution with location parameters η_i and spread parameter μ. Note that the spread parameters are assumed to be identical. The cumulative density function F_i is therefore

$$F_i(x) = \frac{1}{1 + \exp \mu(\eta_i - x)} \;.$$

When we use this assumption in (8.30) it becomes

$$\bar{x}(R_{i-1}) = -C(R[i-1], R[i]) - (C(R[i], H) - C(R[i-1], H)) +$$

$$\bar{x}(R_i) + \frac{1}{\mu}\ln\left[1 + e^{\mu(\eta_i - \bar{x}(R_i))}\right]$$

$$= \frac{1}{\mu}\ln\left[e^{\mu(\bar{x}(R_i) - C(R[i-1],R[i]) - C(R[i],H) + C(R[i-1],H))} + \right.$$

$$\left. e^{\mu(\eta_i - C(R[i-1],R[i]) - C(R[i],H) + C(R[i-1],H))}\right] . \quad (8.31)$$

Note the obvious similarity to the inclusive value of the nested logit model.

Equation (8.31) again gives the reservation price in a recursive form. When we write (8.31) for $\bar{x}(R_i)$ and substitute it into the right hand side of (8.31) we get

$$\bar{x}(R_{i-1}) = \frac{1}{\mu}\ln\left[e^{\mu(\bar{x}(R_{i+1}) - C(R[i-1],R[i]) - C(R[i],R[i+1]) - C(R[i+1],H) + C(R[i-1],H))}\right.$$

$$+ e^{\mu(\eta_{i+1} - C(R[i-1],R[i]) - C(R[i],R[i+1]) - C(R[i+1],H) + C(R[i-1],H))}$$

$$\left. + e^{\mu(\eta_i - C(R[i-1],R[i]) - C(R[i],H) + C(R[i-1],H))}\right] .$$

Repeating this substitution and noting that $\bar{x}(R_n) = -\infty$ yields the following general form for the reservation price:

$$\bar{x}(R_{i-1}) = \frac{1}{\mu}\ln\left[\sum_{j=i}^{n}\exp(\mu(\eta_j - C(R[j],H) + \right.$$

$$\left. C(R[i-1],H) - \sum_{k=i}^{j}C(R[k-1],R[k])))\right] . \quad (8.32)$$

The reservation price (8.32) is mathematically equivalent to the inclusive value of the corresponding nested logit model. At each level we sum the contributions of all the alternatives below this level. For each of these alternatives the costs are made up of two parts:

1. the difference in the costs of returning home from the respective alternative (i.e. $R[j]$) and the alternative for which the inclusive value is computed (i.e. $R[i-1]$);
2. the costs of following route R from alternative $R[i-1]$ to the respective alternative ($R[j]$).

The choice probabilities of the spatial search problem are given by (4.6) in chapter 4. Because we have moved to a maximization problem they need to be rewritten as

$$P(R[1]) = 1 - F_1(\bar{x}(R_1)) ,$$

$$P(R[i]) = [1 - F_i(\bar{x}(R_i))]\prod_{j=1}^{i-1}F_j(\bar{x}(R_j)) \quad \forall \; i > 1 .$$

8.4. Search, Spatial Interaction, Discrete Choice

Substituting (8.32) for the corresponding reservation price and defining

$$V_1 = \eta_1 - C(R[1], H)$$
$$V_j = \eta_j - C(R[j], H) - \sum_{k=2}^{j} C(R[k-1], R[k]))) \quad \forall \ j > 1 \ , (8.33)$$

yields

$$\begin{aligned} P(R[1]) &= 1 - \frac{1}{1 + \exp(\mu(\eta_1 - \bar{x}(R_1)))} \\ &= 1 - \frac{\sum_{j=2}^{n} \exp(\mu(V_j))}{\exp(\mu\eta_1) + \sum_{j=2}^{n} \exp(\mu(V_j))} \\ &= \frac{\exp(\mu V_1)}{\sum_{j=1}^{n} \exp(\mu(V_j))} \ , \end{aligned} \quad (8.34)$$

for the first alternative, and

$$\begin{aligned} P(R[2]) &= F_1(\bar{x}(R_1))\left[1 - F_2(\bar{x}(R_2))\right] \\ &= \frac{\sum_{j=2}^{n} \exp(\mu(V_j))}{\sum_{1=2}^{n} \exp(\mu(V_j))} \left[1 - \frac{1}{1 + \exp(\mu(\eta_2 - x(\bar{R}_2)))}\right] \\ &= \frac{\exp(\mu(V_2))}{\sum_{j=1}^{n} \exp(\mu(V_j))} \end{aligned}$$

for the second alternative. In the same way we can construct all the other choice probabilities. In general we get for $i > 0$

$$P(R[i]) = \frac{\exp(\mu(V_i))}{\sum_{j=1}^{n} \exp(\mu(V_j))} \ . \quad (8.35)$$

This is just the choice probability of the logit model. It is easy to see that the denominator of (8.35) and (8.34) is the sum of the nominators of all the choice probabilities as defined by (8.34) and (8.35). Therefore the probabilities sum to one.

With the proper assumptions we can construct a special version of the spatial search model that is equivalent to a standard logit model. This result is of particular importance for empirical applications of the spatial search model. It allows us to use logit-model software for estimating spatial search models and to build on the extensive statistical and econometric literature about discrete choice models. We will discuss some of the econometric aspects that arise in this context in section 8.5.

8.5 Notes on the Econometrics of Spatial Search

As we see from (8.33), the "deterministic utility" term V_i consists of three elements:

1. the location parameter, η, of the price distribution,
2. the costs of going home from the respective alternative, and
3. the costs of going from alternative 1 to the respective alternative along route R.

The cost of going from home to the first alternative, $C(H, R[1])$, is common to all alternatives and therefore drops from the model. For notational purposes we may as well add this term to each deterministic utility. In this case, (8.33) simplifies to

$$V_i = \eta_i - C(R[i], H) - \sum_{k=1}^{i} C(R[k-1], R[k]))) \quad \forall \quad i > 0 \ .$$

The choice probabilities remain unchanged.

In the usual way, we can make the first element, the location parameter, a function of some explanatory variables. This allows us to describe the alternatives in terms of some additional characteristics and to integrate their influence upon search into the model. Moreover, we can test hypotheses about their importance for the evaluation of the alternatives with econometric methods. The equation for the deterministic utility component therefore becomes

$$V_i = \boldsymbol{X}_i \boldsymbol{\beta} - C(R[i], H) - \sum_{k=1}^{i} C(R[k-1], R[k]))) \quad \forall \quad i > 0 \ ,$$

where $\boldsymbol{X}_i$ represents a vector of explanatory variables that describe alternative i and $\boldsymbol{\beta}$ a vector of unknown parameters. We can estimate and test the elements of $\boldsymbol{\beta}$ in the usual way. We have to keep in mind, however, that our argument is based upon a *price* distribution. This allowed us to integrate the cost components at the various levels of the search process. As a consequence, the have to interpret V_i as being measured in monetary terms.

The third element in the above listing of components of deterministic utility depends upon route R. Therefore, we can measure this element only when we know the searcher's route through the alternatives. The structural equivalence between the spatial search model and the logit model therefore only applies to the stopping component of spatial search. The solution of the routing component has to be observed.

8.5. Notes on the Econometrics of Spatial Search

In order to apply our model empirically, we need to collect the following information about each individual's search process:

1. information about the route; i.e., the full sequence of all n alternatives.
2. information about the respective elements of the cost matrix.
3. information about relevant characteristics of the individual as well as the relevant characteristics of all n alternatives.
4. information about which alternative the searcher has selected.

Because the summation in the denominator in the equation for the choice probabilities (8.35) runs from 1 to n, we have to have information about *all* alternatives. This includes alternatives the individual does not search because he/she terminates search before. This brings us back to the discussion of how to determine the relevant alternatives in section 4.4. There, we have found (theorem 4.6) that a search problem can have irrelevant alternatives only when its price distribution is bound from above. Since the logistic distribution is unbounded, in strict theoretical terms we will always have to take into account all alternatives in the world when applying a search model based on this distribution.

In practical terms, however, we will have to restrict ourself to a certain set of alternatives. It can be determined either by asking the searcher which alternatives he/she considers to be relevant or by cutting off the search sequence at a certain point. When using the second strategy we can either ignore the remaining alternatives or try to approximate their possible impact by use of a "residual alternative". In either case, we need to be aware that we introduce some error into our computations. Since the costs of getting to the alternatives add up through the search sequence, the error tends to be small beyond a certain point in the search sequence. Nevertheless, it will not vanish completely. The problem is similar to the one we have encountered in the intervening opportunities model where we rescaled the choice probabilities because of the alternatives beyond the cut-off point.

From the first three elements of the above list and a temporarily given parameter vector we can compute the choice probabilities for all alternatives. We can use these and the information about the searcher's final choice to compute the likelihood of the sample. The likelihood function of the spatial search model based on set of assumptions is just the standard likelihood function of a discrete choice model that we have derived in section 8.3.

Note that it is sufficient to know which alternative the searcher has selected. We do not need to know the price offer at this or any other alternative. Also, the explanatory characteristics of the alternative that are contained in the vector X_i represent only the alternative in general – the location parameter of the price distribution – but do not relate to the specific price offer the searcher receives. As long as we stay within the framework of the spatial search model as we have developed it in this book, information about the specific price offers is useless in the estimation process. The reason is that in our model the reservation price is a scalar rather than a random variable. Therefore, and based on the assumption of a utility maximizing individual[20], whenever the searcher accepts/rejects an offer we know that the price quote must have been below/above the reservation price. How much the price quote differed from the reservation price is irrelevant for the search process.

The same argument also applies for the search process as a whole. The expected cost of the whole spatial search process is a scalar as well that can be computed a-priorily. It depends upon the unknown vector of parameters, but does not contain any random influence. So, the probability distribution for the various routes to be optimal is degenerated and yields one for just one route[21] and zero for all the other. Consequently, a likelihood function based on the choice of route would be discontinuous and would not allow us to discriminate between various parameter values. Therefore, in our model we cannot estimate the parameters based on information about the route[22].

In this respect the econometrics of our search model differ considerably from those discussed by Lerman and Mahmassani (1985). They too investigate the relationship between search and discrete choice models, and its empirical implications. Lerman and Mahmassani, however, apply Manski's (1973) argument for the causes of observational error, that has become quite common in random utility models. He views the random component to be the result of (1) omitted variables, (2) taste variations, (3) measurement errors, and (4) use of instrument variables. Based on this argument Lerman and Mahmassani (1985) treat *both*, the price offer and the reservation price, as a random variable. By doing so they ignore the intrinsic relationship between the price offer distribution and the reservation price that was a major element of our discussion throughout the book. Instead, they "assume that the analyst has resolved the problem of specifying the search mechanism for the particular type of search under study and is able to specify the search rule up to some set of unknown

---

[20] Of course, we can use information about the price offer for testing the validity of this assumption.

[21] In the unlikely case that k routes yield exactly the same expected costs their probabilities are $1/k$.

[22] Again, we can use the route information for testing the basic assumptions of our search model.

parameters" (Lerman and Mahmassani, 1985, p. 1010).

Based on this quite problematic basic assumption Lerman and Mahmassani discuss general maximum likelihood estimators for various informational situations; among them the case that the order of the search sequence is not observed and the case of only partial observation of the alternatives involved. In an appendix Lerman and Mahmassani derive tractable special cases for specific distributional assumptions. They are based on the assumption of normally or Gumbel-distributed random components that give rise to specific versions of probit or logit models. The latter relationship is the one we have discussed above.

8.6 Summary

In this chapter we have discussed the relationship between spatial search and spatial interaction models. In particular we have focused upon three types of spatial interaction models: gravity models, intervening opportunities models, and discrete choice models applied to spatial interaction.

Section 8.1 was devoted to a brief review of the gravity model. We have discussed different versions of the model and its derivation from an entropy maximization framework as one way of motivating the functional form of the model. In section 8.2 we present the intervening opportunities model. Since this model is less important in spatial analysis than the gravity model or the discrete choice model we keep this discussion very brief. The inclusion of the intervening opportunities model is mainly motivated by its conceptual similarity to the spatial search framework. Section 8.3 briefly presents discrete choice models. This family of models is of no particular spatial origin. However, its conceptual framework can easily be applied to problems of spatial analysis and many analysts have done so in the past. Its advantage over traditional spatial interaction models lies in its well developed microeconomic foundation. When applied to a homogeneous group of decision makers, the logit model, the most important type of discrete choice model, leads to the same interaction pattern as the production-constrained gravity.

This relationship is of particular importance in our context. It is discussed in the first part of section 8.4. Since we can show that under the proper distributional assumption the spatial search model is equivalent to a logit model, the above mentioned relationship also links the search model to the gravity model. All these structural links are discussed in section 8.4. Also in this section we discuss the relationship between the spatial search model and the intervening opportunities model. This relationship differs from the other in the sense that the intervening opportunities model corresponds only to a highly restrictive version of the spatial search model.

The spatial search framework is therefore much more general than the intervening opportunities model.

Discrete choice models and the spatial search model differ in their applicability in empirical investigations. While the spatial search model, as we have developed and discussed it here, is mainly of theoretical importance, the empirical and econometric aspects of discrete choice models are well developed and the models have been applied in many different contexts. Therefore, the structural relationship between the two models that we have found in section 8.4 should proof to be valuable in empirical applications of the spatial search model. In section 8.5 we discuss some of the empirical and econometric aspects of this relationship.

Chapter 9

Conclusions and Future Research

Now that we have reached the end of our discussion of spatial search, we want to take an inventory of what we have achieved. Because we have dealt with a rather new topic in Regional Science, we have probably raised more questions than we were able to answer. We will summarize those that seem to be particularly promising for more research in the future.

In chapter 1 we have mentioned that it is our main goal to provide a comprehensive discussion of spatial search. We have followed this goal by looking at our main topic from various perspectives: from Economics, Operations Research, Mathematics, and, most prominently, Regional Science. We have borrowed and combined concepts from all these disciplines in order to gain a better understanding of spatial search, its structure, complexity, and implications for the theory of the space economy. The basic assumptions that defined what we mean by spatial search are clearly micro-economic. Throughout our presentation we use the idea of economic actors who attempt to maximize utility. This ties our discussion closely to micro-economics, particularly to economic search theory. The fact that we place our economic agents in an explicitly spatial context brings in concepts from Operations Research, Geography, and Mathematics. We use graphs to characterize the spatial structure of a spatial search problem, find that the agent can choose between different routes through the respective graph, and derive results about the mathematical complexity of the spatial search problem therefrom. The traveling salesman problem, an important concept in Operations Research, plays an important role in this step. Also our discussion of heuristics for the spatial search model in chapter 5 is closely linked to the respective Operations Research literature.

Throughout the book we tried to maintain a Regional Science perspective. It is most pronounced in chapters 6 to 8. There we investigate the implications spatial search has for some important Regional Science concepts. Since we cannot reconstruct all Regional Science theories, we concentrate on three prominent elements: market areas and location, agglomeration, and spatial interaction models. When we use spatial search as the underlying micro-economic concept in these theories, some of their well-known theoretical results change quite dramatically. By no means does our discussion exhaust the Regional Science theories that may yield interesting theoretical results when reformulated based on spatial search. It was our intention in this part of the book to demonstrate some interesting examples. However, it is not only these three chapters where we maintain a Regional Science perspective. The idea of an economic agent acting in a spatial context is fundamental to the other chapters as well.

The version of spatial search that we define in chapter 4 and use throughout our presentation is relatively simple. By assumption we eliminate some of the extensions and complications that play a prominent role in economic search theory and that have been discussed in chapter 2. In particular ignoring recall in a spatial search context may appear quite restrictive. Other researchers (e.g., Miller, 1993; Gillen and Guccione, 1993) have decided to allow for recall in a spatial search context. Looking back we feel that the number of theoretical results we were able to derive justifies this simplifying assumption.

Despite its simple structure, our spatial search problem turns out to be quite complex. We derive a number of results that clearly show how complex a problem can become when one takes into account spatial relationships in a serious way. Our most important result in this respect is theorem 4.1, where we demonstrate that the general spatial search problem is *NP-complete*. This means that the spatial search problem belongs to a class of highly complex decision problems. Other results in chapters 4 and 5 emphasis this perspective. There we find that it is difficult to theoretically justify the elimination of alternatives as well as to reduce the complexity of the problem by simplifying its spatial structure. Only when we impose highly restrictive constraints upon the spatial structure the spatial search problem becomes computationally tractable.

These results bear a number of consequences for our discussion and for future work. First, they justify our decision to keep the spatial search problem as simple as possible. Second, they raise the question of how agents deal with such type of decisions in reality. It seems that because of the complexity of the spatial search problem, heuristic approaches play an important role. In chapter 5 we discuss some aspects of the analysis of heuristics and procedures that have been suggested. Also, we propose another heuristic procedure, the k-step l-nearest neighbor heuristic. Third, in order to derive results for market areas, agglomeration forces etc. we have to restrict ourselves to quite simple spatial structures. We apply this strategy in chapters 6 to 8.

When analyzing structure and complexity of the spatial search problem we gain a number of additional insights. It becomes clear that spatial search consists of two interrelated components: a routing component, where the decision maker has to determine the sequence in which to investigate the available alternatives, and a stopping component, where the searcher has to decide whether an alternative produced an acceptable offer or not. The two components are reflected in the proposed algorithm for solving the spatial search problem, and are at the basis of the complexity argument. When we analyze changes in the parameters of the spatial search problem, we find the two components again. While an optimizing agent adjusts his/her stopping behavior continuously (stopping effect), at some points in parameter space he/she changes from one route to another. As a result of these routing effect we observe discrete changes in the spatial distribution of demand as it is characterized by the choice probabilities. These changes may have dramatic effects on suppliers, particularly when demand is spatially concentrated. We note this feature of the spatial search problem in our discussion but do not go into much detail. It may be worth doing so in future research.

In chapters 6 to 8 our results are most interesting in relation to the standard theories. Therefore, in these chapters we always discuss the standard version of the theory first, and then derive results based on spatial search. Since we introduce the complexity of spatial search, in some cases we have to simplify in some other respects. In all three chapters we find strong relationships to the standard theories as well as very interesting deviations. It seems that the concept of spatial search, when adequately simplified, fits into the standard theories but at the same time enriches them.

The idea of spatial search implies a relationship between the various alternatives. On the other hand, because of the spatial structure we take into account, this relationship depends upon the relative locations of alternatives and searchers. This dichotomy becomes evident in the theoretical results we derive in chapters 6 and 7. When we introduce spatial search into a simple model of market areas in chapter 6, size and shape of a supplier's market area become a function of his/her position in relation to all other suppliers. This is in stark contrast to the standard theory, where only the immediately next suppliers are of relevance. It seems that the results of the search based version are more in line with empirical evidence than those of the standard model.

Similar conclusions can be drawn about the discussion of agglomeration forces in chapter 7. The relationship between the alternatives that is introduced by spatial search and the fact that the suppliers compete for customers lead to two counteracting forces in the location decisions of the two suppliers. When transportation costs are large relative to the variability of the price distribution, the competition effect dominates the spatial search effect. This results in the structure of the standard model, where each supplier has his/her own market area that does not overlap with those of the competitors. Spatial search does not occur in this situation. Under our set of assumptions each customer visits only the one supplier with the lowest expected delivered price and buys it there at whatever price is charged. When the market is the perimeter of a circle, the suppliers will locate at opposite poles.

When transportation costs become less important relative to the variability of the price distribution, the search effect takes over. More and more actors find it optimal to consider both suppliers and to engage in spatial search. Market areas begin to overlap. Suppliers find it optimal to locate in closer proximity. When transport costs fall under a certain threshold, the suppliers will agglomerate at the same location. This behavior maximizes their expected sales and minimizes the customer's expected costs. A major aspect of this result is that the search-based model contains the standard model as special case and that the model reflects the transition from the standard locational structure to agglomerated location. It seems to us that this transition is of considerable relevance in retail location.

The discussion in chapter 8 differs from that in the previous two chapters insofar as it focuses upon model structures. We can show that the spatial search model is closely related to gravity models as well as intervening opportunities models of spatial interaction. Also, with proper distributional assumptions we can derive a logit-model structure from the micro-economics of the spatial search model. This links the spatial search model two important classes of models: spatial interaction models, and discrete choice models.

The link to spatial interaction models is important in the sense that it gives us confidence about the macro-structures resulting from spatial search. In a large number of studies spatial interaction models – gravity models in particular – have been found to adequately reflect the interaction patterns of many different activities. Future research will have to determine which of these interaction patterns are the outcomes of spatial search at the micro level.

The relationship to discrete choice models gives the spatial search model access to a well developed operational concept. With proper assumptions we can utilize the extensive econometric literature on discrete choice models for the study of spatial search. This may be of particular relevance for empirical analyses of spatial search behavior.

All these results are new in the literature. Together they demonstrate quite clearly the strengths and weaknesses of the spatial search concept as well as its rich potential as a micro-economic foundation for a theory of spatial economic structure. We have pointed out some directions. More in-depth investigations need to be left for future research.

What are promising areas of future research in the analysis of spatial search? They can be found in all major areas of our presentation.

- As far as structure, basic features and computational complexity of the spatial search problem are concerned more work needs to be done analyzing more complex versions of the model. In particular the question of recall of previously examined alternatives needs to be investigated. Important steps in this direction have been made by Harwitz et al. (1989), and Miller (1991, 1993). Their work has dealt with specific aspects of spatial search with recall. Our presentation may serve as a baseline for a more comprehensive treatment of this and other more complex versions of the spatial search model.

- Our discussion of heuristics for the spatial search problem raises two research questions. First, how do individuals actually make decisions in a spatial search situation? This question is an empirical one that ties into an existing body of literature on individual search behavior and information processing (e.g., Phipps, 1978; McCarty, 1979; Huff, 1981; Clark, 1982; Saunders and Flowerdew, 1987; Saunders, 1990; Herzog et al., 1993). This literature concentrates on the implications of search for different areas, information questions, or tests only some aspects of search behavior. An empirical test of the spatial search model as we have developed it will require a considerable amount of information. In particular information about what alternatives are considered to be relevant, the sequence in which the searcher intended to search alternatives after the one where search stopped etc. Because of this controlled experiments in a laboratory environment may be a promising alternative.

- The second research question that follows from our discussion of heuristics is an obvious one: What other heuristics for the spatial search model can be developed and how do all these heuristics compare with respect to computing time, expected costs, and other performance criteria. Obviously, this question relates to the literature on computational problems and heuristics' performance for other *NP-complete* problems (e.g., Ball and Magazine, 1981; Golden and Steward, 1985; Johnson and Papadimitriou, 1985; Karp and Steele, 1985).

- Chapters 6 to 8 use just three Regional Science concepts for investigating the implications of spatial search and do so with fairly specific model structures. It seems worthwhile to investigate other model structures and to analyze the implications of spatial search for other Regional Science concepts as well.
- Although our main focus was on spatial search as a general microeconomic concept, throughout our presentation we have argued in terms of shopping. Future research should develop this application of spatial search further as well as investigate other possible applications like job-search, migration, search in the housing market, etc. Each area of application raises specific questions about the structure of spatial search and its implications. When following this line of research, steps will need to be taken in order to move toward a spatial theory of search-based markets.
- At the end of chapter 8 we have made a few comments about the econometrics of spatial search, and how the concept may be applied empirically. There, we mainly intended to point out the general direction. More research is needed to develop all the particulars of an empirically applicable version of a spatial search model and to work out all its econometric details. The relationship to discrete choice models may be carried much further, particularly with respect to other types and dynamic versions of discrete choice models.

In this list we mention only those research questions that follow directly from our Regional Science oriented discussion in this book. As was pointed out in chapter 1, however, the concept of spatial search relates to a number of other disciplines that each may be able to generate a similar list of research questions. In Economics, for example, spatial price theory has stimulated considerable development in the theories of product differentiation and imperfect competition (for a review see, e.g., Thisse, 1987; Phlips, 1988; Beath and Katsoulacos, 1991). Because the concept of spatial search can be used to extend and generalize certain aspects of spatial price theory, it may have considerable implications for these areas of Economics.

In our discussion we have found spatial search to be a fascinating concept with interesting features and intriguing implications. As we see from the – probably fragmentary – list above it raises a number of questions for further research. The analysis of spatial search, a fairly new topic in Regional Science, may attract more researchers in the future, and keep them busy for quite some time.

References

Ahlswede, R., I. Wegener, 1987. *Search Problems*, Chichester: Wiley.

Akerlof, G.A., 1970. The market for 'Lemons': qualitative uncertainty and the market mechanism, *Quarterly Journal of Economics*, Vol. 84, pp. 488-500.

Alpern, S., 1974. The Search Game with Mobile Hider on a Circle. In: *Differential Games and Control Theory*, eds. E.O. Roxin, P.T. Liu, R.L. Sternberg, New York: Dekker, pp. 181-200.

Anas, A., 1982. *Residential Location Markets and Urban Transportation: Economic Theory, Econometrics, and Policy Analysis with Discrete Choice Models*, New York: Academic Press.

Arrow, K.J., 1965. *Aspects of the Theory of Risk Bearing*, Helsinki, Yrjö Jahnssonin Säätio.

Axell, B., 1974. Price Disperion and Information – An Adaptive Sequential Search Model, *Swedish Journal of Economics*, Vol. 76, pp. 77-98.

Axell, B., 1977. Search Market Equilibrium, *Scandinavian Journal of Economics*, Vol. 79, pp. 20-40.

Ball, M., M. Magazine, 1981. The design and analysis of heuristics, *Networks*, Vol. 11, p. 215-219.

Bartels, D., 1974. Schwierigkeiten mit dem Raumbegriff in der Geographie, *Geographica Helvetica*, Beiheft Nr. 2/3, pp. 7-21.

Beardwood, J., J. Halton, J. Hammersley, 1959. The Shortest Path through Many Points, *Proceedings of the Cambridge Philosophical Society*, Vol. 55, pp. 299-327.

Beath, J., Y. Katsoulacos, 1991. *The Economic Theory of Product Differentiation*, Cambridge: Cambridge University Press.

Beckmann, M.J., 1972. Spatial Cournot Oligopoly, *Papers of the Regional Science Association*, Vol. 28, pp. 37-47.

Beckmann, M.J., J.-F. Thisse, 1986. The Location of Production Activities, in: *Handbook of Regional and Urban Economics, Vol. 1*, Amsterdam: Elsevier Science Publishers B.V.

Ben-Akiva, M., B. Francois, 1983. μ Homogeneous Genaralized Extreme Value Models, Working Paper, Dept. of Civil Engineering, Massachusetts Institute of Technology, Cambridge, MA.

Ben-Akiva, M., S. Lerman, 1985. *Discrete Choice Analysis: Theory and Application to Travel Demand*, Cambridge: MIT-Press.

Bergman, E.M., G. Maier 1991. Spread and Backwash in the Spatial Diffusion of Development. In: *Regions Reconsidered: Economic Networks, Innovation, and Local Development in Industrialized Countries*, eds. E.M. Bergman, G. Maier, F. Tödtling, London: Mansell, pp. 265-282.

Bergman, E.M., G. Maier, F. Tödtling (eds.), 1991. *Regions Reconsidered: Economic Networks, Innovation, and Local Development in Industrialized Countries*, London: Mansell.

Blau, D.M., 1991. Search for Nonwage Job Characteristics: A Test of the Reservation Wage Hypothesis, *Journal of Labor Economics*, Vol. 9, pp. 186-205.

Bodin, L., B. Golden, 1981. Classification in vehicle routing and scheduling, *Networks*, Vol. 11, pp. 97-108.

Bodin, L., B. Golden, A. Assad, M. Ball, 1983. Routing and scheduling of vehicles and crews: the state of the art, *Computers & Operations Research*, Vol. 10, pp. 63-221.

Bondy, J.A., U.S.R. Murty, 1976. *Graph Theory with Applications*, London: MacMillan.

Brown, S., 1993. Retail location theory: evolution and evaluation, *International Review of Retail, Distribution and Consumer Research*, Vol. 3, pp. 185- 229.

Carlino, G.A., 1978. *Economies of Scale in Manufacturing Location*, Leiden: Martinus Nijhoff.

Carlson, J.A., R.P. McAfee, 1983. Discrete Equilibrium Price Dispersions, *Journal of Political Economy*, Vol. 91, pp. 480-493.

Cho, C-J., 1993. The Measure of Locational Efficiency of Urban Parks: The Case of Chongju, *Urban Studies*, Vol. 30, pp. 1399-1407.

Cho, I., D.M. Kreps, 1987. Signaling Games and Stable Equilibria, *Quarterly Journal of Economics*, Vol. 102, pp. 179-222.

Chow, Y.S., H. Robbins, D. Siegmund, 1971. *Great Expectations: The Theory of Optimal Stopping*, Boston: Houghton Mufflin.

Christaller, W., 1933. *Dir zentralen Orte in Süddeutschland. Eine ökonomisch-geographische Untersuchung über die Gesetzmäßigkeit der Verbreitung und Entwicklung der Siedlungen mit städtischen Funktionen*, Jena.

References

Christofides, N., 1985. Vehicle routing, in: E.L. Lawler, J.K. Lenstra, A.H.G. Rinnooy Kan, D.B. Shmoys, *The Traveling Salesman Problem*, Chichester: Wiley, pp. 431-448.

Clark, W.A.V. (ed.), 1982. *Modelling Housing Market Search*, London: Croom Helm.

DaGanzo, D., 1984. The Distance Traveled to Visit n Points with a Maximum of C Stops per Vehicle: An Analytical Model and an Application, *Transportation Science*, Vol. 18, pp. 331-350.

d'Aspremont, C., J. Jaskold Gabszewicz, J.-F. Thisse, 1979. On Hotelling's "Stability in Competition", *Econometrica*, Vol. 47, pp. 1145-1150.

Deaton, A., J. Muellbauer, 1980. *Economics and Consumer Behavior*, Cambridge: Cambridge University Press.

DeGroot, M.H., 1970. *Optimal Statistical Decisions*, New York: McGraw-Hill.

De Palma, A., V. Ginsburgh, Y. Papageorgiou, J.-F. Thisse, 1985. The principle of minimum differentiation holds under sufficient heterogeneity, *Econometrica*, Vol. 53, pp. 767-781.

Diamond, P.A., 1971. A Model of Price Adjustment, *Journal of Economic Theory*, Vol. 15, pp. 156-168.

Diamond, P., M. Rothschild, 1989. *Uncertainty in Economics, Readings and Exercises*, 2nd edition, New York: Academic Press.

Domencich, T.A., D. McFadden, 1975. *Urban Travel Demand – A Behavioral Analysis*, Amsterdam: North Holland.

Eaton, B.C., 1976. Free entry in one-dimensional models: pure profits and multiple equilibria, *Journal of Regional Science*, Vol. 16, pp. 21-33.

Eaton, B.C., R.G. Lipsey, 1975. The Principle of Minimum Differentiation Reconsidered: Some New Developments in the Theory of Spatial Competition, *Review of Economic Studies*, Vol. 42, pp. 27-49.

Eaton, B.C., R.G. Lipsey, 1979. Comparison shopping and the clustering of homogeneous firms, *Journal of Regional Science*, Vol. 19, pp. 421-435.

Evers, G.H.M., 1989. Simultaneous Models for Migration and Commuting: Macro and Micro Economic Approaches. In: J. van Dijk, H. Folmer, H.W. Herzog Jr., A.M. Schlottmann (eds.), *Migration and Labor Market Adjustment*, Dordrecht: Kluwer, pp. 177-198.

Ferguson, T.S., 1989. Who Solved the Secretary Problem?, *Statistical Science*, Vol. 4, pp. 282-296.

Fergusson, J.G., 1980. Exploration of Coal in the U.K. In: *Search Theory and Applications*, ed. K.B. Haley, L. Stone, New York: Plenum Press, pp. 165-172.

Fetter, F.A., 1924. The Economic Law of Market Areas, *Quarterly Journal of Economics*, Vol. 39, pp. 520-529.

Field, E.A., 1980. Introductory Comments on Exploration and Search Theory. In: *Search Theory and Applications*, ed. K.B. Haley, L. Stone, New York: Plenum Press, pp. 159-164.

Fischer, M.M., P. Nijkamp, Y.Y. Papageorgiou (eds.), 1990. *Spatial Choices and Processes*, Amsterdam: North-Holland.

Fisher, F.M., 1970. Quasi-competitive Price Adjustment by Individual Firms, *Journal of Economic Theory*, Vol. 14, pp. 195-206.

Fotheringham, A.S., M.E. O'Kelly, 1989. *Spatial Interaction Models: Formulation and Applications*, Norwell, MA: Kluwer Academic.

Freeman, P.R., 1983. The secretary problem and its extensions – A review, *International Statistical Review*, Vol. 51, pp. 189-206.

Friedman, M., L.J. Savage, 1948. The utility analysis of choices involving risk, *Journal of Political Economy*, Vol. 56, pp. 279-304.

Gal, S., 1980. *Search Games*, New York: Academic Press.

Gal, S., M. Landsberger, B. Levykson, 1981. A Compound Strategy for Search in the Labor Market, *International Economic Review*, Vol. 22, pp. 597-608.

Gannon, C.A., 1973. Central concentration in simple spatial duopoly: some behavioural and functional considerations, *Journal of Regional Science*, Vol. 13, pp. 357-375.

Garey, M.R., D.S. Johnson, 1979. *Computers and Intractability: A Guide to the Theory of NP-Completeness*, San Francisco: Freeman.

Garfinkel, R.S., 1985. Motivation and modeling, in: E.L. Lawler, J.K. Lenstra, A.H.G. Rinnooy Kan, D.B. Shmoys, *The Traveling Salesman Problem*, Chichester: Wiley, pp. 17-36.

Garofoli, G., 1991. Local Networks, Innovation and Policy in Italian Industrial Districts. In: *Regions Reconsidered: Economic Networks, Innovation, and Local Development in Industrialized Countries*, eds. E.M. Bergman, G. Maier, F. Tödtling, London: Mansell, pp. 119-140.

Garofoli, G. (ed.), 1992. *Endogenous Development and Southern Europe*, Aldershot: Avebury.

Gibbons, A., 1985. *Algorithmic Graph Theory*, Cambridge: Cambridge University Press.

Gilbert, E.N., 1989. A solvable routing problem, *Networks*, Vol. 19, pp. 597-594.

Gilbert, J., F. Mosteller, 1966. Recognizing the maximum of a sequence, *Journal of the American Statistical Association*, Vol. 61, pp. 35-73.

Gillen, W.J., A. Guccione, 1993. Search and Fetter's Law of Markets, *Geographical Analysis*, Vol. 25, pp. 165-170.

Gilmore, P.C., E.L. Lawler, D.B. Shmoys, Well-solved special cases, in: E.L. Lawler, J.K. Lenstra, A.H.G. Rinnooy Kan, D.B. Shmoys, *The Traveling Salesman Problem*, Chichester: Wiley, pp. 87-143.

Golden, B.L., W.R. Steward, 1985. Empirical analysis of heuristics, in: E.L. Lawler, J.K. Lenstra, A.H.G. Rinnooy Kan, D.B. Shmoys, *The Traveling Salesman Problem*, Chichester: Wiley, pp. 207-249.

Golledge, R.G., H. Timmermans, 1988. *Behavioural Modelling in Geography and Planning*, London: Croom Helm.

Graitson, D., 1982. Spatial competition a la Hotelling: a selective survey, *Journal of Industrial Economics*, Vol. 31, pp. 13-25.

Greenhut, M.L., 1956. *Plant Location in Theory and Practice*, Chapel Hill, NC: University of North Carolina Press.

Greenhut, M.L., 1957. Games, capitalism and general location theory, *Manchester School of Economic and Social Studies*, Vol. 25, pp. 61-88.

Greenhut, M.L., G. Norman, C.-S. Hung, 1987. *The Economics of Imperfect Competition. A Spatial Approach*, Cambridge: Cambridge University Press.

Håkanson, H. (ed.), 1987. *Industrial Technological Development: A Network Approach*, London: Croom Helm.

Haley, K.B., L. Stone, 1980. *Search Theory and Applications*, New York: Plenum Press.

Hall, J.R., S.A. Lippman, J.J. McCall, 1979. Expected Utility Maximizing Job Search, in: *Studies in the Economics of Search*, eds. S.A. Lippman, J.J. McCall, Amsterdam: North-Holland, pp. 133-155.

Harwitz, M., P. Rogerson, B. Lentnek, 1989. Spatial price search: optimal policy in the plane. Paper presented at the annual meeting of the Regional Science Association, Santa Barbara, CA.

Haynes, K.E., A.S. Fotheringham, 1984. *Gravity and Spatial Interaction Models*, Beverly Hills, CA: Sage.

Heal, G., 1980. Spatial structure in retail trade: a study in product differentiation with increasing returns, *Bell Journal of Economics*, Vol. 11, pp. 565-583.

Herzog, H.W.jr., A.M. Schlottmann, T.P.Boehm, 1993. Migration as Spatial Job-search: A Survey of Empirical Findings, *Regional Studies*, Vol. 27, pp. 327-340.

Hey, J.D., 1974. Price Adjustment in an Atomistic Market, *Journal of Economic Theory*, Vol. 18, pp. 483-499.

Hey, J.D., 1979. *Uncertainty in Microeconomics*, Oxford: Martin Robertson.

Hirshleifer, J., 1989. *Time, Uncertainty, and Information*, Oxford: Blackwell.

Hirshleifer, J., J.G. Riley, 1992. *The Analytics of Uncertainty and Information*, Cambridge: Cambridge University Press.

Hoffman, A.J., P. Wolfe, 1985. History, in: E.L. Lawler, J.K. Lenstra, A.H.G. Rinnooy Kan, D.B. Shmoys, *The Traveling Salesman Problem*, Chichester: Wiley, pp. 1-15.

Holahan, W.L., 1975. Welfare Effects of Spatial Price Discrimination, *American Economic Review*, Vol. 65, pp. 498-503.

Hotelling, H., 1929. Stability in Competition, *Economic Journal*, Jg. 39, S. 41-57.

Huff, J.O., 1981. Patterns of residential search; paper presented at the Annual Meeting of the Association of American Geographers, Los Angeles, CA.

Huff, J.O., 1984. Distance-decay models of residential search, in Gaile, G., C.J. Wilmott (eds.) *Spatial Statistics and Models*, Dordrecht: Reidel, pp. 345-366.

Hughes, G., B. McCormick, 1989. Does Migration Reduce Differentials in Regional Unemployment Rates? In: J. van Dijk, H. Folmer, H.W. Herzog Jr., A.M. Schlottmann (eds.), *Migration and Labor Market Adjustment*, Dordrecht: Kluwer, pp. 85-108.

Isard, W., 1956. *Location and Space Economy*, Cambridge, MA: MIT-Press.

Isard, W., 1967. Game theory, location theory and industrial agglomeration, *Regional Science Association, Papers and Proceedings*, Vol. 18, pp. 1-11.

Isard, W., 1969. *General Theory: Social, Political, Economic and Regional*, Cambridge, MA: MIT-Press.

Isard, W., M.F. Dacey, 1962. On the projection of individual behavior in regional analysis, *Journal of Regional Science*, Vo. 4, pp. 1-34.

Isard, W., T.A. Reiner, 1962. Aspects of decision making theory and regional science, *Regional Science Association, Papers and Proceedings*, Vol. 9, pp. 25-34.

Isard, W., T.E. Smith, 1966. A practical application of game theoretical approaches to arms reduction, *Peace Research Society, Papers*, Vol. 4, pp. 85-98.

Janko, W.H., A. Taudes, W. Frisch, 1993. Simultane Alternativensuche und Datenpräzisierung, Diskussionspapiere zum Tätigkeitsfeld Informationsverarbeitung und Informationswirtschaft, Nr. 13, Wirtschaftsuniversität Wien, Vienna, Austria.

Jayet, H., 1990a. Spatial search processes and spatial interaction: 1. sequential search, intervening opportunities, and spatial search equilibrium, *Environment and Planning A*, Vol. 22, pp. 583-599.

Jayet, H., 1990b. Spatial search processes and spatial interaction: 2. polarization, concentration, and spatial search equilibrium, *Environment and Planning A*, Vol. 22, pp. 719-732.

Johansson, B., 1991. Economic Networks and Self-Organization. In: *Regions Reconsidered: Economic Networks, Innovation, and Local Development in Industrialized Countries*, eds. E.M. Bergman, G. Maier, F. Tödtling, London: Mansell, pp. 17-34.

Johnson, N.L., S. Kotz, 1970. *Continuous Univariate Distributions*, Boston: Houghton Mifflin.

Johnson, D.S., C.H. Papadimitriou, 1985. Performance guarantees for heuristics, in: E.L. Lawler, J.K. Lenstra, A.H.G. Rinnooy Kan, D.B. Shmoys, *The Traveling Salesman Problem*, Chichester: Wiley, pp. 145-180.

Kadane, J.B., 1980. Industrial Applications of Search Theory. In: *Search Theory and Applications*, ed. K.B. Haley, L. Stone, New York: Plenum Press, pp. 205-210.

Kahle, E., 1990. *Betriebliche Entscheidungen: Lehrbuch zur Einführung in die betriebswirtschaftliche Entscheidungstheorie*, Munich, Vienna: Oldenbourg.

Kamann, D.J., 1991. The Distribution of Dominance in Networks and its Spatial Implications. In: *Regions Reconsidered: Economic Networks, Innovation, and Local Development in Industrialized Countries*, eds. E.M. Bergman, G. Maier, F. Tödtling, London: Mansell, pp. 35-58.

Karp, R.M., J.M. Steele, 1985. Probabilistic analysis of heuristics, in: E.L. Lawler, J.K. Lenstra, A.H.G. Rinnooy Kan, D.B. Shmoys, *The Traveling Salesman Problem*, Chichester: Wiley, pp. 181-205.

Kivell, P.T., G. Shaw 1980. The study of retail location. In: *Retail Geography*, ed. J.A. Dawson, London: Croom Helm, pp. 95-155.

Kolesar, P., 1980. An Application of Search Theory in Medizine: The Detection of Glaucoma. In: *Search Theory and Applications*, ed. K.B. Haley, L. Stone, New York: Plenum Press, pp. 199-204.

Koopman, B.O., 1980. *Search and Screening, General Principles and Historical Applications*, New York: Pergamon Press.

Krugman, P., 1991. *Geography and Trade*, Leuven, Cambridge, Mass.: Leuven University Press.

Latham, W.R., 1976. *Locational Behavior in Manufacturing Industries*, Leiden: Martinus Nijhoff.

Lerman, S.R., H.S. Mahmassani, The Econometrics of Search, *Environment and Planning A*, Vol. 17, pp. 1009-1024.

Lerner, A.P., H.W. Singer, 1937. Some notes on duopoly and spatial competition, *Journal of Political Economy*, Vol. 45, pp. 145-186.

Lippman, S.A., J.J. McCall, 1979. *Studies in the Economics of Search*, Amsterdam: North-Holland.

Luce, R.D., H. Raiffa, 1957. *Games and Decisions*, New York: Wiley.

MacMinn, R.D., 1980. Search and Market Equilibrium, *Journal of Political Economy*, Vol. 88, pp. 308-327.

Maddala, G.S., 1983. *Limited-dependent and Qualitative Variables in Econometrics*, Cambridge: Cambridge University Press.

Mai, C., 1984. Demand Function and Location Theory of the Firm under Price Uncertainty, *Urban Studies*, Vol. 21, pp. 459-464.

Maier, G., 1985. Cumulative Causation and Selectivity in Labour Market-Oriented Migration Caused by Imperfect Information, *Regional Studies*, Vol. 19, pp. 231-241.

Maier, G., 1990. The Economics of Information in the Context of Migration. In: *Labour Migration* ed. J.H. Johnson, J. Salt, London: David Fulton Publishers.

Maier, G., 1991. Modelling search processes in space, *Papers in Regional Science*, Vol. 70, pp. 133-147.

Maier, G., 1993a. The Spatial Search Problem: Structure and Complexity, *Geographical Analysis*, Vol. 25, pp. 242-251.

Maier, G., 1993b. Economic Integration in Central Europe: Cross-Border Trips in the Vienna-Bratislava Region. Paper submitted to the first virtual conference on "East-West Integration in Central Europe"; available via anonymous FTP from "ftp.wu-wien.ac.at" as file "/pub/cerro/virtconf/maier.txt".

Maier, G., M.M. Fischer, 1985. Random Utility Modelling and Labour Supply Mobility Analysis, *Papers of the Regional Science Association*, Vol. 58, S. 21-33.

Maier, G., P.A. Rogerson, 1986. Discrete Choice, Optimal Search and Spatial Interaction Models: Some Fundamental Relationships, *IIR-Discussion* 31, Interdisziplinäres Institut für Raumordnung, Wirtschaftsuniversität Wien.

Maier G., F. Tödtling, 1992. *Regional- und Stadtökonomik: Standorttheorie und Raumstruktur*, Vienna: Springer.

Maier, G., P. Weiss, 1990. *Modelle diskreter Entscheidungen: Theorie und Anwendung in den Sozial- und Wirtschaftswissenschaften*, Vienna: Springer.

Manski, C.F., 1973. *The Analysis of Qualitative Choice*, unpublished PhD dissertation, Department of Economics, Massachusetts Institute of Technology, Cambridge, MA.

Markowitz, H.M., 1959. *Portfolio Selection: Efficient Diversification of Investments*, New York: Wiley.

Marschak, J., 1968. Decision-making: economic aspects, *International Encyclopedia of the Social Sciences*, Vol. 4, New York: Macmillan, Free Press, pp. 42-55.

Massam, B.H., 1980. *Spatial Search: Applications to Planning Problems in the Public Sector*, Oxford: Pergamon Press.

Mattson, R.J., 1980. Overland Search for Missing Aircraft and Persons. In: *Search Theory and Applications*, ed. K.B. Haley, L. Stone, New York: Plenum Press, pp. 87-92.

McCarty, K.F., 1979. *Housing search and mobility*, Santa Monica, CA: Rand Corporation Report R-2451-HUD.

McFadden, D., 1978. odelling the Choice of Residential Location. In: A. Karlqvist, L. Lundqvist, F. Snickars, J.. Weibull, *Spatial Interaction Theory and Residential Location*, pp. 75-96, Amsterdam: North Holland.

McKenna, C.J., 1985. *Uncertainty and the Labour Market*, Brighton: Wheatsheaf.

McKenna, C.J., 1986. *The Economics of Uncertainty*, Brighton: Wheatsheaf.

McKenna, C.J., 1987a. Theories of Individual Search Behaviour, in: *Surveys in the Economics of Uncertainty*, eds. J.D. Hey, P.J. Lambert, Oxford: Basil Blackwell, pp. 91-109.

McKenna, C.J., 1987b. Models of Search Market Equilibrium, in: *Surveys in the Economics of Uncertainty*, eds. J.D. Hey, P.J. Lambert, Oxford: Basil Blackwell, pp. 110-123.

Miller, H.J., 1991. *Dynamic Programming and Stochastic Network Approaches to Modeling Spatial Search*, unpublished manuscript, Department of Geography, University of Utah.

Miller, H.J., 1993. Modeling Strategies for the Spatial Search Problem, *Papers in Regional Science*, Vol. 72, pp. 63-85.

Molho, I., 1986. Theories of Migration: A Review, *Scottish Journal of Political Economy*, 33: 396-419.

Morgan, P.B., R. Manning, 1985. Optimal Search, *Econometrica*, Vol. 53, pp. 923-944.

Morse, P.M., 1977. *In at the Beginnings: A Physicist's Life*, Cambridge, MA: MIT-Press.

Mortensen, D., 1986. Job Search and Labor Market Analysis, in *Handbook of Labor Economics*, Vol. 2, eds. O. Ashenfelter, R. Layard, Amsterdam: North-Holland.

Mott, J.L., A. Kandel, T.P. Baker, 1983. *Discrete Mathematics for Computer Scientists*, Reston: Reston Publishing Company.

Müller-Funk, U., 1993. Probleme des optimalen Stoppens mit Nebenbedingungen, in *Informationswirtschaft - Aktuelle Entwicklungen und Perspektiven*, eds. W. Frisch, A. Taudes, Heidelberg: Physica.

Mulligan, G.F., 1984. Agglomeration and central place theory: a review of the literature, in *International Regional Science Review*, Vol. 9, pp. 1-42.

Mulligan, G.F., T.J. Fik, 1989. Price Variation in Spatial Oligopolies, in *Geographical Analysis*, Vol. 21, pp. 32-46.

Neumann, J. von, O. Morgenstern, 1944. *Theory of Games and Economic Behavior*, Princeton: Princeton University Press.

Nelson, P., 1974. Advertising as Information, *Journal of Political Economy*, Vol. 82, pp. 729-754.

Nelson, P., 1975. The Economic Consequences of Advertising, *Journal of Business*, Vol. 48, pp. 213-241.

Norton, R.D., 1992. Agglomeration and Competitiveness: from Marshall to Chinitz, in *Urban Studies*, vol. 29, pp. 155-170.

Parker, R.G., R.L. Rardin, 1988. *Discrete Optimization*, Boston: Academic Press.

Phipps, A.G., 1978. *Space searching behavior: the case of appartment selection*, unpublished PhD Dissertation, University of Iowa, Iowa City, IO.

Phlips, L., 1988. *The Economics of Imperfect Information*, Cambridge: Cambridge University Press.

Pickles, A., P. Rogerson, 1984. Wage Distributions and Spatial Preferences in Competitive Job Search and Migration, *Regional Studies*, 18: 131-142.

Pooley, J., 1992. A vehicle routing algorithm for the less-than-truckload vs. multiple-stop truckload problem, *Journal of Business Logistics*, Vol. 13, pp. 239-258.

Porter, M., 1990. *The Competitive Advantage of Nations*. New York: The Free Press.

Pratt, J.W., 1964. Risk aversion in the small and in the large, *Econometrica*, Vol. 32, pp. 122-136.

Pudney, S., 1989. *Modelling Individual Choice - The Econometrics of Corners, Kinks and Holes*, London: Basil Blackwell.

Pyke, F., W. Sengenberger (eds.), 1992. *Industrial Districts and Local Economic Regeneration*, Geneva: International Labour Organization.

Reinganum, J.T., 1979. A Simple Model of Equilibrium Price Dispersion, *Journal of Political Economy*, Vol. 87, pp. 851-858.

Richardson, H.W., 1973. *Regional Growth Theory*, London: MacMillan.

Richardson, H.W., 1978. *Regional and Urban Economics*, Harmondsworth: Penguin.

Richardson, H.R., 1989. Search Theory. In: Search Theory: Some Recent Developments, eds. D.V. Chudnovsky, G.V. Chudnovsky, New York: Dekker, pp. 1-12.

Rogerson, P., 1982. Spatial Models of Search, *Geographical Analysis*, 14: 217-228.

Rogerson, P., 1990. Spatial Search for the Lowest Price, *Geographical Analysis*, Vol. 22, No. 4, pp. 336-347.

Rosenfield, D., R. Shapiro, 1981. Optimal Adaptive Search, *Journal of Economic Theory*, Vol. 25, pp. 1-20.

Rothschild, M., 1973. Models of Market Organization with Imperfect Information: A Survey, *Journal of Political Economy*, Vol. 81, pp. 1283-1308.

Rothschild, M., 1974. Searching for the lowest price when the distribution of prices is unknown, *Journal of Political Economy*, Vol. 82, pp. 689-711.

Sahni, S., T. Gonzalez, 1976. *P*-complete Approximation Problems, *Journal of the Association of Computing Machinery*, Vol. 23, pp. 555-565.

Salop, S.C., 1977. The Noisy Monopolist: Imperfect Information, Price Dispersion and Price Discrimination, *Review of Economic Studies*, Vol. 44, pp. 393-406.

Salop, S.C., 1979. Monopolistic Competition with outside Goods, *Bell Journal of Economics*, Vol. 10, pp. 141-156.

Samuels, S.M., 1985. A Best-Choice Problem with Linear Travel Cost, *Journal of the American Statistcal Association*, Vol. 80, pp. 461-464.

Saunders, M.N.K., 1990. Migration and Job Vacancy Information. In: *Labour Migration*, J.H. Johnson, J. Salt (eds.), London: David Fulton Publishers.

Saunders, M.N.K., R.Flowerdew, 1987. Spatial Aspects of the Provision of Job Information. In: *Regional Labour Markets*, M.M. Fischer, P. Nijkamp (eds.), Amsterdam: North-Holland, pp. 205-228.

Schmenner, R.W., 1982. *Making Business Location Decisions*, Englewood Cliffs: Prentice Hall.

Schneider, M., 1959. Gravity Models and Trip Distribution Theory, *Papers of the Regional Science Association*, Vol. 5, pp. 51-56.

Shiriaev, A.N., 1977. *Optimal Stopping Rules*, New York: Springer.

Smith, D.M., 1971. *Industrial Location: An Economic Geographical Analysis*, New York: Wiley.

Smithies, A., 1941. Optimum location in spatial competition, *Journal of Political Economy*, Vol. 49, pp. 423-39.

Spence, A.M., 1974. *Market Signaling*, Cambridge, MA: Harvard University Press.
Stafford, H.A., 1979. *Principles of Industrial Facilities Location*, Atlanta: Conway.
Stahl, K., 1982. Differentiated products, consumer search, and locational oligopoly, *Journal of Industrial Economics*, Vol. 31, pp. 97-113.
Stevens, B.H., 1961. An application of game theory to a problem in location strategy, *Regional Science Association, Papers and Proceedings*, Vol. 7, pp. 143-157.
Stigler, G., 1961. The economics of information, *Journal of Political Economy*, Vol. 69, pp. 213-285.
Stigler, G., 1962. Information in the labor market, *Journal of Political Economy*, Vol. 70, pp. 94-105.
Stone, L.D., 1989. A Review of Results in Optimal Search for Moving Targets. In: Search Theory: Some Recent Developments, eds. D.V. Chudnovsky, G.V. Chudnovsky, New York: Dekker, pp. 13-32.
Stouffer, S., 1940. Intervening Opportunities: A Theory Relating Mobility and Distance, *American Sociological Review*, Vol. 5, pp. 845-867.
Thisse, J.F., 1987. Location Theory, Regional Science, and Economics, *Journal of Regional Science*, Vol. 27, pp. 519-528.
Thompson, A., R. Caves, 1993. The Projected Market Share for a New Small Airport in the North of England, *Regional Studies*, Vol. 27, pp. 137-147.
van Lierop, W., 1986. *Spatial Interaction Modelling and Residential Choice Analysis*, Aldershot: Gower.
Webber, M.J., 1972. *Impact of Uncertainty on Location*, Cambridge: M.I.T. Press.
Webber, M.J., 1977. Pedagogy again: what is entropy, in *Annals of the Association of American Geographers*, Vol. 67, pp. 254-266.
Webber, M.J., 1980. *Information Theory and Urban Spatial Structure*, London: Croom Helm.
Weber, A., 1909. *Über den Standort der Industrien*, Tübingen.
Wilson, A.G., 1967. A Statistical Theory of Spatial Distribution Models, in *Transportation Research*, Vol. 1, pp. 253-269.
Wilson, A.G., 1970. *Entropy in Urban and Regional Modelling*, London: Pion.
Wilson, A.G., R.J. Bennett, 1985. *Mathematical Methods in Human Geography and Planning*, Chichester: Wiley.
Wilson, R.J., J.J. Watkins, 1990. *Graphs, an Introductory Approach*, New York: Wiley.

Studies in Contemporary Economics

B. Hamminga, Neoclassical Theory Structure and Theory Development. IX, 174 pages. 1983.

J. Dermine, Pricing Policies of Financial Intermediaries. VII, 174 pages. 1984.

Economic Consequences of Population Change in Industrialized Countries. Proceedings. 1983. Edited by G. Steinmann. X, 415 pages. 1984.

Problems of Advanced Economies. Proceedings, 1982. Edited by N. Miyawaki. VI, 319 pages. 1984.

Studies in Labor Market Dynamics. Proceedings, 1982. Edited by G. R. Neumann and N. C. Westergard-Nielsen. X, 285 pages. 1985.

A. Pfingsten, The Measurement of Tax Progression. VI, 131 pages. 1986.

Causes of Contemporary Stagnation. Proceedings, 1984. Edited by H. Frisch and B. Gahlen. IX, 216 pages. 1986.

O. Flaaten, The Economics of Multispecies Harvesting. VII, 162 pages. 1988.

D. Laussel, W. Marois, A. Soubeyran, (Eds.), Monetary Theory and Policy. Proceedings, 1987. XVIII, 383 pages. 1988.

G. Rubel, Factors Determining External Debt. VI, 264 pages. 1988.

B. C. J. van Velthoven, The Endogenization of Government Behaviour in Macroeconomic Models. XI, 367 pages. 1989.

A. Wenig, K. F. Zimmermann (Eds.) 3, Demographic Change and Economic Development. XII, 325 pages. 1989.

J. K. Brunner, Theory of Equitable Taxation. VIII, 217 pages. 1989.

E. van Imhoff, Optimal Economic Growth and Non-Stable Population. IX, 218 pages. 1989.

P. S. A. Renaud, Applied Political Economic Modelling. XII, 242 pages. 1989.

H. König (Ed.), Economics of Wage Determination. XI, 373 pages. 1990.

C. Dagum, M. Zenga (Eds.) Income and Wealth Distribution, Inequality and Poverty. Proceedings, XIII, 415 pages. 1990.

A. J. H. C. Schram, Voter Behavior in Economic Perspective. X, 274 pages. 1991.

J. B. Woittiez, Modelling and Empirical Evaluation of Labour Supply Behaviour. VI, 232 pages. 1991.

R. Arnason, T. Bjorndal (Eds.), Essays on the Economics of Migratory Fish Stocks. VIII, 197 pages. 1991.

Ch. Czerkawski, Theoretical and Policy-Oriented Aspects of the External Debt Economics. VII, 150 pages. 1991.

D. Stern, J. M. M. Ritzen (Eds.), Market Failure in Training? VII, 233 pages. 1991.

M. Savioz, New Issues in the Theory of Investment. XVI, 216 pages. 1992.

W. Franz (Ed.) Structural Unemployment. X, 132 pages. 1992.

N. Blattner, H. Genberg, A. Swoboda, (Eds.), Competitiveness in Banking. VIII, 315 pages. 1992.

M. Carlberg, Monetary and Fiscal Dynamics. VIII, 194 pages. 1992.

H.-J. Wagener, On the Theory and Policy of Systemic Change. VIII, 234 pages. 1993.

E. Wurzel, An Econometric Analysis of Individual Unemployment Duration in West Germany. V, 244 pages. 1993.

W. Gebauer, Foundations of European Central Bank Policy. VI, 258 pages. 1993.

G. de Wit, Determinants of Self-employment. XII, 194 pages. 1993.

W. Smolny, Dynamic Factor Demand in a Rationing Context. VIII, 242 pages. 1993.

A. Haufler, Commodity Tax Harmonization in the European Community. XIV, 216 pages. 1993.

N. Blattner, H. Genberg, A. Swoboda (Eds.), Banking in Switzerland. VIII, 330 pages. 1993.

H.-J. Wagener (Ed.), The Political Economy of Transformation. VIII, 242 pages. 1994.

G. Steinmann, R. E. Ulrich (Eds.), The Economic Consequences of Immigration to Germany. X, 178 pages. 1994.

F. P. Lang, R. Ohr (Eds.), International Economic Integration. X, 264 pages. 1995

G. Maier, Spatial Search. VIII, 254 pages. 1995